Death in a Nutshell
An Anthropology Whodunnit

Armchair Anthropology Series
Book One

by

Roxanne Varzi

First Edition

Library of Congress Control Number: 2023913037
Varzi, Roxanne
Title / by Roxanne Varzi—1 st ed.
p. cm.
ISBN: 979-8-9886844-0-4
[1. Murder Mystery—Anthropology—Dioramas—
Museums—Dyslexia—Neurodiversity—National Parks—
Natural History Museum
[Fic]-

For Rumi, who always spots the red herring no matter how I devise the plot.

Dear Princess Beatrice,
thank you for all of
your dyslexia
advocacy!
Rj.
2023 - UC Irvine

Very few of us are what we seem.

- Agatha Christie

Disclaimer

This is a work of fiction. Any resemblance the characters bear to persons living or dead is coincidental, apart from Jack Horner, who appears with permission as a fictionalized version of himself. Aside from the fact that he has dyslexia, is Emeritus at Montana State University, and discovered the Maiasaura, everything else—including his dialogue—is entirely fictional. I wrote Jack Horner into this story before I coincidentally met him when he mentored my son at the Eye-to-Eye after-school program for students with Dyslexia. Pure serendipity!

Certain long-standing institutions, agencies, and public offices are mentioned, but the characters and the events involved are wholly imaginary.

The information about anthropology is an accumulation of the author's experiences, which includes a Ph.D. in anthropology from Columbia University and teaching positions at NYU, the University of London, and the University of California Irvine.

The information about bisons and muddy cars should be used with discretion.

A Note on the Field Notes

The field notes are offered here as an opportunity to delve deeper into anthropology through Alex's observations as a student of anthropology. They are meant as a brief introduction and can be read or skipped with no consequence to the storyline.

A Note on Perfection

Because no one is perfect and my dyslexia Kryptonite is spelling, I've left behind a few spelling errors. You will understand why when you get to Page 105 (No Peaking!)

Chapter One

She met her death in a pink linen sundress and spotless white apron, the ties of which splayed out alongside her like limbs floating carelessly in a pool of blood. Pink eyeshadow shimmered brilliantly across her half-opened eyes that gazed-up at the crystal chandelier—brightly lit in anticipation of dinner guests who would never taste the juicy roast beef still cooking in the shiny red stove. A starched gingham kerchief lay inches from her bashed and bloodied blonde head.

Had the kerchief begun the evening around the hostess's neck or the killer's?

Alex shone her flashlight around the remains of the picture-perfect mid-century dinner-party that never was and wondered if the guests had ever arrived. Had they come, seen the fresh blood that pooled around their hostess's head, and left without leaving a single print on the recently polished floors? Who alerted the police? Who called off the dinner party? Did an early arrival kill her with a whack to the back of her head? Showing up early to a dinner party was considered rude in the 1950s.

Only a pink suede kitten-heel, knocked from her tiny, elegant, plastic foot, suggested a struggle. A matching pink lipstick outlined the curvature of slight surprise frozen across her lips.

Alex studied the starched white napkins that dotted the length of the mahogany table—untouched. Long-stemmed glasses stood empty, their bulbous bellies ready to receive the decanted wine still-breathing on the sideboard. The lusterware shimmered, unblemished.

Had the detectives noticed the gingham kerchief that, surely, began the evening somewhere around the woman's neck?

Alex's breath fogged the protective glass screen between her studious gaze and the tiny dead protagonist whose party had gone awry. She backed away from the scene and looked around at the other little houses. She was alone in the gallery and felt as if she had stumbled into a deserted neighborhood on the wrong side of town. Even the guard, who had given her a flashlight to view the low-lit exhibit, had abandoned her. Alex shivered despite the heat from the humming radiators. She wiped her glasses with her t-shirt and moved to the next miniature murder house.

This one had the aura of innocent disarray left by a child called away mid-play. A miniature man lay sprawled on his back, one leg dangling uncomfortably over his couch. The elbow patches on his well-kept cardigan and the knee patch on his overalls suggested that, though appearing cash-poor, he still cared about his appearance. The overturned buckets on his front porch and the fall leaves tracked inside were not in keeping with a fastidious farmer who would mend his own clothes. No, he'd had a visitor and, given his unnatural posture on the sofa, not of the friendly kind. Alex was impressed with how the artist conveyed in a single brush stroke of red that the wood-burning stove was still warm—which, in turn, suggested that someone had recently fed it a log, also suggesting that the man's body was still warm. A dog (his dog—?) sniffed at the man's pocket. What had the dog found? A treat? A familiar human scent?

Alex tilted her head to get a better look, but, no matter at what angle she held her flashlight or contorted her neck, no matter how close she got, nothing could afford her more than a bird's-eye view. Aside from peering and peeking, she could not fit her adult body into the little house. These intricate worlds were meant to be seen and not inhabited. And (given the lack of any contextual information) not meant to be solved. She glanced around for a gallery guide, an exhibit label, or a solution to the crime scene but found little to help explain the mystery. There was nothing more frustrating for an anthropologist than a museum exhibit without a full narrative. Where was the backstory? Where was the information that would help her make sense of these little dollhouse scenes reduced to an artistic moment frozen in time? Where were the life histories? Who were these people? Why had they been killed? And why was she not privy to this information? An anthropologist was no different from a detective. And Alex wanted answers.

Alex took a deep breath, turned off the flashlight, returned it to its place, and exited the exhibition of "Murder Is Her Hobby."

She paused at the gift shop, tempted to go inside—knowing it was a bad idea given the credit-card debt she was already accruing—when she noticed an oversized hardcover entitled *Nutshell Murders*.

"Aha!" she said to herself, "That's where we find the answers," and she entered the shop.

The heavy, expensive, coffee-table book was wrapped in a thin plastic cover.

"No display copy?"

"I am afraid not," the salesperson answered regretfully.

Alex handed over her credit card and purchased the book. Never one to wait, Alex tore off the plastic wrap and turned to the page with the farmhouse murder.

"Thought so," Alex murmured—the dog knew something. She turned the page and ... "Nothing?!" Alex exclaimed—the salesperson looked up, alarmed.

"Where are the solutions?" Alex asked as she thumbed the surrounding pages. "Why aren't they here?"

"Frances Glessner Lee created the *Nutshell Studies of Unexplained Death* to help solve these particularly difficult cases. She started a department of legal medicine at Harvard in 1936 and donated the entire collection to them. Today they continue to be used by the Baltimore medical examiner's office to train and test detectives. The solutions, if there are any, are well-guarded secrets," the woman explained. "Would you like a refund?" she asked.

"No, thank you," Alex said. She had an idea.

She was eager to leave the museum and return to her friend Kit's house.

She pushed hard on the heavy doors and stepped out of the dark museum and into the bright day. D.C. was a lunch city, and the hustle and bustle of workers headed out to the delis and cafes was already in full swing.

Alex ran down the Renwick Gallery stairs and across Lafayette Square where the trees were turning orange and red. The musty, cool scent in the air that signaled a change in seasons made Alex nervous—fall was her deadline to begin her new project.

Anti-gun protestors were gathered in front of the White House. Alex paused briefly to pull her long brown hair into a bun, hoping to blend in with the tourists that milled about the area. But a woman she had met at an earlier protest spotted her and motioned for Alex to join them.

"Alex!" the woman called.

Alex called back, "Next time; got to run!"

D.C. felt like a swamp in early Fall, and Alex was sweating when she reached her friend Kit's parent's tall, narrow red-brick Victorian townhouse on Mass Avenue. Kit was Alex's best friend and in her Ph.D. cohort at Columbia. All the students in their cohort had completed their coursework, exams, fieldwork, and were now writing their dissertations. All except Alex, whose first field project had crashed and burned. While Kit was starting a fellowship at the Smithsonian, Alex was couch-surfing at Kit's to save money while she applied for grants.

"Hello?" Alex called out, walking inside.

Everyone was out.

Alex helped herself to a vegan cupcake and a Nespresso with almond milk and got to work on her laptop. She logged into the American Anthropologist fellowship database and typed "Rockies" in the search engine.

The fellowship ad had annoyed her when she saw it the

day before because it was listed under cultural anthropology when, she thought, it was clearly physical anthropology or even paleontology. Alex spent hours that summer wading through correctly labeled fellowships that she had exactly one chance in a million of even interviewing for, let alone getting. So to stumble on one more unclear ad that would take her three times that of an average reader to read and discard was maddening. She was twelve months away from having to mark anthropology down on her tax returns as a hobby. She desperately needed a fellowship and a new field site before Columbia University kicked her out of the Ph.D. program. But now, after seeing the Nutshell Murder exhibit at the Renwick, she was sure that stumbling on *that* ad was an act of providence. In Alex's cosmology, there were no coincidences; things happened for a reason. Kit would tell her not to get her hopes up so quickly, but she couldn't help herself. Alex found the ad and uploaded her application.

"This is it!" she said to the empty room and hit "Send."

Chapter Two

Three Weeks Later

Alex nestled into the backseat of the Lyft car and took out her phone and opened the camera app. She scrutinized her bloodshot eyes and smeared gold eyeliner that made her look like someone who had stumbled out of an all-night rave. *They don't call it a red-eye flight for nothin'*, she thought. Her hair looked like a child's after she'd touched a big metal ball at a science museum: an unruly mess of static electricity. She rubbed the sun freckles that spotted her nose despite a summer spent indoors applying for grants. She had as many freckles as rejection letters: Fulbright, the National Science Foundation, the Wenner-Gren, the Social Science Research Foundation, and more.

"First time in Bozeman?" The driver startled her.

"Yes, first time out West," Alex answered.

"You'll love Bozeman. Everyone does. Did you know it's the fastest growing micropolitan in the US?"

"Really?" Alex took out her notebook and wrote: *Micropolitan?? Polis: city. Where are all the people???*

"The indigenous folk call it the 'valley of flowers.'"

Alex wrote, *No evidence of Flowers under all this snow—of first-nation institutions—the Crow nation?? [Look-up later.]*

"Yeah, history grad student, MSU. Easy money ferrying folks from one end of campus to the other. The city, the campus, is bigger than it looks," he explained.

"History? Cool." Alex refrained from mentioning that she, too, was a grad student.

"Yeah, mostly Greek and Roman and some Bozeman," He laughed at his joke. "Bozeman was a crossroads for Native American migrations: Shoshone, Nez Perce, Sioux, Blackfeet, Flathead, and the local Crow Nation. It was a mining town named after the explorer John Bozeman. He created the Bozeman Trail in the 1800s—great hiking town, by the way."

"Oh," Alex replied vaguely; she was not a hiker. She gazed out the window where the sun rose behind the short brown mountains, lending the field an ethereal look.

"Museum of the Rockies," he announced. The sleek cement-and-steel building looked more like the Museum of Modern Art than the Natural History Museum in New York City, but the dinosaur sculpture in front made it clear what kind of artifacts were on display.

"That was fast," Alex remarked.

"Streets are empty at this hour," he explained.

"Empty is the operative word." A scattering of single-story cabins dotted the snowy field surrounding the museum.

"This is all campus. Montana State University. And this is Old Museum Road," he said, turning onto the deserted road that ran the boundary of the field.

"Not many houses," Alex commented.

A tall, dilapidated farmhouse with sinking gables and rotting wood sat like a scab at the center of the field.

"What's that?" Alex hoped it wasn't her cottage. It was downright creepy.

"The Tinsley House. William Tinsley built it when he came out during the Civil War to work for the Wells Fargo State Company. The Tinsley family had money. There's a dining room, parlor, four bedrooms, children's playrooms, and a master bedroom."

"It was a plantation?"

"No, why would you think that?"

"*Master* bedroom." *Language is power, it has history, it can subjugate as well as inform*, thought Alex. She was too tired to get into the controversy around the term *master bedroom* or how important it was to choose words carefully. Language was a minefield, and it's not like she wasn't blowing things up all the time. His intentions weren't bad; she laid her teaching cap aside and gazed out the window.

"Oh?" He thought for a moment and then continued his spiel. "It's a living-history farm."

"A what?"

"You know, one of those places where you can experience nineteenth-century living, right down to the authentic outhouse and water pump. The kiddos love it. Volunteers demonstrate how to weave on the loom. Amateur actors bring in costumes for the kids to role-play life as early settlers. They plow the fields, cook chicken potpies using the real chickens they keep in the coop." He smiled at her in the rearview mirror

and said, "Don't worry, they don't kill the chickens in front of
the kiddos. The house is a whole lot of fun, but not until
summer. No heat in winter."

* * *

Alex stood at the front door of the Blue Cabin and re-read the
email instructions sent to her by her new mentor and supervi-
sor, Dr. Diana Bakerson. Her glasses were fogged from the
cold, humid air. Even her phone seemed to be glitching in reaction to the weather.

Keys to your cabin are hidden under a bag of sod that you may
or may not have to unearth from snow, depending on the
weather, which is unpredictable at best.

Alex squatted down and lifted the corner of a heavy, wet plastic
bag of what may or may not have been sod when a slim, well-
dressed woman in a chic camel-hair coat and tall black boots
appeared out of nowhere and startled her.

"Diana Bakerson," the woman announced.

Alex's new mentor was as unpredictable as the weather.

Alex jumped up and stammered, "I was looking for the
key."

Diana leaned in and gave her an unexpected double-
cheeked kiss. Her eyes twinkled despite her serious expression.
The corners of her lips were slightly turned-up as if to give a
wry smile.

"Here," Diana said, swiftly sticking a skeleton key into the
keyhole. "Rot," Diana exclaimed, squinting her dark gray eyes

at the keyhole. Her head shook as she struggled with the stuck key. Not a strand of her jet-black hair fell from her perfectly pinned chignon.

"Come," Diana commanded after finally dislodging the key and pushing open the door. She slipped the key back into her tote. Alex did not dare ask if her key was indeed waiting for her under the bag of sod. She was already intimidated by her new mentor.

"*Voilà*. The Blue Cabin." Diana led Alex into the living room. There was a sizable fireplace, a couch, a coffee table, and a tall empty bookshelf, which Diana dragged her finger along to inspect for dust. "You must be thirsty," Diana said, taking off her coat and reaching to take Alex's.

"Yes," Alex handed Diana her coat and smoothed her hair, wishing she had a hair clip. She had not expected to see anyone until the next day.

"Come see your kitchen; it has a fabulous view of the field," Diana said, leading Alex. "All that is museum land out there." Diana pulled the cord too hard and broke the blinds. "Sorry, it's stuck, but at least it's open."

Alex gazed out at the expanse of snow and horizon. Her heart skipped a beat when she realized there was no need to shut the blinds; she was alone for miles. She took a deep breath. The view was fantastic, and she wondered how something so beautiful could also feel so terrifying.

Diana fiddled with the water tap. It sputtered, choked, and finally spat out a sludgy brown liquid before gifting fresh, clear water.

"Been a while since anyone's stayed here," Diana apologized. As if on cue, they heard the front door slam shut.

"Were you expecting someone?" Diana asked, offering Alex a glass of water.

"Me? No. You're the only person I know in Bozeman," Alex said.

"Odd." Diana marched into the living room.

Alex set down her glass and followed.

"Marta?" Diana startled a petite, dirty-blonde woman hanging her jacket on a hook by the door.

"I clean for visitor," Marta said, fixing her large green eyes on Alex.

"Ah," Diana said, "Yes, here she is ... this is Alex, our visitor." Diana turned to Alex and explained, "Marta is the museum's all-around helper."

"Anything you need," Marta smiled tightly.

Alex smiled, trying to place Marta's accent, it was not like anything she had heard before, and Alex heard a lot of different accents in New York City.

"Actually, you could help Alex out," Diana said, thinking aloud.

"Yes?" Marta studied Alex.

"Alex is an anthropology graduate student."

Marta bristled slightly.

"She is interested in recent transplants to Bozeman."

"No, I never have transplant," Marta shook her head vehemently.

"No, no." Diana laughed, "Not organ. She is studying new residents in Bozeman." She turned to Alex, "Marta's been with us for about a year. She's perfect for your project." And back to Marta: "Alex is making mini dioramas of people's lives in Bozeman."

"Oh, museum artist like you," Marta sounded relieved.

"Yes, but not a physical anthropologist, like our paleontologists. Alex is a cultural anthropologist."

Marta scrunched her face.

"Barely an anthropologist," Alex offered. Was she imagining Marta's disapproval? Maybe Kit had been right, and Alex did need a break from anthropology.

"Cultural anthropologists study living people, contemporary, you know—in the moment," Diana smiled encouragingly. *Con-tempo*: "with time." Latin was Alex's secret decoder. Time was out of joint as far as Alex was concerned. She was woozy from jet lag and wondered if it would be impolite to sit down.

"We make dinosaur dioramas; she makes human dioramas." Diana winked at Alex.

"I understand." Marta accepted Diana's explanation, "You want tour?" she asked Alex.

"That would be great." Alex was utterly unprepared for what was swiftly becoming her first ethnographic fieldwork interview. Maybe her luck was changing? First, a scholarship, then—mere hours after arriving at her field site—her first informant.

Alex hated the term "informant." It sounded so dry, so illicit, so wrong. "Subject" was not any better. Informant implied a person was spying on and betraying their own people. Subject alluded to a power dynamic where the anthropologist was more powerful and smarter—an observer on high.

"OK, I show you bathroom?" Marta asked, and Alex's heart sank. This was not the tour of Bozeman she had hoped for.

Marta pointed out the bulbous claw-footed bathtub as if she were revealing a rare museum sculpture. What was rare and sculptural and genuinely worthy of a museum was the antique ceramic heater in the bedroom that Marta called "too old."

"No," Alex muttered with admiration.

"It is pain. I have same in my cabin. You must feed the wood to stay warm."

"Actually," Diana cleared her throat, "This one is all show. There's a thermostat," she assured Alex.

Marta saved the best part of the one-bedroom cabin for last.

"Come." Marta led her to a dark, narrow set of stairs that Alex hadn't noticed when they'd passed by earlier.

"An attic?" Alex followed Marta up the creaky stairs.

"The house, it talks," Marta whispered, as if it could also listen.

"Wow!" Alex stepped into the bright, beautiful loft. Marta smiled, pleased. Alex, like Marta, did not take this loft for granted. "Breathtaking."

Marta joined Alex at the window.

"It appears out of nowhere, like magic," Alex said, in wonder.

"This place?" Marta asked.

"The snow. When it first starts to flutter. One minute, the sky is clear, and, the next, it's like someone picked up a giant snow globe and started shaking it."

"Snow globe?"

"I'll show you. I'm sure we can find one in Bozeman," Alex smiled.

"My cabin. You come day-after-tomorrow?" Marta pointed in the distance to a small cabin nestled in a pine grove near the museum.

"Yes. Thank you."

With that, Marta said goodbye. "You stay," she said, when Alex tried to follow her.

A few minutes later, Alex watched from the window and saw Marta dart across the field, barely bundled in a battered leather jacket and a bright-red wool hat—thin protection. Marta, too, was out of her element.

14

. . .

When Diana had left, Alex plopped down on her couch and texted Kit:

It's legit! My cabin is amazing! It comes with a Subaru Forester!!! Mentor met me at the door, already have my first field interview!!!

Kit texted back:

Too good to be true.

Alex sighed and opened her notes app to dictate her first impressions when Kit's video call interrupted her.

"Do they know about your dollhouse method?" Kit asked without saying hello.

"They're not just dollhouses. They're re-constructed crime scenes."

"So ... really, Alex? Miniature dollhouses. Is this the new project?" Kit's wary tone made Alex anxious. Despite her new fellowship, they both knew, like a baby, a dissertation was expected to be delivered by a specific date, and Alex's project had been gestating too long for Columbia's rules. It was eight years to defense or bye-bye. Alex had less than two years to complete her fieldwork and write her dissertation.

"The houses are inspirational," Alex explained.

"Do they know that? The museum people who gave you the grant?" Kit asked.

"Yes. Besides, what difference does it make? A dollhouse is a dollhouse." Alex frowned.

"My dad didn't think a dollhouse was ever just a dollhouse. He wouldn't let me have one until we found one with black dolls resembling me. Do dollhouses even count as ethnography?"

"Count? Zora Neal Hurston, Margaret Mead? They wrote plays, made films. Why can't I make a dollhouse? It's material culture. I'm down to the wire here. I can't afford not to do this fellowship."

"I know," Kit said gently, "But, Alex, it's just weird. No one's heard of the funders. You need to reach out to your disability ally ask for more time. Don't they grant that to students with learning disabilities?"

"Not everyone gets a prestigious Smithsonian internship."

Kit glanced behind her at the gallery entrance, where a big banner announced: *African Arts*.

"Every time I walk in here, I wonder if I was an opportunity for them to put a black face in their newsletter. Who says I'm not filling a savage slot?" Kit whispered, looking around the empty gallery. "Would I have this fellowship if I had applied in European decorative arts instead of African art?"

The Savage Slot is a singular slot that people of color can occupy. Alex wrote all about it for her first-year proseminar paper in visual anthropology. She used Spike Lee as an example. When Spike made films about Black folk, that was cool, but *Summer of Sam*—how dare he write about a white serial killer. Lee had left his savage slot.

"Alex, stop letting one little mistake ruin everything. Nobody blamed you."

"Talk about armchair anthropology. I'm a fraud."

"It wasn't your fault."

"A good anthropologist would have known not to ask, not to push, not to put her in danger. I didn't do my research."

"You were studying filmmakers in New York City, not the Middle East. How were you to know that—"

"Look, I don't need a big win," Alex—who had desired a big win academically her whole life—lied to Kit. "I need to be redeemed."

"I know," Kit soothed. "You'll find another internship.

Don't go hiding in a pile of bones in Montana because the humans got a little too complicated."

"A *little* complicated? She trusted me." Alex moaned, then added brightly, "I have a good feeling about this fellowship."

"I don't," Kit said. "Got to go," she said, and she signed off.

Field Note

Wasn't expecting a welcome party. In the old days, a whole village or tribe would appear to welcome Margaret Mead to her field site. And, on her return home, a flock of journalists would appear to capture an iconic shot of her stepping off a plane or waving from a steamer. Anthropology used to be newsworthy.

Perhaps because Mead wrote books *and* made films. Nowadays, anthropology is buried in a textual cemetery, waiting for an audio-visual spirit to wake it up. We, plebes, are discouraged from partaking in modalities like filmmaking until we have mastered writing. And academic writing is not so easy with dyslexia. Visuals, now that's another story.

No one pigeonholed Margaret Mead—nor did it take a village to break the mold, as it does now. Even Zora Neal Hurston, a black woman in a white man's world, did not cower in the shadow of tradition as a grad student at Columbia in the 1920s—no, she spun her field data into plays. It helped that her advisor was Franz Boas, the father of American anthropology and founder of Columbia University's Anthropology Department. He not only encouraged her but was a rebel in his own right when in 1894 he made a speech at the American Association for the "Advancement" of Science, calling anthropology out as a "political justification for the suppression of the American Negro."

Papa Boas (as he was known to his mentees) didn't always get it right. For one thing, he had Zora out in the streets of New York City, recording skull measurements with calipers to disprove the eugenicists. She also helped him record life stories —the wax-cylinder recordings stolen from the convertible he left idling on 116th and Amsterdam. Distraught, he exclaimed it was as if he had never been on the trip (kind of like losing your Instagram account).

I won't let Zora's or Frances Glessner Lee's efforts go to waste. Rest easy, spirit-mentors; I'm going to make ethnographic models! That sounds silly. Dollhouses. OK, let's call them Nutshells, as Glessner Lee did. Wait—is that plagiarism? Is it morbid? Am I conjuring spirits of violent death? Wonder what Professor Whiner will say? Best ask for forgiveness rather than permission ... or is this a one-way ticket out of my Ph.D. program? Zora Neal Hurston recorded life stories and turned them into plays, and here I am preparing a fight with my advisor over dollhouses. Anthropology has serious short-term memory; has Zora already been forgotten? How did Mead and Hurston manage to shake-up anthropology while I am here in the twenty-first century, shaking in my boots every time Professor Whiner emails me with a big fat "Can't happen." "Not possible," and, my favorite, "Won't count when you're a professor going up for promotions."

Professor Whiner told me to include everything in my field notes: theory, thoughts, observations, and interviews.

"Pretend you're teaching, Alexandra." He said it as if all I'll ever do is pretend.

Teaching is the holy grail after four years of coursework; Ph.D. exams; a year or two in the field (before which we study the history, background, and language of our field site); and a year writing a dissertation.

My fieldwork: Foreign Immigration to Bozeman, Montana.

What was I thinking?

Good question. An anthropologist starts by asking, "What do I want to know?"

Why are people immigrating to Bozeman? *Are they?* I hope so; otherwise, I'm in big trouble—my Ph.D. committee did not press me on this point, as I was getting a grant (albeit from an organization that no one has ever heard of—Cloudsplitter, whatever that means). Given the unbelievable fiasco of my first fieldwork attempt, the ivory tower elders were happy to see me off doing ANY research.

OK, immigration to Bozeman. Here we go: Is it an economic, cultural, or political move? Why Bozeman? Is it even a choice?

Remote, less population density. Employment opportunities? Yellowstone is only an hour away from Bozeman—what role does the National Park play in immigration? Is it a destination or an employer?

Non-profit organization involvement? Government subsidies? Refugee relocation? Are they documented or undocumented? Does immigration status play into the decision to come here in the first place or to stay?

How do the locals feel about the immigrants? Are they welcomed with open arms or with suspicion and contempt?

Will people receive me with open arms or with suspicion and contempt?

Chapter Three

An Anthropologist's ethnography begins with an arrival story. And Alex was already mentally penning hers as she trudged across the snowy field in soaking-wet fake Ugg boots.

Anthropologist arrives at Marta's door and ... runs. Alex wanted to turn and flee. She felt like a child pretending to be a social scientist. *Act as if,* she reminded herself.

Ironically, her first experience of imposter syndrome was in a summer acting camp. Acting, after all, was about pretending to be someone you were not. Alex loved improv. It was fun, and she was naturally good at it. And, it was, finally, a school activity that would make her mother, Cora, proud. But, like all good things, the improv week ended, and she was handed a script and asked to perform her worst nightmare: to read aloud.

Alex stumbled over simple words that any seventh grader should decode with ease. Words like decibel, decide, and decipher. Anytime a C showed up, Alex was in trouble. She could not remember when a C should sound like an S. Her heart pounded, and she prayed not to be called on to read. She desperately desired to disappear under Harry Potter's invisibility cloak. But someone had not only seen her but had seen right through her.

"You were enjoying yourself; what happened?" asked Professor Lilian, her gray curls bouncing as she approached. She was a retired theater professor who volunteered at the camp. She was short and slim and tough as nails. Alex was mortified.

"So?" Lilian peered at Alex over her bright-green reading glasses.

"I can't read," Alex blurted. She was sure she would be banished from camp—which was fine with her, preferable, even. Instead, Lilian pulled Alex into a hug.

"Oh, dear. Reading can be taught; talent and creativity are another thing."

While Alex's Broadway career was over before it started, her tutelage with Professor Lillian had just begun. Alex spent the next four years meeting Lilian in the city to see plays and to read Shakespeare aloud. It was Lilian who taught her Stanislavski's principle of acting as if.

And now, if her imposter syndrome told her that she was posing as an anthropologist, then acting as if was all she could do until she was comfortable being an anthropologist.

"If, as Shakespeare tells us, 'All the world's a stage'—then do as Shakespeare suggests and play on," Lilian once advised.

Which is exactly what Alex did. She acted as if she knew what she was doing and knocked confidently on Marta's door.

Marta greeted her warmly and asked her to remove her shoes before stepping inside onto a stunning blue rug that covered the entire floor of the one-room studio. It was a perfect circle overlaid by intertwining rings of pink and mustard. Little white dots fell over the rug like a scattering of snow or a field of white wildflowers. It was a singular piece one might find in a high-end carpet boutique and not something to tread on with muddy shoes.

"Spectacular." And expensive, Alex thought. She wiped her glasses on her t-shirt and bent down to examine the rug.

"Donation," Marta shrugged.

"From?" Alex looked up at Marta, hoping her question would elicit a name, not a place.

"Jasmine Anarpour," Marta freely offered. Alex's fellowship was called The Anarpour Foundation Fellowship. She knew the CEO was named Kamran Anarpour but had never met him. Was Jasmine *that* Anarpour? Wealthy enough to toss a rug like this or close enough to be a friend of Marta's to gift it? Understanding the exchange of gifts and goods in a community was a fundamental requirement of ethnographic research. She made a note to re-read Marcel Maus's *The Gift*. Maus would say that every gift begets an obligation. A gift is based on reciprocity. And, if Maus was correct, then who owed Marta this level of debt or kindness? What was or who was being reciprocated?

"Tea?" Marta asked.

"Please," Alex accepted. She handed Marta a gift, this one in exchange for information.

"Oh," Marta looked embarrassed.

"It's a token of appreciation for your time," Alex offered.

Marta gingerly unwrapped the package.

"You shake it," Alex instructed with an apology, "It's a snow globe—Big Sky. They only sell ski slopes."

Marta dutifully shook the snow globe, and a smile broke across her lips.

"You make dollhouse?" Marta set down the fluttering snow globe.

"Yes, of your home, and, when I'm done, we talk about it." Alex looked around and wondered if there was anything other than the rug to comment on or to add to the model. Marta's cabin was a study in sparsity. From what Alex could see, there were no paintings, posters, or pictures anywhere.

Marta looked at Alex skeptically. "How this dollhouse helps you? I play with it?"

"Well, it's kind of like play. It's an opportunity for you to see how I build your life, and then you come in and correct it." Alex explained.

"Correct my life?" Marta chuckled.

"No, you correct my interpretation of how I see your life. Social scientists are people, and we have opinions—you know, subjectivity? Anyway, we color our research with our biases and our own life circumstances. This is not an entirely Archimedean view of the world."

"Yes, Archimedes, I know," Marta said as if to suggest that everything Alex had said until now was complete gibberish.

"It's called shared anthropology. Have you seen *Nanook of the North*? Maybe you saw it at the museum?"

Marta shook her head. It was a youthful gesture. Marta appeared younger than her worn expression and outdated clothes suggested.

"Around 1920 Robert Flaherty, an adventurer with a camera, filmed Inuits, showed them the film, then asked if he got it right. If it was realistic."

"And he listened?" Marta smiled slightly.

"No." They both laughed. "As a matter of fact," Alex confided, "He forced them to trade their guns for fishing spears and toss their cigarettes. No white-man-influence in front of the camera."

Marta raised her perfectly threaded eyebrows. Alex made a mental note to ask Marta about Bozeman's beauty salons.

"I know. I know: so colonialist. Anthropology preserved the primitive for posterity."

"'Preserving primitive'—this means?" Marta tilted her head.

"Recording history before things changed. Film cultural evolution as it was happening."

"But change was done, no?"

Alex continued: "Yes. You cannot stop events from happening by filming them. Anthropologists believed these cultures were less evolved, and to study them was to witness evolution before their very eyes. Totally racist. You know the word stereotype?"

Marta shook her head.

"It means duplicating images—stereo, two, double, duplicate. When members of one group see people in another group as the same, it's an oversimplification. To take away a person's uniqueness is to take away her humanity."

"Oh." Marta said and frowned. "So it is fake?" she asked. "The documentaries, they are not real?"

"They are, but we can never capture more than an imprint nor the full essence of the 'Real.' Once the camera arrives, it changes everything. People start acting; even animals have been seen to sniff around and play with a hidden camera." Alex spoke quickly when she was excited, and her thoughts were too fast to process. "Sorry, I get carried away." Alex apologized.

"Why you apologize? You like teaching, I think. Please, explain your project," Marta encouraged her.

"Right. So, the idea of shared anthropology is when the

anthropologist listens to the 'native' or the informant or the subject—there is no good word—for feedback to verify their observations. Thirty years after Flaherty, Jean Rouch shared his films with his subjects; unlike Flaherty, Rouch listened to their feedback."

"How?" Marta's interest was piqued.

"Well, for example, in his film about hippo-hunters in the Niger Valley, he had added dramatic music as the hunters were sneaking up behind the hippo. Imagine them with their spears at the ready," Alex raised her arm and mimed the scene. "When he showed the hunters the scene, they yelled, 'Music scares hippos!'" Alex yelled for emphasis. Marta laughed.

"He took the fake music out of the film," Alex concluded.

"I like Mozart." Marta offered and stood. Alex's cue to leave.

* * *

Alex dumped her coat and boots by the front door. Her brain was moving a mile a minute, and she needed to dictate before she forgot anything Marta had told her.

"*Dicte*: a thing said. Diction, discourse, dictate, Dicta-phone," she intoned to no one. Alex loved playing with language and word roots. It was one of the few things she enjoyed during years of tutoring for her dyslexia. She took out her phone and began dictating her notes.

Field Note

Mozart...is that really all I got out of Marta? A love of Mozart? Economic exchange. The rug. Marx. I need to revisit Marx. Karl Marx is so utterly complicated.

Marcel Maus is much easier. He observed that tribal societies in the Pacific Northwest believed a person's spirit, or *hau*, is embedded in the gift they give, just as a worker's spirit, according to Marx, embeds in the commodity they produce. Unlike a commodity, a gift can be traced back to an individual, whereas a veil of money obscures a worker's identity.

Whew.

Commerce is not a direct exchange like a Gift. This is why Marx calls a commodity "fetishized labor." It hides the worker's labor by replacing the face of the worker (direct exchange) with money—the commodity fetish. For Marx, money deflates the workers' value and the soul they put into their work. It fetishizes the commodity by making it appear what it is not by hiding a person's blood, sweat, and tears—in short, their soul.

A pair of shoes does not show the value of the laborer, but instead the value only of exchange or what the seller can get for them. A pair of tennis shoes contains an entire social history that catapults people into unequal social relations with one another, wherein the laborer, who is hidden in the commodity, is not paid the surplus value of the exchange. Gifts can create a weird social-power dynamic. Think about the time you got a gift for which you could never reciprocate ... my mom called those the "we-can't-accept-that" gifts because no one wants an unequal relationship. (Well, almost no one; I would have taken some of those gifts, no questions asked).

For both Maus and Marx, it's all a problem of excess, surplus, and the negative energy trapped in the unfairness of low-paid workers and over-priced shoes.

Surplus wealth, what's accumulated beyond subsistence needs (like Jasmine's), can cause some serious social problems in a community—reliance on a wealthy benefactor, jealousy, indebtedness, and inequality are some reasons the tribes Maus studied chose to burn excess wealth in a potlatch.

Was giving Marta an expensive rug a potlatch-like gesture by Jasmine? Was it a power play, or was it an actual gift? Was it symbolic burning of excess, surplus, wealth—or was she giving away a piece of her soul? It's an important distinction, though I'm not sure yet why.

Too many assumptions, Alex. Need data.

Everything is about power and where it's located. Power haunts visual images, dances in language, and spins in objects. In capitalism, objects accrue value and power beyond their material value. And sometimes, there's cultural capital. A jug unearthed from a Roman burial site has a much higher value than one you'd buy at Ikea—even though the Ikea one is more useful and, by some standards, more pleasing to the eye. Why? Because we have given the Roman jug cultural capital by assigning debris left behind by a fallen empire (aka antiques) value beyond its material worth. Marx called this confusion of object and subject a fetish.

The Roman jug is a fetish.

Like in the Nutcracker ballet, the doll (a fetish object) comes to life and takes power over Clara.

Is Jasmine the Nutcracker? Wait, is Jasmine Drosselmeyer? Seriously, Alex, where are you going with all of this?

Has this gift encaged the recipient or freed the giver?

Chapter Four

The sun slipped behind the Bridger Mountains while Alex listened to Mozart's violin concertos and carefully glued a miniature felt rug to the floor of Marta's model house. She pressed down on the rug until it dried.

Objects contain power, hold secrets, and weave social webs. This rug tied Marta, the museum custodian, to Jasmine Anarpour. Who was Jasmine? A wealthy, powerful Bozeman elite, if her name was anything to go by.

Objects are magical—some more than others. Alex examined her little creation. It had all the basics: four walls, a roof, and the rug that would transform the simple box into a home.

But it did not. Her model cabin lacked the aura of the original. Like a poster of an impressionist painting, it was a cheap imitation of the original. Alex sighed and rubbed her eyes. What seemed like such an innovative idea a month ago now felt like a big mistake.

Frances Glessner Lee's original Nutshell houses had auras. They were downright haunted by spirits. What animated those houses? What lurked within?

How did she impart the lingering of those murdered spirits? There was an art to depicting the haunting. An art to suggest an unsettling left by the dead. But how? Was it the dim museum lighting or the echo of visitor footsteps bouncing off the empty walls of a large space hosting tiny objects? She could not discount the museum environment. Think like an artist, an architect, an anthropologist, a murderer.

Was that a creak on the stairs? Alex caught her breath and looked around. The dark had crept up on her, and now, beyond sunset, the only light source was a small plastic desk lamp trained on her dollhouse.

The wind hissed at her closed window. The world outside was a dark expanse of uninhabited space. She needed curtains.

She heard another scrape on the stairs.

The cabin was surely settling, she told herself. It was adjusting to the retreat of the warm sun on its shingles. It could be ice or snow expanding and contracting with the temperature change. Simple explanations that did not slow her racing heart. She set down her glue gun, stood, and stretched. A friend had once told her that it was important to greet a house when entering and to talk to it occasionally. Whether her friend had learned this from an ethnography, the field, or was simply superstitious, didn't matter. "Break-time!" Alex announced to the empty cabin.

. . .

She made herself a cup of tea and took it to the living room, where she caught up on her field notes and FaceTimed Kit.

"Hello, beautiful!" Kit blew an air kiss to Alex.

"Kit!" Her friend's smile soothed her. Alex squinted into the screen, an unwilling participant in a bumper-car ride as Kit swerved in and out of the crowd. "Slow down; you're making me queasy."

"Sorry; too much motion? Want me to call you back?" Alex said no and repositioned her phone temporarily to avoid the disorienting video.

"Never liked hand-held films," Alex added. "Where are you?"

"Lafayette Square. Running home."

"Aren't you indoors?" Kit paused to examine Alex.

"Yeah, why?"

"That heavy anaconda around your neck that's about to squeeze the life out of you."

Alex shivered in response: "It's freezing in here."

"Haven't found anyone to keep you warm yet?" Kit joked.

"Funny."

"Does everyone have their head in the sand?" Kit asked.

"Ha, ha. You mean snow? Not everyone here is a paleontologist."

"What else do they do? Farm?" Kit asked demurely. "Lots of wild animals out there, no? Work at Yellowstone National Park? Didn't a bison recently attack someone out there? Doesn't seem safe."

"As a matter of fact, I briefly met a tall, dark, mysterious Ranger. Diana, my mentor, introduced us. We ran into him when we were out getting coffee."

"Is it already time for me to come rescue you? Alex and a man with a gun. Will your first date be an anti-gun rally, or don't they have those in Bozeman?"

"He has dimples." Alex said smiling.

"Oh, lord. Time to come home," Kit insisted.

"I like it here."

"You mean your nice cabin. Surely not Bozeman?"

"Bozeman's great. Not everyone who leaves New York withers up and dies."

"You sure about that?" Kit asked skeptically.

"I don't miss the city," Alex surprised herself. "How many times have you been pushed or bumped today? I don't miss the lines, being shoved on the subway, the smell of trash in the summer, the wet black snow in winter. Bozeman is clean and cobble-stoned. There are charming storefronts, and people are friendly. Tomorrow, I'll wake up and go hiking in pristine snow."

"Hiking?" Kit howled.

"And the food ... I had bison chili for dinner last night," Alex said.

"What about the poor Vegans?" Kit, a lifelong Vegan, rolled her eyes.

"They've repurposed a cattle ranch into a Vegan spa retreat."

"Coffee? There is no way the coffee is city-quality." Kit was sure she had Alex.

"Delectable. And...wait." Alex peered closely into the screen, "Please tell me you're not at Nat Geo?"

"How's the dollhouse project going?" Kit changed the subject.

"Glessner called them Nutshells, *Les Petites Morts*."

"She did not!" Kit laughed wildly. "Not in the 1950s, she didn't."

"Tiny murders. I thought you'd appreciate my French. I've been practicing on Duolingo to visit you in Togo next year."

"It's not a direct translation." Kit laughed.

"Well, that's what they are." Alex answered defensively.

"It's a verb."

"Killing small?" Alex was annoyed with Kit's private joke.

"Sorry, tell me more about the tiny deaths," Kit giggled as she entered her parent's house on Mass. Ave.

"They're called Nutshells."

Kit walked into the study her parents had set aside for her in their rambling home. Everything in Kit's study screamed success: from her Togolese masks acquired during her summer fieldwork to the new iMac computer to her framed MPhil.

Alex's Master of Philosophy diploma was still rolled-up in its mailing canister that bore the address of a place where she no longer lived. After three years of grad school, Alex felt even less well-equipped for the job market: she didn't type any faster —not a single letter faster per minute—and was convinced she read slower than before grad school. She got nothing out of all those dry academic books filled with material and words that she couldn't visualize. Reading was hard for someone with her type of dyslexia when the words did not conjure images. *Cat*, Alex could visualize, but *functionalism*, *structuralism*, and *rhizomatic*? Forget it.

"So, what's your object du jour?" Kit interrupted Alex's thoughts.

Alex was thinking about Claude Levi-Straus; she loved this idea of structuralism, how the Giza pyramids and the Mexican ones could be built across cultures without any contact, without any sharing of ideas, that eventually humans would re-invent the wheel ... in a circle of infinite regression.

"Hey, Alex, what's buzzing in the hive?" Kit coaxed Alex back.

Alex smiled. No one else credited Alex's mind for being active when it took off to those places not on the attention menu. Kit knew she was deep in thought and not checked out as everyone assumed of people with ADHD. Over the years, many of Alex's teachers called her "sluggish," implying that she didn't have any thoughts. The problem was that she had too many ideas simultaneously, which were incredibly hard to organize.

"Huh?" Alex snapped out of her daydream.

"The object?" Kit reminded her.

"Oh, yeah. A rug. It's her only possession with character. There's no detritus."

"'Detritus,' she says," Kit joked. She knew how much Alex liked to play with language.

"Trash. Junk, things tossed about. Nada. I was hoping for a little fun—stacks of paper or a lost sock. A moment when my interviewee looks at the dollhouse and says, 'So that's where I left my keys.' Nope, she's a model of sparsity."

"So, she's clean—isn't she a cleaning woman?" Kit threw her coat on the hot pink couch that Alex had slept on for two weeks.

Marta didn't have any strewn clothes, not even a throw pillow on her couch, thought Alex.

"She's hiding something," Alex insisted.

"You're being paranoid. Have you asked your mentor?" Kit asked.

"Seriously? You mean 'Professor Get-it-done-or-get-out'?"

"No, not Whiner. Forget Columbia. The new one, your fellowship mentor," Kit said.

"Diana? Yes, I asked her how to make a diorama of nothing-ness," Alex said.

"And?" Kit flopped down on her couch.

"She said, 'You mean like a tundra?' Then she asked me if my first subject was a hibernating bear. 'Don't be moving into my territory, missy.' Diana joked but seemed serious."

"Are you?" Kit wondered.

"Am I what?" Alex asked.

"Moving into her territory?"

"Come on, Kit. Don't be silly. I'm researching human behavior, though Marta acts like a hibernating bear who has swallowed a huge chunk of life and is holding it deep inside her. Imagine a home with no personal items. No books, no papers, no photographs. Even an Airbnb has a magazine lying around, right?"

Alex smiled. She imagined an Airbnb ought to have magazines lying around, but she had never stayed in one.

"That's a tough one. Remember my dad's colleague Bernice, who came to Thanksgiving dinner?"

"Of course," Alex said—as if Alex could forget meeting legendary Sweet Honey in the Rock singer, activist, and historian Bernice Johnson Reagan: she was a titan. Smithsonian's Folkways recorded her singing bible songs as a child and again later in her adult years as an integral voice of the civil-rights movement. She was also a formidable historian.

"She says history is not only what's in the records but also the missing parts. So, this empty space, Alex. If something isn't there—well, that's important information. Why isn't it there? Remember, archives are created by the victors."

"What's that supposed to mean?"

"If her home is an archive, then what was pillaged? What did she lose? And why?"

Good questions, thought Alex. She needed to dictate notes.

Field Note

Marta doesn't even have a poster. Everyone can afford a poster. The museum offers free posters of old exhibits in a bin outside the gift store. It's like she has a thing against visual imagery. Maybe she's a snob about art and won't accept a reproduction?

Walter Benjamin writes that replicating a piece of art causes it to lose its initial value—it's spirit, it's hau, or what he called, it's aura.

Photography is the art of lost originals.

And, yet, some believe a portrait contains the sitter's soul.

What becomes of a soul when the photograph is copied?

And where are all those souls who are Marta's kin?

How can someone live in this image-regime without a single photograph? Who can't afford to print a photo? People still print and proudly display their pictures. My cousin sends me a yearly calendar of family pictures.

With cheap means of reproduction (a printer) and camera at our fingertips (most phones)—we create our own archives; we no longer must cede visual history to the wealthy and the powerful.

That was not always the case. Until the invention of cheaper, easier-to-use cameras like the Kodak pocket camera, visual history, like any historical archive, was created by the powerful, the wealthy, and the victorious, who had access to expensive equipment.

Susan Sontag said it best: "In America, the photographer is not simply the person who records the past but the one who invents it."

The intimate family photograph, or what came to be known as the "Kodak moment," was born of the Kodak pocket camera. Why? Because it had roll film and was easy to operate. The cheap Kodak cameras enabled more newspapers to send journalists out to photograph human-interest stories and important headlines.

Do we even have headlines anymore? There's no top or bottom; we scroll. We move around a page; we change mediums from moving to still to sound.

I digress.

The onset of personal photography gave us historical and ethnographic records of intimate spaces—they made the Kodak moment part of a public archive through the practice of keeping family albums. Some of those family albums like that of the Persian Qajar King Nasr al-din Shah became important historical records. We would not have had access to the Persian Harem, where the women and children resided, had the king not been an early adopter of photography and not gifted cameras to his wives to play with in the Harem.

I'm a little obsessed with Iran. I read all about Iranian cinema, looking for all the ways I could have avoided royally messing-up my fieldwork interview with the Iranian filmmaker.

What I learned: the camera invades, intervenes, and changes everything. Photographs can incite change by bearing witness. And they can be as easily used to harm and to powerfully persuade people for both good and bad ends. So how do anthropologists deal with this problem? We remedy, or fix this by recognizing the subjectivity and agency of the person that we are studying. We do not turn them into objects. I told Marta this and she said: "Agency? I do not work with agency. I am hired on my own." I explained that agency is a person's right to be themselves. To speak for themselves, to have autonomy, to be a full person without someone else or entity governing their very being. I mean, we're governed on so many levels, but we still have the right to speak out. And her response: "And anthropology, it helps with the agents?"

It's a simple solution: we let people speak for themselves. We do away with voiceovers or intertitles to explain another person or their culture.

Jean Rouch and the French New Wave ushered in this moment when Rouch placed microphones on friends in Paris to film an intellectual conversation about the world. One friend left the conversation, still mic'ed, and talking to herself. Rouch caught her off-guard and recorded a private moment.

Shortly after, the McDougalls (a husband-wife anthropology team) came along and introduced us to the idea of observational cinema in their famous Doon School Chronicles, where the camera was constantly rolling as they followed and filmed the boys' daily lives, from teeth-brushing and morning yoga to fighting on the field and eating dinner. The McDougalls often caught each other on camera, gingerly stepping over a camera cable as they moved their cameras around in silence.

Innovations like video and sync sound made filmmaking mobile. They also introduced subtitles, so we understood what the boys were saying to the camera and to each other and didn't just hear the anthropologist's commentary in voice-over. Anthropologists went from sounding like sportscasters to providing a real slice of life.

So much to think about. For one: where are Marta's photos?

Chapter Five

Alex avoided passing the creepy Tinsley House by crossing the field the long way and entering the Museum's main entrance. The MSU student on desk duty barely looked up from her book to nod at Alex.

"Marta starts work early," Alex commented.

"Huh?"

"The marble floors," Alex explained, "They're spotless."

"Yeah, they reflect the morning light. The architect must have planned it," the student muttered.

"It's quiet this morning," Alex referred to the open but empty gift store.

"Yeah, show just started. Everyone's in there." The student pointed toward the small planetarium and screening room and went back to her book.

The kitchen, an unofficial staff hangout, smelled faintly of coffee but was otherwise unoccupied. Alex glanced at the wall clock and hit her forehead with the palm of her hand. "Shoot!"

She rushed back to the lobby and asked the MSU student if she had seen Diana.

"We were supposed to meet in the kitchen." Alex left out that she was late.

"Check the Wolf Exhibit."

Alex took off at speed, taking a shortcut through the Dino Hall, where Jack Horner, the chief paleontologist, whose life inspired the fictional Jurassic Park series, stood amidst a flurry of activity.

"Look at what our team uncovered," Jack called to Alex as she attempted to slip by. Alex ducked under the low-hanging fragments of bone and skull.

"You're safe. Nothing's going to fall on you. The bones stay suspended while we decide where to place them. What do you think?" Jack asked.

"Me?" Alex asked, pointing at herself.

Jack nodded.

"Looks like a child's mobile," Alex offered. "You know, the ones they hang in cribs?"

Jack laughed. "The team is debating whether to fill the missing pieces or leave empty space."

"Empty space allows for the imagination," Alex glanced at the clock.

"And...?" Jack encouraged her; he was a natural teacher.

"We don't know what was happening to this creature," she ventured, unsure whether it was a dinosaur or a woolly mammoth. "A diorama should lead you down a path ... but not take you all the way," she offered tentatively, and then with more confidence, "You know, it offers ideas, hints, but leaves the rest to the viewers' imagination."

Jack Horner smiled.

"An educated imagination, of course," Alex stammered.

"Come work with us!" Andy, the art director, exclaimed. Was he being serious or affable?

"I'm a doctoral student in Social Cultural anthropology at Columbia. I'm here on the Anarpour Foundation Fellowship," Alex introduced herself.

"Ah, the Ph.D. can wait. The discoveries are happening now," Jack said.

Columbia would not wait, yet this was not a bad idea, given she was on the verge of being kicked out.

"I'd love to, but Diana is waiting for me."

"Say no more," Jack drew back so she could pass.

Alex folded her hands in gratitude. "Can you tell me how to get to the Wolf Exhibit?"

"Diana won't allow anyone to see her magnum opus until the big opening. Are you sure she wanted you to meet her there?"

Alex nodded faintly.

"In that case, just take a left as you leave the hall," Jack directed her.

Alex thanked him and ran out of the hall and to the left, where she saw an enormous banner with the image of two large, yellow wolf eyes announcing Diana's show.

Alex stepped into the cold Exhibition Hall.

"Diana?" Alex called out into the dark. The scent of toxic

shellac hung heavily in the air. She moved in further, and the strong scent of resins and paint gave way to a mossy and peaty smell of musty fur pelts. It reminded her of a childhood embrace at a gravesite—of tears on a musty mink coat—the soft, silky, pungent odor of death.

She could barely make out the outline of the diorama in the low light. It was neither contained by glass nor roped off. Unlike her reproduction of Marta's home, this diorama had a strong aura. The temptation to step inside was visceral—the compulsion to approach and touch the terrifying creature that had stopped dead in its tracks was irresistible. She did not resist. She stepped up and inside the diorama and was immediately flooded by memories of a hot and humid summer day in another museum with a similar diorama.

The strong scent transported her to that hot summer day in New York. She remembered every detail of that day, from waking up tired and cranky after a week of Special Ed summer school to being angry instead of grateful when her mother, Cora, announced a trip to the city.

"You promised me free time." Alex imagined herself back in Brooklyn, talking to Cora, holding onto a cereal box for dear life, should that too be snatched by her mother, who was awake uncharacteristically early for a Saturday morning.

The musty museum smell, the low light, and the dead animals playing out the role of their life behind velvet ropes and glass walls brought it all back. She could see that whole day so clearly.

"Teddy's coming." Cora jangled Teddy's mom's car keys—bartered in exchange for bringing along the twelve-year-old neighbor. There was no going back. Alex groaned. Teddy was annoying at best and unbearable at worst.

"Not so fast," Cora said when Alex reached for the passenger door. She handed Alex the car keys.

"But the city? Can't we go to the Brooklyn Art Museum?" Alex cursed the mailperson who delivered her driver's permit. As if spending a second meager summer vacation trapped in a bright red Driver's Academy smart car with Mr. Allen and his onion breath, practicing parallel parking and signaling five pauses before a turn, wasn't punishment enough. The summer before she had failed the test by turning right from a far-left lane. Driving was not for her.

"We don't own a car. The subway is faster. What's the point of practicing?"

"Independence," was all Cora said.

Alex slipped into the driver's seat, pushed it back to accommodate her long legs, and adjusted the side mirrors.

"That's my girl. You'll thank me one day."

Now Alex wished she could. She wished she could re-live that day, right down to the barely air-conditioned lobby of the American Museum of Natural History—even Teddy's annoying tour of the Hall of Mammals where his high-pitched voice, breaking from both excitement and puberty, announced, "If you drive through Yellowstone Park with a shiny car, a bison will charge."

"Really? Why is that?" Cora feigned interest: her attention was already elsewhere, for good.

"They see their reflection and take it for another bison," Teddy explained.

"Well, that *is* interesting," Cora winked at Alex.

"So, if you go, muddy your car," Teddy concluded.

Alex rolled her eyes. "Be nice," Cora mouthed.

Alex was engrossed in a kaleidoscope of greens, reds, and oranges of the Amazon butterfly casement when a docent, undercover in her neatly ironed pink Oxford and Khakis, announced a family craft activity.

"Never too old to make a diorama." The woman smiled

broadly at their little group. The other option was to return home to their third-floor, un-air-conditioned Brooklyn Brownstone. Heat rises. Alex accepted the shoebox.

"Go crazy, kiddo!"

Alex and Teddy dug into the large tub filled with miniature plastic trees, bushes, elk, wolves, bighorn sheep, bears, and bison. There were twigs, pebbles, glitter for the streams, a spray to make snow, and little pieces of wood to create trails.

Alex spent hours combing through pieces of pebble, tiny conifers, and twigs from which she created an elaborate landscape in miniature. Inspired by the Yellowstone National Park Diorama of a bison at Old Faithful, she created a mini geyser—a fumarole. Alex recalled a school science experiment with baking soda and vinegar which at the time had seemed silly and remedial. Now she sheepishly asked the docent for these supplies. And, spurred by Alex's enthusiasm, the docent procured a box of baking soda from the janitor and a packet of vinegar from the cafeteria, which Alex used to create an explosion from the mouth of her little mud mound.

"Brilliant." Cora pointed at the glitter Alex used to convey a stream.

"Let's go," whined Teddy, who had long abandoned the activity. Cora hushed him and wearily shifted her weight from foot to foot—fatigued. "I've never seen her this focused."

Heaven was Cora gushing over Alex's little diorama the same way her schoolmates' parents beamed at their child's Spelling Bee medal. Something Alex would never win.

On their way home, Cora made a detour through Chinatown and double-parked the car in an alley behind an Art Supply Store. "Two minutes," she promised.

She returned with a large plastic shopping bag dangling from one hand and an oversized box cradled close to her chest.

That evening, Alex tore open Cora's gift and began constructing her first and last dollhouse.

Filled with awe over her daughter's emergent skill in creating dioramas, Cora took every opportunity to take her daughter to flea markets in search of tiny furniture and dolls. She taught Alex how to sew curtains and expertly handle the glue gun. Those six months were magical because Cora took a lot of time off from work. Alex remembered her mom's smile, her hands wrapped around a hot mug of tea, legs curled under her as she sat next to Alex on the floor, watching and listening to Alex show her every new detail of her magical house—a house she built for herself and her mother, a place of infinite space. And time. Six months later, cancer took Cora, and Alex was done with dollhouses.

Alex squeezed her eyes tight and willed herself back from Brooklyn to Bozeman.

She stood quickly and swayed. She had stayed too long. She needed to find Diana, before Diana found her here.

She tip-toed cautiously back out of Diana's snowy world, stopping briefly to pet the wolf's soft head. She brushed by trees and rubbed the pine needles between her fingers to take in the scent when, like a faulty fake Christmas tree, the branch detached and fell.

"No!" Alex exclaimed.

"Who's there?" A guard appeared at the entrance. Alex jumped behind a large exhibition crate. Diana would be none-too-pleased to find her messing with her diorama, and Alex could not upset her new mentor.

"Just me," Diana answered the guard and flipped on the diorama lights.

"Oh, no," Alex muttered under her breath. Being exposed was the last thing she needed. Hopefully, Diana would be quick, and Alex would not have to hide for long.

Alex peeked out at the brightly lit snowy tundra where, minutes ago, she had been standing next to the Yellowstone alpha female. Lit up and from a distance, the space was no longer a box filled with realistic props but the scene of a bright, still day, after a major storm, amid which, brazenly and boldly, stood a single white wolf.

She watched Diana step into the frame of her fantasy world of fir trees and streams, and Alex understood why Diana chose to work alone. This was a place where the world outside, with all its demands, ceased to exist. A place where no one dared to disturb her.

Diana turned her back, and Alex prepared to bolt when a sharply dressed, handsome man—a weathered man with eyes as deep and dark blue as the wolf's—appeared. Alex held her breath and squeezed her eyes closed. She did not want to witness Diana's assignation if that was what this was.

"Look, Pete, we've already spent the better part of my morning on the catalog of your photography for the show. Now I have real work to do." Diana pointed to the exit.

"You must have loved dollhouses as a kid," Pete stepped in, undeterred.

"Nope," Diana answered tersely, "A diorama is not an enlarged plaything. We will have your photographs hung exactly as you have already specified. No need to hang around."

Definitely not a lovers' quarrel, thought Alex.

"The wolves move in packs, Diana," he said, stroking the wolf's head.

"I'm expressing the vulnerable lone wolf exposed to the

poachers." Diana stepped before him as if to protect the wolf from a poacher.

Pete put his hands up like a naughty boy and stepped back. He paused to look around. Alex crouched down lower and hoped they could not hear her fast-beating heart.

"Diana," Pete patronized her, "everything changes when a wolf enters the Yellowstone ecosystem. The deer move to higher ground to escape the wolf; the over-grazed meadows regenerate; the willow trees grow back; the beavers build dams. It's a cascade effect. When the wolf arrives, there is change."

"Don't I know it? Now shoo."

"What's that?" Pete pointed at the tree stump covered in fake snow where Alex had sat moments before. Alex held her breath, hoping she had not left evidence of her transgression behind.

"It's an animatronic spy-cam, or what we affectionately call a crittercam," Diana sounded pleased.

"Enlighten me." Pete barely repressed a flash of anger.

"Surely, you've seen them. They're hidden cameras disguised as animals. Haven't you enjoyed Animal reality TV? Super cute. This one was made-to-order. It's a tree stump."

"Yes, I can see that."

"Oh, good! I wasn't sure if it was obvious. Can you tell it's a camera? The audience should know it's a hidden camera." Diana pointed to a tiny termite hole, a peephole on the side of the stump where the camera lens was propped. Alex prayed it was off.

"Are you seriously," Pete faltered, "intending to use that stupid contraption, that gimmick? You're an artist; surely you can see that it's destroying the scene. As a professional photographer," he took a deep breath, "I lie in wait. I would never use one of those things."

"Well, you're not lying anywhere in my diorama. This is a stage set for one—a wolf. This exhibition isn't about you."

"Really?" He frowned at Diana.

"The photographs you took of the wolves are a separate part of the exhibit. The Diorama is about wolves. No one—not you, or your telephoto lens, can get this close to a wolf. I want to see the wolf's underbelly."

"Some things are not meant to be seen," Pete said.

"Really? Tell that to the zoologists, the scientists." Diana patted the little tree stump and delivered her final punch. "This one is special, a recent innovation. Instead of video like the other animatronics, it shoots stills."

"The photographs in this exhibition, the ones I took, were not taken by a damn mechanical contraption."

"Really?" Diana pointed to his Nikon.

Pete was about to speak but held his tongue when Marta appeared with a tray of coffee and cookies.

"Saved by coffee. Thanks, Marta." Diana motioned for her to place the tray on the table next to the chair with Pete's Nikon.

"Come have coffee; we can discuss this later," Diana said. She helped herself to a cup of coffee from the tray. Marta poured a cup and handed it to Pete, who said, "What—no cream?" Marta startled.

"I was joking," he began, but Marta had already gone to retrieve the cream from the tray. He followed her to the tray and set his cup next to his camera so she could pour the cream.

"Not too much," he said, meeting her gaze. Marta's hand shook, and she spilled the cream.

"Watch the camera," Pete snapped. Marta turned and ran.

"Watch your tone with my employees, mister."

"What? She nearly—"

"You scared her."

"Yeah, I have that effect on women. Look, Diana, we're done here." He retrieved his camera and coat. "Ditch the crittercam."

"Or what?" Diana threw a handful of fake snow on the little mechanical stump. Pete stomped out, leaving Diana alone below an ominous shadow cast by an artificial tree in the path of an unsuspecting wolf.

Field Note

The museum is in the throes of mounting a large exhibition by a famous nature photographer. It's a great example of art being elevated to science by the mere context of the science museum. Photography is in a constant pas-de-deux between art and science, and today I got to hear an actual fight about it between the photographer and Diana. I couldn't have asked for a better ethnographic moment—only I wasn't supposed to be there, and I don't have a signed release to write about what I heard.

I love the history of photography. It begins with a tiny hole —like one a termite might have made in Diana's tree stump ... was it really a camera, or was Diana bluffing?

Anyway, a pinhole camera funnels light in a straight line through a little hole to relay an inverted reflection of the outside world. Pinholes are lots of fun to make and easy to use. Maybe I'll make one this weekend from my oatmeal drum and photograph the field.

The first pinhole cameras, or camera obscuras, were large round drums that looked like planetariums and were used to view eclipses by everyone from the fifth-century Chinese philosopher Mo-Ti to Aristotle and Leonardo da Vinci (who was dyslexic, by the way, or so they think). While they were an innovation of science, it wasn't long before artists found a use for them. The most famous is the Dutch painter Vermeer, of *Girl with a Pearl Earring* fame, who used it to project his subjects onto a canvas and traced and then painted the reflected image. Was he a cheat or a brilliant innovator?—jury's still out.

Photography got going (pun intended) when Edward Muybridge invented a way to freeze movement in sequences.

Muybridge's invention enabled humans to record dynamic events that had hitherto been too fast to capture, like the split-second change in the gait of a speeding horse.

Between 1878 and 1886, Muybridge lined up his cameras alongside a racehorse track; he attached parallel strings to the camera that the horse tripped as it passed. He created the first frozen frame of each step of a gallop.

The strings were messy and difficult to set up. Muybridge's innovation was soon surpassed by Étienne-Jules Marey's photographic gun—invented in 1882. With each shot of his chronophotographic gun, Marey, a bird watcher, captured 12 distinct images per second. Marey changed science by capturing the flights of fast-moving animals, insects, and birds.

Chapter Six

The night air bit at Alex's thighs as she headed across the slippery tundra-like field. It reminded her of skating across the outdoor ice rink at Rockefeller Center, minus the people and the buildings. Black tights did not cut the cold in Bozeman as they did in New York. At least she had a hat and gloves. She had anticipated a month of fall weather before she received her first paycheck. Montana, she now knew, was on a whole other schedule. Her imitation Uggs were already falling apart after a week. She slipped and slid to the restaurant, cursing herself for saving a few bucks by buying her duck boots online.

All around her, the field was silent, save for an occasional whistle of wind. The mountains were dark and stout, like trolls gathered in a circle, closing in and ready to pounce. In the distance, she could make out the big red barn that stood alone on the edge of town, far enough to feel isolated but close enough to be a popular hangout, especially for the museum workers who were only a short walk away.

A figure paused and turned toward Alex, waiting.

"Alex! Are you OK?" Alex was relieved to hear Diana's voice call out in the dark.

"Yeah," Alex called back. "Why?"

"You missed our meeting. I was worried."

"I emailed you. I got lost and ..." Alex stopped short of lying.

"Sorry, busy day, haven't checked email in hours. I'm glad you're OK." Diana studied Alex, concerned.

OK? Alex wanted to say that she was freezing and out of breath, and her glasses were fogged. Diana exuded comfort, warmth and fashion in her tall leather duck boots, long down coat, and stunning emerald-green scarf.

"Need to acclimate," Alex's teeth chattered.

"Take it." Diana unwrapped her scarf and wrapped it around Alex's neck. "And keep it. Looks better on you with those gorgeous honey-colored eyes."

"I couldn't," Alex blushed.

Diana opened the door, and Alex melted right into the warmth billowing out of the café.

The Back Barn was like an old English pub with comfortable velvet wing chairs and two large fireplaces. A sleek collection of metal-framed, large-format, black-and-white wildlife photographs adorned the walls. These were no cheap posters. They had both an edition number and a signature: original prints. Aura intact.

"Pete Holgan is the photographer—annoyingly impressive," Diana said. "Sit."

Alex obeyed and sank into the soft leather sofa in front of the fire. The waiter arrived with two deconstructed virgin blackberry juleps.

"This place is heaven," Alex said, accepting a drink. The cozy pub cum gallery was as much an upscale family place with parties of young, hip, outdoorsy parents, and their energetic children as it was a college bar or local art scene.

Soon, a crowd of young, eager museum interns colonized their cozy corner. A frazzled waiter brushed past and spilled the remains of a drink on Alex. He apologized and promised to return with napkins when Diana's friend Will, the local ranger, arrived in time to hand her a monogrammed handkerchief.

"How chivalrous; didn't know they still made these." Alex dabbed at her sticky wet arm.

"Better for the environment." Will flashed deep dimples and a five-o'clock shadow. He was more handsome than Alex recalled.

"Wasn't expecting you. What a nice surprise." Diana patted the space on the couch between her and Alex.

"Looking for a stray." Will declined to sit and instead scanned the room. His green eyes matched his Ranger uniform. He was tall and lean and possibly muscular under his heavy winter coat. And he carried cotton handkerchiefs and no gun.

"Was wondering why you were in uniform at this hour," Diana said. Alex knew little about rangers other than what she had seen on TV. She had no idea that being a ranger was a nine-to-five job; she assumed they were always on duty—just in case.

"My cue to leave," Will said when the jazz musicians started their warm-up.

"Don't like jazz?"

"Love jazz, don't like . . ." Will's voice trailed off; his gaze moved to the door, through which the handsome photographer had just entered.

Pete Holgan was accompanied by a slim woman with large brown eyes and saucer-like eyelids that were dusted with shimmery bronze eyeshadow. Inches of thin gold bangles jingled up her arm as she shimmied out of her cashmere coat and brushed back her long black hair. She wore a thick gold wedding band.

"Oh, hell, I forgot about him." If Diana were a cat, her hair would have stood straight up. "Assuming that's your stray?" Diana asked Will.

"Drinks were not on Pete's itinerary," Will assured Diana.

"Neither was the museum this afternoon. No one warned me he was in town. He showed up unannounced."

"Not my monkey, not my circus," Will answered.

The dirty glasses on the waitress's tray shook, "Pete Holgan! He, like, single-handedly saved the wolves," she gushed.

Diana rolled her eyes, "Oh please."

"I'm off," Will said.

"Didn't you just say you loved jazz?" Alex projected over the music.

"Don't like crowds," Will answered.

"Crowds or not, you better be at my opening," Diana told him.

"OK, I'll come if she's coming," Will smiled at Alex.

"Alex is my mentee; she has to come."

"Really? OK, if she's not one of the museum's attempts to bring *culture* to Bozeman with their Anarpour fellowship."

"Why is that?" Alex asked, her cheeks burned.

"Wannabe artists leave unproductive lives elsewhere to flock here and freeload off our generous donor. This year, there's a paleo poet," Will laughed.

Alex's face burned hotter.

"Maybe he's good. Aren't you being a little harsh?" Alex gritted her teeth. She hated any kind of confrontation. She would be the first to agree with Will about the ridiculous paleo poet, but she knew her dollhouse project was next. Luckily, she was saved by a rush of excitement as Pete approached and ordered the waiter to bring everyone another round, "On me."

"No, thanks," Will said. "I am only here to remind you about tomorrow. Early start. And turn on your darn phone. I've been calling you all night."

"Will," Pete's beautiful companion pecked Will on the cheek. "When did you arrive?" she asked.

"Just leaving," Will said.

The band announced a break.

"I'll walk you to the door," the woman threaded her arm through Will's and led him away.

"Wait," Will turned back to Alex, "Diana says you have not been to the park? We'll be at the post-office near the Norris trail tomorrow morning, eight sharp, if you want to join us." He smiled and left.

Diana winked at Alex. "Cute, huh?"

"Not my type." Alex feigned indifference. "So, he's a Park Ranger?"

"You're curious?"

"Not my type," Alex sipped from her empty glass.

"And therein, anthropologist, lies the problem with types."

"Touché."

"Ever heard the story about the tiger hunt?" Pete took advantage of the band's break to hold court.

"No?"

"Jasmine," Pete called to his date, who was returning after seeing Will out, "Storytime."

"Jasmine?" Alex asked. *That* Jasmine Anarpour, donor of

61

rugs and fellowships? Pete had begun his story. Alex would have to wait to ask Jasmine about the rug she gave to Marta.

"This tale is of a Chinese villager, high in the mountains, who goes off to hunt a tiger."

Every detail from the animal's piercing eyes to each stripe on the lean, muscular tiger's body came alive as Pete performed his story.

"The villager deftly advances on the beautiful, endangered animal. And ...," Pete paused for dramatic effect, "Right when we expect him to shoot...he unsheathes—not a gun but a camera." Pete brought his story home to wild applause.

"Brilliant," exclaimed the waitress who had lingered, tray-in-hand, to listen.

"Cameras shoot to save." Pete smiled broadly at his audience and rested his eyes on Alex, studying her reaction. He knew that he had unsettled her. Photographers were, after all, experts in faces.

"It's a happy story," Pete informed her.

"Cameras don't always shoot to save." Alex was annoyed to be singled out.

Pete smiled. A good anthropologist hides in the background, watching, waiting, and observing. A good anthropologist blends in and makes herself a fly on the wall. The best observers disappear as they remain watching. An anthropologist is a human camera. But, tonight, things were not as they appeared.

"How so?" Diana reached for the peanuts.

"Huh?"

"Cameras, not shooting to save?"

"Nothing," Alex muttered.

"Do elaborate," Jasmine said, her voice thick, deep, and heavily accented.

"It's nothing. It reminds me of Marey's chronophotographic gun," Alex explained.

"What's that?" the waitress asked.

"It was a revolver rigged with photographic plates; in place of bullets it shot images," Pete answered. "Ten or twelve images per second, is that correct?" Pete asked Alex.

"Wow, how?" Diana was impressed.

"It used a metal shutter. It was the first moving-image camera," Alex told them.

"You know a lot about cameras," Jasmine mused.

"I'm doing a Ph.D. in visual anthropology. We study the history of documentary."

"Hmm," Jasmine purred.

"Photography began out of the barrel of a gun back in the 1880s. Hence the term 'shooting film.'" Alex was aware that she was being tested.

"How interesting." Jasmine stood, leaned over Pete, whispered something in his ear, and pecked him on the cheek. Then she swiftly said, "Good night," and was gone before Alex could properly introduce herself.

"Time for bed," Alex swiftly gathered her coat and gloves, hoping to catch Jasmine.

"Shall I walk you?" Pete stood.

"Diana?" Alex asked Diana hopefully, but Diana waved her off, "The night is young, my dear."

"Those Uggs are more slipper than boot," Pete said to Alex's back. She ignored him, quickly put on her coat, and went outside.

"You might need a little help." Pete followed her out. She turned to look at him.

Was he the kind of man who would lay down his coat for a woman to cross a puddle? Or the kind who would help an Ugg-wearing anthropologist across the ice if it would lead to her bed?

"No, thanks; I'm right around the corner." Alex slipped on her gloves, gave him a little wave, and headed out onto the lightly snow-covered street.

"The blue cabin? You rented it from the museum?" he called after her.

"You're no stranger to these parts?" Alex turned to see if he was following her. "The cabin came with my fellowship."

"And you came alone? Lucky girl, having that whole cabin all to yourself." Pete crossed the street and walked toward her.

"Yup." Alex took a step back. Her heart raced.

"Be careful," Pete said, "They say the museum cabins are haunted by an angry tetradactyl." He laughed and marched right past her toward the closed museum and Marta's cabin, where a Yellowstone Ranger's Jeep was parked.

Field Note

Am I turning Marta into a fetish object by placing a model doll of her in a dollhouse?

Being aware of the subject/object divide is important in anthropology. We allow people their own agency by permitting them to speak for themselves, to represent their own emotions and histories and not to type, or stereotype, them. How can I make Marta the captain of her own fate? By giving her a voice.

Vox, voice, box; do not place my vox in a box.

Who says people with dyslexia can't rhyme? Initially, Cora didn't think I had dyslexia because I could finish the sentence in a Dr. Seuss book as she read it aloud to me when I was a toddler.

I love rhyming, I love Latin. I can rhyme, but I cannot, for the life of me, conjugate a Latin verb. Latin still helps me with my dyslexia—when I can play with it and not worry about getting the details right.

Allow Marta to narrate her own story. Now, if she'd only speak!

What's the difference between my little dollhouse models

and model houses you can walk into, like the Tinsley House? Does walking in give one more autonomy, authority, and agency?

No, even the Tinsley House turns you into a voyeur or, worse, an object. It affords no more sense of stepping into someone else's shoes than a dollhouse does. You don't become someone else by wearing their clothes and pretending to bake in their oven. Even AI fails there. No VR goggle is going to allow you to truly experience another person's reality. Can we ever truly experience another person's reality? Especially if it were so long ago? So very different from our own?

The point of the Nutshells is to allow the viewer to get a bird's-eye view of another person's life, to be a fly on the wall observing the probable past.

The original Nutshells, Glessner Lee's, allowed detectives to see more than what happened (dead body on floor) but what might have happened (live body being strangled and thrown to the floor).

Like neorealist films, which are not pure documentary but scripted to show what has the possibility of existing and not just what does exist, anthropologists edit the script. See, Zora was more honest in writing plays. Nothing is devoid of fictional crumbs and musings. Memory is never one hundred percent accurate. And, if you have my memory and handwriting, neither are field notes. And I can hardly dictate in front of my interviewees. And it's not always appropriate to record the interviews.

Anyway, the point is that a detective plays with the evidence in a Nutshell. They move people around: they place a doll so she is peering from around the corner, hiding behind a couch. They put them in places they could have been at the time of the murder based on the evidence from the investigation: interviews, clues, and other observations to help solve the case. Sort of like anthropology. There's a lot of guesswork, or what anthropologists call "cultural critique"—the conclusions we reach based on observations and fieldwork. Or what the very self-assured scientists would call a conclusion, but I don't believe in those; culture is fluid and ever-changing. Unlike archeologists, paleontologists, and detectives who examine the past and predict what happened, we social-cultural anthropologists catch people in the act, in the moment, and hope that we understand what we are seeing. Sometimes we deign to predict the future.

Looking is more than observing the other. It's about power and controlling the narrative. And, in this power dynamic, Marta is holding fast to the narrative; she has the upper hand and...she's hiding something.

Chapter Seven

The previous evening's snow had lightly dusted the gabled roof of the historic Yellowstone Park post-office—a building that resembled an oversized yellow Victorian dollhouse. Alex pulled into a barely plowed parking spot in front of the building and waited for Will. Was she late? It was unusual for her to arrive anywhere first. Maybe she had the wrong day? Or the wrong place. No one staffed the park entrance booth as she drove in. Nor had she seen a single car coming or going as she drove tentatively along the slippery park road.

She glanced at her watch and was about to leave when a

white Tesla Model X pulled in beside her car. Alex thought, *That vehicle is perfectly camouflaged for snowy terrain.* Had she driven past it?

Will emerged from the car and ambled over to greet her. "You made it!" Alex said.

Pete opened the passenger door of the Tesla and asked, "You invited company?"

"Good morning," Alex said tentatively, stepping out of her car.

"Can you believe she hasn't been in the park yet?" Will said to Pete, "I knew you wouldn't mind." Pete collected his gear, shut the door, and turned to Alex. "Where's your camera? Aren't you a photographer?"

"Not really." Alex slipped her cold hands into her jacket pockets. "My phone's my best camera these days," she added.

"Come on." Will chirped his car lock. "We'll start at the terraces." He pointed ahead to where the frozen landscape dimmed under a descending fog.

The smokey white steam from the fumaroles had already obscured the boundary of earth and sky when they arrived at the base of the terraces.

"Wow," Alex said, "It's like a giant, bubbly Zen fountain."

"Magmatic carbon dioxide reacting with limestone," Will explained, "When hot-spring fluids emerge from the subsurface into the pools on Mammoth terrace, pressure release causes them to de-gas--like opening a soda can. It drips down and forms these famous terraces. We call them Mammoth Hot Springs."

"What a backdrop," Pete said in a reverent hush. "Just stunning. All I do is click, and it's gorgeous."

"It's all about the machine," Alex commented under her breath. "One simply could not get a bad shot here even if they tried," she said, louder.

"Take your time; I'm going to show Alex the upper terraces," Will said to Pete, motioning for Alex to follow.

"Wait," Pete called after them, "Shouldn't you leave me with bear spray or something?"

"They're hibernating," Will shouted back. He and Alex laughed as they walked away.

"So much for being the big nature lover," Alex whispered to Will when they were out of earshot.

"If they're hibernating, why did we see carrion on the side of the road?" Pete yelled.

"The man notices everything," Will joked in a more muted voice. "There are plenty of other animals who don't hibernate. Including humans," Will called back to Pete whose camera was already glued to his face and pointed to where a fox emerged from the snow, a wisp of snow on her nose, red furry tail up.

"Hope he got his shot. That will be a good one," Alex said, and added, "He's a piece of work," She quickened her pace to keep up as Will loped effortlessly over the terrace path.

"Yeah, if it weren't for the wolves, I would not be out here in the freezing cold escorting him from one natural wonder to the next. His photographs make a difference. Thanks for keeping me company."

"Thanks for inviting me." Alex said.

She turned to join Will and slipped slightly. Will caught her elbow before she fell into a bath of boiling water.

"Stay on the boardwalk."

"Boardwalk?" Alex looked down and saw a hint of wood peek through the snow. "So this isn't a random slog through a geography of boiling pots—lids off, boundaries obscured, ready to boil whatever or whomever is unfortunate enough to fall in? There's a boardwalk."

"That's an extreme scenario."

"Is it?" Alex really did want to know. She changed the

subject. "Photography is powerful. It sways people, and they in turn sway politics."

"Montana needs a lot of swaying. Not everyone wants to conserve the Yellowstone wolf pack," Will said solemnly.

"Does Pete? Or are the wolves simply another pretty picture to be taken and sold?"

"I don't know. People do two kinds of projects here: they either shoot propaganda—not that that is a bad thing, especially if it aims to save the wolves—or they shoot documentaries."

"As long as they're not shooting each other," Alex half-joked, "And, sometimes, they're one and the same."

"How so?" Will asked.

"Well, documentary isn't so far off of propaganda; you have to try hard not to let your own subjectivity or an agenda intrude. It's about how we frame things. Sorry—I talk a lot when I'm nervous."

"You're nervous?" Will asked, moving closer, which only made her jitters worse.

"Bears," Alex white-lied.

"You never know," he laughed. "You might scare them off with all this academic chatter." Sensing Alex's discomfort, Will added, "I'm joking, please continue."

"Take Pete Holgan's book," Alex started, pausing to collect her thoughts before continuing, "It's called *Freeze Frame*. It's a pun. A photograph freezes a moment in time, forever as an image."

"Like those Mammoth mummies they found in the Antarctic, perfectly frozen baby mammoths, depicting one moment in time?" Will asked.

"A photograph is flat. But a Mammoth specimen is rife with layers of time, starting with food remnants in a stomach or a broken bone. We learn about its life as it moved through time, rather than one image in time. That one moment, its death, is preceded by loads of evidence of other moments which are not so evident in a photograph." Alex paused to catch her breath. "Unless it's an X-ray," Alex added thoughtfully. "Film is a different story because of movement," she continued.

"Moving images," Will offered.

"Exactly. The still image doesn't move like film does, at a rate of 24 frames per second."

"Wow, our brains process 24 photos consecutively in a second?" Will marveled.

"Yup. A photograph allows you to pause and contemplate the image before it moves right past you. A photograph embodies stillness. Something poses; it stops. Cinema is all about movement and speed—something passes; it moves—like a wolf."

"But the camera is a technical piece of equipment. It is a mechanical eye, no? It records exactly what it sees. Especially a good one," Will suggested.

"True, and often times, it sees things that we don't even remember being there." Like a person that we didn't notice in the background, Alex thought. But then, this came down less to memory than to attention. She would have to think more about this.

"I will say this: Pete is stellar at still and silent. Amazing focus," Will said.

He stopped suddenly, staring down intently at the snow.

"What is it?" Alex asked.

"Did you see anyone on the road when you were driving in this morning?"

"No. Why?" She looked around, confused.

Will straightened and took-off as close to a run as one could in a foot of snow. Alex tried to run after him but could not see past the heavy steam in the cold air. She was unsure how it was humanly possible for Will to keep that pace. Finally, she caught up to him at the end of the trail where he was again examining the snow.

"What is it?" she asked, out of breath.

"Footprints. Relatively fresh. Tourists never come this far into the park in the winter unless they are on snowshoes or cross-country skis. Haven't seen any tracks—car or otherwise, this morning."

"Oh."

"Wait here," Will said, "The trail gets trickier up ahead. I need to follow this trail to the end. Can't believe I missed the tracks."

"Two sets?" she asked, wiping off her glasses with the corner of her cuff. Between the steam from the nearby fumaroles and the humidity of the oncoming storm, it was nearly impossible to keep her lenses clear.

"I hope so. Survival would be twice as likely. No one wants to find a lone hiker cooking in a boiling soup of death. I'd better hurry to catch these hikers before they freeze. Start heading down; I'll catch-up," Will said and left.

Alex wiggled her frozen toes. It was already too late for her, new duck boots or not. She navigated the path slowly and carefully, walking on feet that felt like wood pegs. The sky darkened, and the impenetrable fog obscured her path back to her car. She bumped into a guardrail and was thankful to be saved from falling into a fumarole. She slid her gloved hand along the rail to guide her through the fog and down to the last terrace, where she paused to catch her breath. The air was thick with sulfur and lightly falling snow. She wrapped her scarf around her nose and mouth and surveyed the misty world below. She could just make out Pete who was back at the car and looked like he was rummaging through Will's backpack. Whatever for?

"Hey," Will emerged from the fog and startled Alex. "You noticed it too?" His handsome jawline tensed.

Alex was about to mention Pete's snooping when Will said, "I was halfway up the Norris Trail when I saw the two prints were going in different directions from the same feet. The hiker has been up and back. Come and gone."

"Thank goodness," Alex said, relieved. Somehow the moment to mention Pete had passed.

They made their way down the terraces to Pete, who was right where they had left him. Had she imagined him at the car going through Will's pack?

"He's a calm one," Alex whispered to Will, "To be staring out at nothing as a storm tiptoed up behind him."

"Pete!" Will shouted, startling Pete.

"Bundle of nerves if you ask me," Will told Alex and smiled.

"What the...?" Pete asked.

"Better get a move on if we're going to find the wolves. Looks like snow."

"What else is new?" Pete asked and put away his camera.

"Climate change." Will motioned for them to follow him back to the cars.

"Don't Kamran Anarpour and his minions, or millions, have the climate under control? By the way, speaking of Kamran, I am staying for the opening."

"What about your project in the park? I thought you were on a tight deadline. I re-arranged my schedule to bring you back to the park next week."

"Well, now you have time off," Pete flashed his public smile and walked ahead to the car.

"Come with us," Will said to Alex, "We are off to find the cubs. We'll take my car and come back for yours. The roads further into the park are difficult to navigate in the winter unless you are familiar with them."

After half a mile of slipping and sliding along a fire road,

Will pulled the car over onto the shoulder and yanked the emergency brake. "If we are going to see the cubs today, this will be the place," Will said, exiting the car.

"He knows this place blind," Pete told Alex as they watched Will swiftly and expertly wind his way into the wild.

"What's out there?" Alex asked, reluctant to leave the warm car.

"A small stream cuts through the frozen brush. Can't see it, must feel it." Pete said. He changed his lens quickly and expertly, grabbed his camera bag. "I'm off," he said and left to join Will.

Alex stayed in the car with the heat on. She watched Will and Pete follow the ribbon of thin ice barely visible under the frosting of fast-falling snow. They moved like Butoh dancers, fearlessly feeling their way through the thickening air. One misstep and they would be knee-deep in the freezing-cold Yellowstone River.

The men advanced into the mist while Alex did some exploring of her own. Since the guys had their backs turned to the car, Alex reached for Will's backpack, unzipped it, and peeked inside. There were headlamps, maps, snack bars well past their expiration date, four aluminum packages of electrolyte gel, a small first-aid kit, three battery packs, and bear spray. She zipped it up and placed it back where she'd found it. Had Pete taken what he was looking for, or didn't he find what he was after? Should she mention it to Will?

Field Note

Does Pete get the perfect shot or does he touch up his photos? Watching Pete shoot has me thinking about Sergei Eisenstein's concept of montage—juxtaposing visual images and layering sound and rhythm. Eisenstein pulled on all the senses: sound, timing (a heartbeat), juxtapositions, dialogue, and symbolism to elicit fear, happiness, patriotism, and love. He was a master at editing and introduced the world to the idea that, when two disparate elements, or images with their own individual meaning are brought together, they create a third meaning. He learned this as an advertiser practicing the art of collage.

He knew the power of an image and understood even in the 1920's with rudimentary cameras and editing equipment how easily it could be manipulated. The Soviet social-realist film-makers were lifting images from their original contexts, manipulating, altering, and fabricating fake news, or what they called propaganda, well before Photoshop was even invented.

I've been thinking about my research design and how I'm going to pull this whole thing off. An Anthropologist arrives, looks, listens, and analyzes her observations, what she thinks is going on, (her analysis) and then she "writes-up." We include the bits of information that support our argument and leave out what does not—it's no different from editing film. So can't ethnography just as easily be faked? Oh, many an anthropologist has been accused of doing just that. Anyway, I don't want to make a film as a final product. It's not that I prefer still photography or moving images necessarily. I think they can both be just as easily adulterated as propaganda or used as anthropological material. A documentary film would be much easier to pass off with my PhD committee than a dollhouse. But there's something about the dollhouse and creating it from scratch that makes it feel more real. The surrealists understood that the further one stepped away from reality the closer one got to it. Maybe that's why I prefer fiction to textbooks. Anyway, I digress.

I do love photography as a method of ethnography. Photography as a tool helps us remember. It's like recording interviews. But for me it's less about memory and more about focus. I tend to hyper-focus on just one aspect of a scene; a photo freezes the action so I can focus on details that otherwise move too quickly for me to notice.

It's like what Walter Benjamin says when he talks about viewing a painting versus watching a film. The painting allows us to hyper-focus or meditate on one moment because it is not moving.

And this is exactly what the nutshells offer. A moment to slow down time, to move time to our own pace, to meditate on murder.

Take Degas' dancer: the painting freezes her in a pose that allows us to admire her lines, her grace, the colors of the scene. We can embody the moment. Whereas in a film she would be moving too fast to appreciate each gesture. Unless of course she is in a very, very slow French art-house film where you think you're watching a still shot until you see a leaf just barely, ever so gently, move by an invisible breeze. Yes, photography, film that I can pause or rewind and rewatch, or slow down, helps me see the things that are happening around the edge of where my mind had previously decided to focus. But that's only after the fact, when watching a moment that has passed and already become a digital archive. Photography cannot aid me in the moment. It failed me when I was interviewing an Iranian filmmaker as her minder listened in the background. I didn't notice him until months later...when I had heard what happened to her, and re-watched the footage. Her back was to him, I was facing him. I should have noticed. Hyper-focus is my ADHD superpower that allows me to focus on one thing so intensely that everything else recedes in the background. It's great for writing notes, for studying, but not so helpful otherwise. What am I missing in the background???

Chapter Eight

Alex finished spraying the edges of Marta's dollhouse cabin with faux snow, set down the spray gun, and nearly jumped out of her skin with fright.

"I'm not that scary, am I?" Will asked, standing over her. "I called out—you didn't hear me," he gestured toward her headphones. "I was worried."

Alex pushed her headphones off. "How did you get in here?"

"Your door was open."

"Open or unlocked?"

"Open."

"Really?" She stood up and ran downstairs.

"I closed it," Will called after her. He followed her to the front door, where she stood, looking around wildly.

"I swear I closed it," Alex said, checking for her laptop. "Nothing was stolen."

"Maybe it blew open?"

"I locked it; I always do." Was he lying or had she really been that careless? Or had someone... she did not finish her thought.

"Ready to go?"

"Yes," Alex lied. She had forgotten Will's invitation to brunch. Alex took her jacket from the rack and slid on her duck boots. She patted her pockets, "Testicles, spectacles..." Alex incanted an old New York joke as she opened the door.

"What?" Will laughed.

"Oh, it's something to help me remember things as I walk out the door."

"What kind of things?" Will gave her a sideways glance.

"You know ... remember to take the keys."

"You're a good candidate for a smart lock."

"Yeah, if I were any better at remembering numbers. Keys are easier." Alex went back inside the house for her keys.

"Don't forget your spectacles."

"Or my testicles." She came back out and locked the door, "Let's go. Where are you taking me anyway?"

"Feast, a culinary delight, nestled in the mansion mile in the hills right outside of town."

"Never noticed a restaurant out there," Alex said, trying to remember if she had seen one the last time she drove out that way for a walk.

"It looks like a stray mansion if you miss the discrete restaurant sign," Will told her.

. . .

81

The maître d' at Feast personally ushered them to the front of the line. "Usual spot, Will?"

"Something more private today, Xav," Will answered.

The man pointed to a small table by a large bay window. "We have many reservations for brunch ... it's not very..."

"That's perfect, Xav," Will said.

"Of course," Xav said, motioning for Will and Alex to follow.

"Miss," Xav said, pulling out a chair for her.

"Fancy," Alex remarked after the maître d' had seated them. "You should have warned me."

She pulled a book out of her large bag and handed it to Will.

He was about to open *The Nutshell Murders* when the waiter appeared and placed two large menus on the table. Will declined his menu. "The usual, times two." Will said.

The man nodded at Will and turned to Alex, "To drink, Madam?"

"Oh, I get to choose for myself?" Alex half smiled at Will.

"The Spinach Benedicts are to die for." Will explained, "She'll have real eggs."

Alex examined the meticulous menu and the astronomical prices and added, "And a virgin peach mimosa."

The waiter left with their order, and Will moved the place settings to make room for the gallery guide. He opened it and paged through it while Alex described her project.

"Imagine every mundane detail of a murder scene in miniature: a sock falling off a foot, saliva on the corner of a dead mouth, unraked leaves at a front door, paw prints leading away from the side door. Imagine tiny pill jars lining a medicine cabinet or little dirty undies in a hamper. And every object is hand-made to scale."

"She made all those tiny objects?" Will asked, studying the miniature houses. "Impressive."

"She didn't. She hired a carpenter to make everything, including the house. She could afford to. She was Chicago elite; we are talking enormous wealth."

"She outsourced?"

"Yeah, with very exact instructions. She once asked for a rocking chair to rock at the same angle as the one on which it was modeled. Imagine counting out the rhythm of a miniature rocking chair. Or, in the case of a murder investigation, the exact number of steps made by a man's size-eight shoe from the door to the fridge?"

"Murder?"

"I know. It's a little creepy—and there's the risk of life imitating art."

"Is there?"

"No, but...if one were superstitious. My project is obviously not inspired by murder but by the houses, the process."

"One would hope," Will laughed. His phone beeped and he took a quick look before slipping it back into his pocket.

"Anthropology could use a more multi-modal approach. We've done film and text, and paleontologists have done great work with dioramas. Why shouldn't we cultural anthropologists use a more creative and visual approach?"

"And Bozeman?" he asked.

"Hmm," is all Alex said.

"So, really, why Bozeman of all places?"

Money, Alex wanted to admit: *I'm a freeloader.* Bozeman was a last-ditch effort to stay in the game, which is why Will's comment at the Back Barn about the fellowship program being a scam hurt—because it was true. Lesson one in economic anthropology: economics + desperation + training = interesting research project, Alex hoped. If academics were not constantly shifting their project descriptions to meet the criteria for any given pool of money, they would never get funded. Mostly they ended up doing what they wanted to do anyway. But Bozeman was a world away from Alex's original project on feminist filmmakers at risk. Alex studied artistic freedom in despotic regimes. Anthropology was becoming an autocratic country. Rather than explain all this to Will, she said, "Bozeman is in a moment of transition; it's a perfect petri dish for an anthropologist. Cowboys hanging with techies. Do you have a gun?" Alex slipped in her question.

"What?"

"Don't rangers carry weapons?"

"I have a taser for bears and wild animals."

"Humans included?"

"Judging from your anti-gun-violence keychain in the little bowl by the front door, you're not a fan?"

"My keychain? You were looking in my bowl?"

"Thought you'd appreciate my material-culture skills. Paying attention to objects."

"Funny."

The waiter arrived with two glass bowls filled with two beautifully poached eggs floating in a soup of hollandaise sauce and covered with a layer of perfectly steamed spinach.

"So, Bozeman?" Will gestured for her to continue.

"I'm tracking recent urban growth in Bozeman through individual life histories of migration. I interview new arrivals at their home, take notes on their living environments ... you know, look around and ask them about their things, workspaces, and their daily activities. I observe, listen, and then I make this model of their life. The fieldwork part is traditional anthropology, but instead of creating a textual ethnography with my data, I am making 3D models."

"Picture-worth-1,000-words type thing?" Will articulated through a mouthful of spinach.

"More than that. The person I'm studying can come and look at the model and tell me if I got it right."

"To what end?" Will asked looking up from his bowl. A light blush crossed his cheeks and he quickly added, "Sorry, I'm keeping you from eating with all my questions. Please, eat."

Alex took a small bite of spinach and put down her fork and said, "Ethnography."

"Isn't an ethnography a written description of a people, a culture?" Will asked.

"Yes, look at you! You're up on your sociocultural anthropology."

"I've read an ethnography or two. How's the food?"

"Heavenly." She sipped her mimosa, wrinkled her nose, and said, "The worst part is, in the end, I will still have to write-up a report of sorts—a critique, an analysis. No way is Columbia University going to accept a dollhouse in lieu of a 300-page dissertation."

"Carpentry is serious work. How many houses are you planning on doing?"

Alex mopped-up the last of her hollandaise sauce with a piece of freshly baked sourdough bread. How could she admit that, after Marta, there were no other prospects—yet? She should have studied the immigration and gentrification numbers before she chose Bozeman. So far, Alex had encountered ski tourists and college students, but very few immigrants. Diana had offered herself as the next subject, on the basis that she was the sole East Coast Jew for miles. But she had been in Bozeman too many years to count as a recent resident. Diana was as local as it got.

"So why did this woman do murder dollhouses? I still don't get it," Will asked.

"Frances Glessner Lee was desperate to go to medical school at Harvard, which wasn't an option for women in the 'thirties—not even wealthy elite ones." Alex toyed with a last crust of bread, "Anyway, Frances did not let the unfairness of F students at Harvard getting the jobs as coroners get in her way."

"This bothered her? Who wants to be a coroner?" Will was amused.

"As fate would have it, which, by the way, is the only way women get ahead—"

"Says the superstitious anthropologist. Go on."

"She got sick and landed at the same posh convalescent home as a family friend who happened to be a famous medical examiner. They sat together for hours while he regaled her with all sorts of tales from the medical-exam rooms and inquests. He shared his frustration with the inadequacies of the criminal-justice system and explained how necessary it was to show the jury the actual crime scene. Or at least something more useful than a drawing or a photograph." Alex paused and with a far-off look added, "Like armchair anthropology; ethnographies take readers to places they may otherwise never see."

"I like that," Will met her eyes, and she blushed.

"Frances suggested, instead of taking the jury to the crime scenes, that they bring the crime scenes to the jury."

"Hence the dollhouses. Brilliant."

"And... the detectives still working on a case could sit and stare at the scene and move people around while they deliberated. They could see multiple rooms at once, which helped create a timeline of events and alibis."

"Like a man in the kitchen getting a glass of water while someone plunged a knife into his wife's back in the upstairs bedroom?" Will joked. Alex frowned.

"Exactly. Unless you split a screen in a documentary, you

cannot show two things happening simultaneously. The doll-house solved this problem."

"Why not lay out the photographs on a timeline?" Will played the devil's advocate.

"They did, but the dollhouses were better. They were visceral."

"For you, too?"

"Photography is invasive and too easily posted to social media."

"Someone should tell Pete," Will said.

"The dollhouses are recreations rather than reproductions. They are more protective of the subject's privacy. The person is not as easily identified as a doll as they would be in a photograph," Alex explained.

Will waved the waiter over and ordered coffee and dessert. "The usual." Will nodded for Alex to continue.

"*Any* camera, moving or still, comes between people. Think of photo-journalists as doing a hit-and-run. There's no need to sit, talk, and get to know the other person. Or ask them about their dessert choice," Alex added and smiled. "Doing ethnography is like being in a long, dysfunctional marriage, whereas photography is over in a flash. Besides, video wouldn't do the trick anyway," Alex continued, "because you would need to shoot a ton of different scenarios with people and objects in different positions at different times. The dollhouses, on the other hand, slow down time and space, allowing you to inhabit the crime scene for as long as needed. The detective, or anthropologist, can move the players around like a chessboard."

"I play chess," Will offered. He nodded to the waiter, who placed a plate of multi-colored macaroons and a percolator of coffee and cream on the table. "So how is it like chess?" he asked, pouring the coffee.

"OK, imagine being able to put players where you know

they were and where they could have gone. Take the rook, for instance: it can only move up and down, side to side."

"Right," Will furrowed his brow as if looking at an imaginary chessboard.

"It's not static. It allows for *possible* moves, in addition to the moves people *actually* make."

"Smart."

"It's like neorealist films. They create reality rather than record it."

"What?"

"Sorry," Alex stopped. She sounded like a posturing Ivy league Ph.D. student trying to make an obscure theory plausible. She took a bite of a chewy lavender macaroon.

"Sorry for what?"

"Blabbering on..." Alex said, her mouth still sticky from the macaroon. How soon could she politely reach for another?

"Continue," Will encouraged her. Was he being polite? Or was he interested?

"It's important to be able to see how a social actor inhabits her space. What's possible? What *could* happen and not just what *does* happen. The neorealists created reality with their scripted scenarios. They had no interest in replicating reality. In a documentary film, everything would be a fait accompli. You couldn't move or change anything—you see and record exactly what is in front of you. But with the dollhouse you see what has the possibility to happen. The subject or the anthropologist can change the scenario."

"By moving the dolls," Will added.

"Exactly. You can move the figures around based on new information. Besides, objects are a good aid for intimacy."

"How so?"

"Well, for example, had I not seen or questioned Marta

about her rug, I would never have known that she received it from Jasmine."

Will raised an eyebrow. "Jasmine? That *is* interesting."

"There's a big difference in social relations between a gift versus a donation. So, which is it?"

"Well, Jasmine's not one to give away family heirlooms."

"You know her well?" Alex tried to sound casual.

"I'm glad you chose Bozeman," Will said, avoiding her question slipping the waiter his credit card.

* * *

Back home, Alex immediately called Kit. The call went straight to voicemail.

Kit texted back: *What's up? I'm in the archives; can't talk.*

Alex: *I think I just went on a date with the hot Ranger!*

Kit: *You mean you don't know?*

Alex: *He paid. Beautiful restaurant; the waiter held out the chair for me. And... he listened to me talk shop!*

Kit: *Nice. Meanwhile, they have me labeling masks... This is not why I am doing a PhD. Does everyone think that a fellow is free labor? This is supposed to be prestigious fellowship, I applied to do a small show of Togolese masks.*

Alex: *Stand up to them—that's what you would tell me to do.*

Kit: *Funny, I got the opposite advice from my mentor... Suck it up. You're lucky to have the fellowship. We all start on the bottom, etc., etc. Only that's not true. There's another fellow in South American Arts, and he is assisting a curatorial project.*

Alex: *The fellowship is supposed to help you develop your career skills... they're not even paying you. Isn't your funding coming from the Ford Foundation or the Woodrow Wilson?*

Kit: *I know... tell me more about the Ranger?*

Alex: *He's smart. But doesn't talk much about himself. Or maybe I didn't give him a chance to...*

Kit: *I'm sure there will be another chance?! Need to return to the masks.*

Alex: *Good luck. And tell them what they can do with their masks...*

Kit: *I have a few ideas actually...*

Field Note

It didn't take long after the inception of photography for people to start doubting what they were seeing. The power film once had to cause people to leave a cinema in fear of a train coming out of the screen and running them over was short-lived. At its inception, photography was embroiled in fakery. A famous example is the San Juan Hill footage of Teddy Roosevelt's charge. When the footage arrived from Cuba, it wasn't as dramatic as hoped, so they shot extra footage from a coffee-table book, complete with cigar smoke for battle scenes, to spice things up. Now, even with all we know about the ease with which we can alter images, fake news is consumed—hook, line, and sinker—without blinking an eye. We forget that entertainment is just as easily a lie.

Chapter Nine

Alex assumed the quiet museum was deserted until she walked into the staff kitchen and turned on the lights, startling Marta, who sat alone in the dark, sipping her tea.

"Sorry; didn't know anyone was in here." Alex should have guessed, given the strong scent of floral tea.

"It is Sunday." Marta stated. Her wispy bangs were arranged in a messy attempt to hide dark rings of sleeplessness around her tired eyes.

"I called you yesterday," Alex said. "I was worried about you. "You never called back."

"We have special exhibition; the museum it is busy," Marta replied.

"Yes, Pete Holgan's photography," Alex said.

"No. Diana's diorama is the special part. You work here today?" Marta asked.

"I need supplies," Alex explained.

Marta offered her a teabag and poured hot water into a glass and slid it over to Alex. The water was tepid. Marta had been sitting there a while.

"*PG Tips.*" Alex dipped her teabag in and out of the water. "Haven't seen these since England. Where did you find this in Bozeman?"

"Why Americans do this thing?" Marta asked, watching the tea bag bob up and down.

"What thing?" Alex looked up at her.

"Fussing so much with tea bag. Why so bad to leave bag for brewing?"

"Oh." Alex let go of the thin string. "Beautiful glasses," she changed the subject.

"I bring my own, I like glass for tea." Marta said off-handedly.

Crystal. Expensive, Alex thought. She rubbed her finger along the rim. It released a haunted note.

"Crystal, it is very fine. Too close to fire, and it will break," Marta warned her.

"I imagine so," Alex mused.

"I see the glass break by heat. Shattered by stones. I watch it smashed by fist. Cracked by metal rod." Marta seemed to know every way to break glass. Fire was Alex's favorite.

"Where?" Alex caught Marta's eye. Surviving ones past did not cure one of it.

"Glass blower on the Broadway. The tourists, they watch."

Marta looked away; this was a bad memory that had nothing to do with the glass blower on Broadway.

"Hello," David surprised the women. "Teatime?" His voice was gentle. He took a mug.

Marta studied the paleo poet, David, as he poured himself a cup of tea. In his corduroy pants and wool blazer, David reminded Alex of the scrawny writers who hung out at the Hungarian Pastry Shop near Columbia.

"Nice jacket," Alex said to David.

"Thanks," he said tentatively.

"It is like the ones of my father's students," Marta offered.

"Your father was a teacher?" Given that David was dressed like an overgrown prep-school kid, Alex ventured, "High school?"

"Men. They wear the wool sweaters under the jacket. For the cold weather," Marta explained. She wore a far-off look. "I watch the reading of the poems."

Alex imagined her in a place like the Nuyorican Poet's Café, where nodding heads emerged like dragons from the foggy smoke—back when people could still smoke indoors.

"Nice boys, they pretend I am not there."

"Does your dad still teach?" Alex asked.

Marta glared at Alex, "No, he does not breathe."

"I'm so sorry." Alex said, looking at David for help. "And your mother?" Alex asked carefully.

"She bakes the cakes, and she wraps the teapot in this..." Marta pointed at the teapot.

"Cozy," David offered, still standing tentatively, waiting to be released from the awkward conversation or invited to sit.

"Yes, cozy," Marta half smiled.

"For you?" Alex asked.

"For stupid boys. Interested only in politics. Persuading

people—talking, shouting. Poetry is better than politics," Marta concluded firmly.

Poetry could be political, Alex was tempted to say, but did not.

"My mother, she agrees with boys: poetry is useless and dangerous. My father, he does not agree. He says poetry saves everyone. Poetry kills him. Read to me your poem," Marta demanded. Dave looked for an escape.

"Read me poem. From heart. In my country..." Marta's voice trailed off. She always changed the subject when Alex asked about home. Alex wanted to ask: Where? How far? Did Marta's home still exist? Had it ever existed—this mythic country? Remnants must remain. Land and people did not fully disappear—no matter how hard an enemy tried to kill them off, change the borders, erase the history, or rename the country. A new line may have been drawn somewhere, a name changed, but a line and a name could not eradicate a place. There was a physical place on Earth where Marta came from—solid ground, soil. Alex was about to ask when Marta pre-empted her question.

"Poland?" asked Alex. She was sure that Marta had come from somewhere else prior to Poland. But Marta ignored her and said, "In my country, poet writes poem on his heart, how do you say this memory forever?"

"Memorize," Alex offered.

"Yes, he sees poem in memory of his eyes."

David cleared his throat. "Sorry, I'm a little nervous." He looked down, as if there were a paper to read from. Instead, he pulled at a loose thread on his cuff.

Marta stood swiftly, took a pair of scissors from the counter, and cut the little piece of loose yarn from David's shirt. She set down the scissors and said, "Poem, please."

David stared at his cuff as if examining a missing limb. He

cleared his throat and recited his poem, "Under the guise of a forensic moon, white and brittle and sharp they bloom ... a knee, an elbow, a neck extended like a loon...flying..."

"To moon?" Marta interrupted. Alex suppressed a laugh.

"What is this sharp and soft at same time?" Marta critiqued David.

"It's a poem about contradictions. You know, the laboratory light?" he implored.

"I work in museum; I know all lights." As if on cue the fluorescent lights flickered.

David continued, "The strong beam of light penetrates the skeleton, the bones; it washes them out, and they look like fragments of the moon. Imagine a pond, the shimmery face of—"

"Moon," Marta concluded with a faraway look. Aside from the bones and the moon, what else was in Marta's pained expression.

"Forensic anthropology," David explained.

"Yes, they are removing the bones from the graves," Marta agreed.

"Not just crimes scenes," David said.

"She's right." Alex said, "What you're describing is physical anthropology, paleontology, archeology—but forensic anthropology deals with crime scenes." No wonder Marta bristled when Alex mentioned anthropology. She was thinking forensics.

"Yes, well," David muttered.

The problem was not Marta's English but David's poetry.

"So, why archeology?" she asked David. She wanted to add, *And how is it you have a degree in Archi and know nothing about the other four fields of anthropology?*

He told them about growing-up in the Montana ski town of Big Sky where his parents were ski instructors. How the land around their house was teeming with fossils that David, who was homeschooled, spent hours collecting. When it came time to go to college David had no aptitude for the prerequisite subjects to study paleontology. Numbers were beyond his scope. From statistics to calculus, each subject failed him as he had failed them. So, he engaged paleontology like an unrequited love, from afar—as a poet. This fellowship was not a coup because of the money, but because, for the first time in his life, he was surrounded by his tribe. He loved paleontology with a passion.

"That's why I became an English major." David explained.

"My father tells students they must get hands messy. You know, stick them in the mud?" Marta said.

"I'm a stick in the mud," David agreed, sadly, resolutely.

"Yes. Stick yourself in the mud. You crawl into hole with bones," Marta demanded.

"Graves?"

"You feel flesh is gone; you understand?" Marta's voice cracked. She looked-up and caught Alex staring at her. Alex reluctantly looked away. Something about Marta conjured the Greek term *Alethia*: to reveal, while concealing. Between her long bangs and heavy make-up, Marta did not want to be seen. And yet a revelation of sorts was peeking out at Alex, if only she knew what it was. She desperately wanted to photograph her, but her instinct warned her not to. A photograph would allow her to stare at Marta for hours without being stared back at, without Marta knowing, or hiding.

Marta's phone alerted her to a text. She glanced at it briefly, took her jacket and bag and said, "Late for class."

Alex noted that she used a flip phone, so there was no chance of her storing photos there. How could someone live without an album, a memento?

"Class?" Alex asked, but Marta had already gone.

"Psychology," David said, "Community college."

Field Note

Marta caught me staring at her. I was outright staring at the woman. What is this strong urge to gaze? I regret not taking her photograph; it would have been much easier to study her without having her looking back. Though, according to Roland Barthes, the photograph returns the gaze; it looks back. Am I afraid of Marta looking back at me? Does some part of me fear her scrutiny?

Is staring at a photo any more moral than staring at the real person? Is this curiosity scientific in nature, or is there something I want from her, and to what end?

No wonder anthropologists have a bad rap. We are downright intrusive. Should we look away? No, that's not the answer. The answer is to spend an equal amount of time moralizing why we look and to what end, and—more important—HOW we look. It's a question of power, and where it's located. Are we taking, or giving?

Here we go again with the importance of locating power. I see power as silver matter that moves around... through objects, language, and, yes, the eyes, our very gaze. So, what's in a gaze?

Power. Frankly, it should be called the guilty gaze, because, when we look, we take. It all started with (you guessed it) the male gaze—a term coined by Feminist Film theorist Laura Mulvey. Only this time we're not giving the boys credit for something good. Mulvey argues that women become objects of the men who look at them. The more we de-humanize, the more we can subjugate. To observe is to take power. So much so that some Africans and Middle Easterners believed the camera stole their souls along with their images.

The Geneva conventions has a clause that protects civilians from having their images taken and projected, printed, and abused in war. Imagine, in war, taking a person's photograph is a crime—a human-rights violation. What about the war of everyday life? Ron Haviv, a seasoned war photographer came to speak to our visual anthropology seminar. He is famous for a picture of a soldier in the Balkans kicking the body of a dead (most likely Bosnian) woman, a civilian lying on the sidewalk. What disturbed me most about his visit was not the photograph, but what happened after. Right after taking the picture, he walked into a nearby bar and had a drink with those very soldiers. *That's war*, he implied.

Luc Delahey, another war photographer, photographed a dead man on the side of a road in Afghanistan with no clear indication as to whether the dead man was a civilian, soldier, or Taliban. An anthropologist asked Delahey at a public lecture at the Getty Center why he so blatantly disregarded the Geneva Conventions that protected the right of civilians and of the dead not to be photographed. His reply: "I don't care about morality. People can judge this in a hundred years."

But this wasn't a Robert Capa show being looked at years later, this was current events. War has elevated journalism's depictions of suffering into an art and, unlike Capa's photos, it is happening as the war wages on and when the victim's family and friends are still alive to see their loved ones—many of them innocent civilians in less-than-appropriate condition for viewing, especially by loved ones—reduced to a common curiosity. As Paul Virilio observes: battle changes the line of vision. Or, as Sontag says, "There is shame as well as shock in looking at the close-up of a real horror. Perhaps the only people with the right to look at images of suffering of this extreme order are those who could do something to alleviate it ... or those who could learn from it. The rest of us are voyeurs, whether we mean to be."

Chapter Ten

Downtown Bozeman was a cozy strip of cobblestone and quaint one-story shops including hiking outfitters, ski stores, chocolatiers, delis, the organic coop, the Bare Bones Café, and the Honey Hive, a shop dedicated solely to honey.

Alex entered the honey store and strolled through the sweet-smelling cocoon of octagonal shelves meant to mimic honeycomb, admiring—and desiring—everything from the beeswax candles to the Manuka honey, Sage honey, Honey pops, honey lip balm, honey cream, and creamed honey. The impeccable woodwork and exquisite scent of beeswax and clove shouted *expensive*. Unless the extra o on the Manuka honey tag was a misprint. People did not seriously pay $40 for two ounces of honey. The answer appeared in the form of a question: "No dollhouse for us?" purred Jasmine. Jasmine Anarpour was exactly the type to shell-out $40 for honey. She sniffed a beeswax candle and blocked the end of the aisle. The queen had returned to her hive.

"Oh, hi." Alex casually replaced the honey to the shelf.

"You made one for the cleaning lady."

"She told you?" Alex asked, surprised.

Jasmine ignored her questions and said, "I feel left out."

Alex doubted Jasmine ever felt left out.

"I'm an immigrant," Jasmine added for good measure, turning to walk to the cashier, and expecting Alex to follow.

"You've never seen my house." Jasmine dumped her goods on the counter and unwrapped a lollipop. She took a lick and said, "If you plan to be fair or what you social scientists call representational," she rolled her R, "then, you are going to have to do a mansion here and there."

Alex smiled tightly in response.

Jasmine took another lick. "Come around for tea." Jasmine smiled and handed the cashier her credit card.

"Sounds lovely," Alex answered politely.

"See you in half an hour."

"Today?" Alex panicked, her mind devoid of a ready excuse. It was too late, anyway; Jasmine had already collected her shopping and left the store.

As much as she wanted to ignore what was more a command than an invitation, Alex's curiosity got the better of her.

For one thing, how did Jasmine know about Marta's

Nutshell? No doubt she was on the Anarpour Foundation board and had read Alex's grant proposal.

"You buying that?" The cashier eyed Alex's lollipop. She handed her a dollar for it and turned to leave.

"Wait," the cashier called her back, "You're going to the Anarpours'? Can you take this? It came in for her, special order; I forgot all about it." She handed Alex a small parcel wrapped in plain brown tissue paper and sealed with a honeybee sticker.

Twenty minutes later Alex found herself in the new millionaire development on the edge of town, maneuvering her Subaru up the long and windy driveway to the Anarpour estate, where, like at an English countryside manor, the only place to park was right in front. Before she placed a toe out of her car, a young man appeared to take her keys.

"I'll have her back here when you leave, Miss," he assured her.

Alex walked up the flagstone steps, remembered the package from the honey store and turned to go back for it, when she heard Jasmine ask, "Leaving so soon? Come."

"I—" Alex stepped inside the hall of stained-glass panels. They reminded her of a narrow Oxford college chapel. Stunning. She forgot about the package.

"The foyer," Jasmine said and gestured toward the main house. "Kamran likes beautiful things." As if to demonstrate this fact, Jasmine gathered her thick dark hair and secured it at the nape of her neck with a Cloisonné butterfly clip.

Alex imagined an Anarpour dinner party in the stately dining room with its heavy pistachio-colored silk curtains. If she were the hostess, she would be nervously monitoring guests lest they spill on the gorgeous Persian rug. It rivaled the ones at the Metropolitan Museum. It was an unusual color, like the one in Marta's cabin. They must be a set. The separation of which made Jasmine's "gift" to Marta that much more perplexing.

"Did you know that there's a flaw in every single one of these?" Jasmine asked.

"Really?" Alex asked. Surely Jasmine didn't get a discount on defective rugs.

"Because only God is perfect," Jasmine explained.

"Oh," Alex said. Jasmine did not strike Alex as the spiritual type. She had a mature gravitas that lent her a more worldly and accomplished air, even though she must be close to Alex in age. Academia had a way of arresting development.

"In order to make this point about God's perfection, the weavers leave one hidden mistake that only they know is there. We are all flawed. Only God is perfect."

Jasmine led Alex to the kitchen. "This is where Persian women like to gather." It was outfitted like a culinary studio and had beautiful mossy green subway tiles that Alex wanted in a house of her own one day.

"Sorry it is not as tidy as usual, as you know our cleaning lady has been busy with other projects as of late."

Was Jasmine suggesting that Alex was taking up too much of Marta's time? Did Marta give up a side-job with the Anarpours for Alex? Diana had mentioned off-handedly that Marta spent a lot of time at the Anarpour estate. The implication being that she was seen coming and going more often than necessary for cleaning. Diana sounded as if she might want to spend a little more time at the Anarpour estate herself. In Marta's defense, it was an enormous place for one person to clean.

"She's efficient?"

"Do you mean does she do more than clean?" The mental chess had begun, and Jasmine was winning. Alex's face reddened. "You know little about my husband. His class does not stoop to sleep with a cleaning woman." She said coolly. "Besides," she continued, "he is sleeping with someone else." Jasmine smiled, "Don't look so shocked."

"I was told that she is here a lot." Alex stayed on course.

"Are you investigating or implying? Who told you that, anyway? Ranger Will? He's been seen at your place lately. I'm assuming he's not doing the cleaning?"

"He's not; we aren't." She did not owe Jasmine an explanation.

"Does that mean you're available?" Jasmine extended her arm for Alex's jacket, which Alex held tight to her chest.

"You cold? I can turn up the heat?" Jasmine offered.

"I'm great," Alex said and surrendered her jacket.

"Darjeeling or Persian?" Jasmine asked.

"Um," Alex looked perplexed.

"Tea, my dear. I believe I invited you for tea, no?"

"Never had Persian."

Jasmine laughed, "I bet not. Do you like Bergamot?"

"Not sure, I'm not much of a tea drinker." Alex flushed.

Jasmine leaned into Alex, "I'm wearing it. On my neck. Don't be afraid; come in close, it's subtle. Do you smell it? My ex-lover was mad for it. Something to do with a past life."

It was the scent of Marta's tea in the staff kitchen at the museum.

"Yes, that's great; Persian, please." Alex tugged at her sweater but kept it on. This was not the moment to take it off. Jasmine was braless in a loose black silk top and tight black yoga pants, which explained the ungodly heat.

Jasmine scooped the shiny black aromatic tea into the pot. The scent was stronger than Jasmine's perfume, which Alex guessed she purposely kept faint to lure people in closer.

"Marta and my husband?" Jasmine repeated and laughed again. Alex heard someone walking overhead. Did Kamran work from home? Jasmine poured the boiling water over the tea leaves, set a timer, and placed it and the teapot on a tray next to two delicate glasses.

"Come," she said to Alex and led her out of the kitchen.

Little rays of sun peeked through the clouds and warmed the large glass-covered veranda. Alex finally pulled off her sweater.

"A *Wintergarden*," Jasmine explained with a perfect German accent, pronouncing the W like a V.

The interior wall was papered in a soft salmon and teal butterfly motif that repeated in the customized cushions on the wicker chairs. Each corner of the room was guarded by a large leafy monstera, as if Jasmine had something against right angles. The effect was reminiscent of a nineteenth-century wintergarden where Charles Darwin might take tea.

"The orange plants are tropical milkweed. A big no-no. They mess-up the monarch migration. I keep the glass panels closed October through May to discourage them from lingering."

"It's pretty cold anyway?" Alex said, looking out at the snowy meadow beyond the house. Jasmine agreed.

"Gorgeous," Alex breathed.

"It is modeled on the Palm Café in Vienna, which is tucked into a nineteenth-century art-nouveau greenhouse and home to a butterfly pavilion." Jasmine said and motioned for Alex to sit.

"This must rival the real one." It certainly rivaled the butterfly diorama at the American Museum of Natural History in New York.

"That one has *a je ne sais quoi*. Replicas never rival the real. Don't you agree?" Alex imagined the delicate silk wings immobilized and pinned to fake branches and leaves. Enjoying its beauty made her feel complicit in the cruelty. Did dioramas need to use taxidermized animals? Marx—and Freud—would say yes; the aura was still there, irreplaceable.

"Precisely why my husband's affairs don't bother me. They're short, like the life cycle of a butterfly. Sometimes, they break the tedium. And they never rival the real thing," Jasmine smiled.

"Interesting," was all Alex could think to say. Thankfully the tea-timer rang, and Jasmine said, "Saved by the bell." She reached for the teapot. "In Iran we never pour tea into a cup where you cannot see the color. The color of the tea is every-thing. Do you like yours light or dark?" Jasmine poured the amber-colored tea into a glass cup the shape of a tulip.

"Medium?"

"Cute," Jasmine laughed.

"The butterflies were alive?" Alex asked.

"In the pavilion? Some were, some weren't. They glided about, landing on a head, a shoulder. And, for a patient person, a hand, if held it out long enough."

"Like the patience of a nature photographer."

"Subtle change of subject." Jasmine delicately sipped her tea and studied Alex.

"How so?" Alex set down her cup without drinking; it was too hot.

"Pete Holgan." Jasmine paused for effect. "You want to ask me if I am sleeping with him?"

Alex blinked, embarrassed.

"Now you look like you want to ask me how it was, or do you already know? I saw the way he eyed-you at the Back Barn."

"We didn't ..." Alex cringed at the reminder of Pete's sloppy flirtation.

"Why do people make such a big deal about photographers? Are they artists or merely mechanics? Don't let them fool you. They are not artists."

"I agree." Alex said carefully in case this was a trap.

"Will, on the other hand." Jasmine said and paused for effect. "—I'm joking. Alex, relax."

"When?" Alex asked inaudibly.

"Did I sleep with Pete?" Jasmine expertly changed course. She seemed genuinely sorry to have upset Alex. "Years ago, when he sold his first photo to Kamran. The one of the alpha wolf. When Kamran found out, he was livid. He took the photograph right off the wall and drove it straight to the museum and managed to get a tax write-off for his donation." Jasmine took another sip of her tea. "Let's not speak ill of the dead."

"Dead?"

"That poor wolf."

Jasmine pushed a plate of sweets toward Alex. "Halva, traditionally mourning sweets. We serve them at wakes. We eat them at graves," Her voice caught, "But I like them with my tea."

"For the wolf?"

"For the world. You know I took an anthropology course in undergrad? Loved it. It was refreshingly easy compared to my engineering classes. A nice break for the brain."

"It's funny," Alex was irritated; "every anthropology book about Persians mentions how polite they are."

"Anthropology books generalize. When my family won the green-card lottery, I thought I could finally study what I wanted. In Iran, you see, if you scored high on the college entrance exam, you were stuck in engineering. Americans are obsessed with a lack of women in STEM. In Iran, we were all stuck in STEM. Anyway, my parents were not having it. Thank God for the American electives; I got to take one anthropology class." She paused before continuing, "And I learned a lot about people."

"Really?"

"Yes. Like how to tell when they're out of their element. How to tell when they are snooping around in the guise of science."

"Snooping around?" Alex asked.

"No one mentioned dollhouses in the anthropology course I took. You study where?"

"One elective does not an expert make," Alex informed her.

"Enough to know you're missing a huge demographic by not including me," Jasmine reiterated.

"So, you lured me out here to show me how the other half lives?"

"Certainly not to offend you; my apologies, really." Jasmine retreated tactfully.

"Why *did* you invite me out here?" Alex's heart raced.

"Your dollhouse idea is interesting. It reminds me of Persian miniatures."

"The illuminated manuscripts?"

"You do like the Met. See, we have interests in common. Yes, like Shah Jahan's hunting scene. Much more vivid than Pete's silly storytelling. You would agree?" Jasmine smiled. "You see, one can enter the scene of a Persian miniature, like your dollhouses, from any angle and still not be on the same three-dimensional plane as the other characters. It's like mysticism; not everyone will exist on the same plane despite physically existing in the same scene."

"Right." Was Jasmine suggesting they would never be equals?

"We all have our Archimedean points. Time and space are not necessarily linear or monochronic. You know my favorite anthropology ritual?" Jasmine asked.

Alex shook her head. There was no point correcting Jasmine—telling her that anthropologists study rituals; they don't make them up.

"Marcel Maus's potlatch. What a great work of anthropology. You have read *The Gift*? Imagine. People burning their wealth to create equality in the community. Some days, I want to have a big bonfire and burn it all down. More tea?"

Field Note

Weird—I've never seen Kamran and Jasmine together. How easily she guilted me into being my next dollhouse subject. I never should have agreed. Guilt is quite the motivator. Guilt over my past fieldwork experience and being accused by Jasmine of not being representational. If she only knew about my debacle with the filmmaker. Besides, representational?! Seriously? It's impossible to represent every ethnicity, social class, age group, etc. How can one anthropologist achieve all this? And doesn't it take money to study the wealthy? To hang out like a fly on the wall of a castle demands gold trinkets at the very least. Can researchers be bought by wealth and power? Working on Jasmine's manor will be tricky enough, without the added burden of being accused of Orientalism.

What did Edward Said mean by "Orientalism" anyway? Know your author, Alex. Don't take an Ivy League professor's assigned text as the final authority.

Edward Said:

English Literature Professor at Columbia University. Deceased.

Seminal work: *Orientalism*, 1978. His book on colonial literature and culture birthed the field of post-colonial studies.

Orientalist: Back in the day, anyone who studied the Orient was called an Orientalist. While many Orientalists were philologists who loved their area of study, too many studied and documented the Orient to help their government dominate and subjugate the people in their colonies. The output of these "studies" in the eighteenth century, or what Said referred to as the "Western gaze," is not ethnography but fiction. And yet, it was still used as representational. Take the lascivious scene of a naked "oriental" woman at a bathhouse. No Muslim woman would have allowed herself to be the subject of that painting. But, as the West was ruling over and dominating the "orient" through colonialism, it behooved them to paint a picture of a docile and backward people.

Said defined Orientalism further by suggesting that the "orient" is not the physical space we think of as Asia, South Asia, or the Middle East but an idea—an invention of the European imagination. Why would they invent an idea of an "orient?" It was a device used to "orient" the West vis-à-vis the East and to differentiate the Orient and the Occident, the East and West, Them and Us.

Said was strongly influenced by French philosopher Michel Foucault, who insisted that power resides in discourse. In other words, the way a Westerner speaks (discourse) of the East or pictures it (represents it visually) can take power from the East and put it into the realm of the Westerner who speaks about/becomes the authority on the East.

A great example is French novelist Flaubert's encounter with an "oriental" woman in the harem. She never speaks for herself; she never represents her own emotions, and she certainly would not have approved of the lascivious harem paintings. Even though, as a European male, he was not allowed in the harem, and never spoke to a woman in the harem, Flaubert spoke for her through a fictional narrative he created. So, not only was she a product of his imagination, which often was mistaken for real ethnographic knowledge, but, in speaking for her, Flaubert took away her agency to speak for herself and turned her into a "type." In this case the stereotypical Moslem woman, hidden away from society, and, in effect, muted. By the way, stereo, in front of type, means it is amplified and multiplied... one person becomes representative of many. So, while he mutes her voice, he amplifies his projection of her. To typify is also to classify. Is there one kind of American? Then why should there be one kind of an Iranian? Was I stereotyping Jasmine to assume all Iranians use a tea timer?

I did a little reading on Iran (formerly known as Persia before 1935 when Hitler suggested a name change to honor the Caucasian, Aryan ancestry of Persia). It turns out that, during Flaubert's time, Persian women in the Harem were authoring their own texts (just as they were photographing their own lives). This flies in the face of documentary voice-overs by anthropologists who speak over their subjects—I digress. FYI— to the aspiring visual anthropologists: whether you're speaking for someone in a text, or speaking over them in a film, it's a bad idea!

*Must read: Qajar Princess Taj Al Sultana's memoir of her days in the harem.

Is orientalism a thing of the past? No. It is alive and well in the way we speak of or represent another culture: "Those backward..." The way we picture a culture. Like the four decades Americans only showed veiled Iranian woman (in turn helping the Iranian regime's visual landscape of power). Instead of showing the only woman to ever win the Mathematics Field's Prize—Iranian, by the way, born and raised. In short, not allowing a culture to speak for or picture itself in our media. Until, of course, those women tore off their veils.

Why bother? Will anthropology remain forever a part of the colonial project, or can it be a remedy? If we continue to speak for, represent, or use our findings to subjugate a population, then we continue the colonial project. But, if we learn the language and geography, hang-out, speak to locals, take footage but show it without commentary, accumulate data, analyze, synthesize, present as many "objective" perspectives as possible, and use the voices of the people we speak with, then there's a chance at a non-Orientalist representation. Whew. Take that, Jasmine!

Chapter Eleven

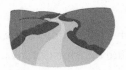

"What?" Alex asked her GPS as it directed her inside Yellowstone Park. She thought park concessions were closed for the season. Leave it to Diana to know about something no one else would. Diana promised Alex the best free spa experience in the world.

"It's a bring-your-own-towel kind of place," Diana had instructed. Which was fine by Alex, whose fellowship money did not stretch to spa days.

"Trust me," Diana had said. But could she?

Alex continued along the park road into the wild and empty expanse. Maybe the spa was an exclusive members-only place, hidden, like a bunker, in the side of a mountain? It was in-vogue to repurpose Cold-War remnants as nightclubs and cafes. What other explanation could there be? There was nothing but mountain and road ahead of her for miles. When the major left-hand turn appeared exactly where Diana said it would, Alex took it into a trailhead parking lot. She parked but kept the car running while she texted Diana. *I'm here. Where's the spa?* Diana was never late. But Alex often was. Had she gotten the wrong time?

She turned off the car and waited. *It's so quiet* she thought as she texted Kit: *If I disappear: last-known location, Yellowstone Park.*

Kit texted back: *Alone with the ranger?*

Alone, Alex was typing when a tap on her window startled her. A tall man whose face was obscured by a big black scarf had emerged from nowhere.

Pete Holgan swiftly unraveled his scarf and Alex rolled down her window.

"Either get out and let's go, or let me in, it's freezing," Pete said. "Assuming you are here for spa day?"

"Yes," Alex answered.

"Then let's go. We're late, they're probably already at the spot. It's a short hike," Pete opened her door. "Get out."

Alex emerged from the car and surveyed the empty parking lot. If the others were here, where were their cars? And how had Pete arrived?

"Diana invited you?" she asked Pete, doubtfully.

"Oddly, yes."

"How did you get here?"

"Friend dropped me."

A sharp cold wind hit her face and Alex bemoaned her clothing choice. She was barely dressed for the short walk up from the car to the entrance of a five-star spa, let alone a hike.

"Let's go," Pete said.

"Famous last words." Alex doubted Diana, the queen of temperature-controlled worlds, who rarely attended a nature setting that wasn't of her own making, had intended on coming.

"You'll warm-up once we get in the water," Pete promised.

"You've been here before?" Alex asked.

"Many, many times."

Alex was not reassured. For all she knew, he could be planning to throw her in a fumarole. To what end? New York instilled in her the idea that a lone man was a dangerous man. Pete was far too smart to try to pull off murder in broad daylight. Why are people murdered in the dark? Or are they? Surely not. Alex's mind raced.

Pete moved ahead effortlessly in his hiking boots, while Alex bumbled behind, careful not to slip on the snow-covered gravel.

"Diana didn't mention the dress code." Alex called to him.

"Ah, there is no dress code where we are headed."

"I'm freezing; this isn't funny."

"You'll be warm soon enough. You're my ride home; you can't ditch me, and I'm not leaving Yellowstone without a dip."

Alex caught-up to Pete who sat smugly on a snow-covered bench in front of a puddle passing for a hot spring.

"*This* is the hot springs?"

"Yes."

"It's barely a stream." She had imagined something less rugged and certainly less like a watering hole for a thirsty bison.

"It's the Yellowstone River hot springs. Ladies first." Pete unzipped his jacket and motioned for Alex to do the same.

"Where's Diana?"

"I have a pretty good guess."

Great!—he knew all along that she was not coming.

"Come on," Pete encouraged her.

"No way am I going in first."

"You're not dressed properly for any other activity here—clothes off, woman."

Alex reluctantly unzipped her jacket.

"These natural hot springs are popular among the summer workers who keep them a secret from the tourists. This makes you a local," Pete said, as if inducting her into a secret society. Did Marta come here? Pete peeled off his final layers—a long-sleeved wool shirt, jeans and socks and then tiptoed into the water's edge, before relinquishing his boxers.

"I can't do this." Alex called down from the ridge above him. She was still fully clothed and freezing.

"Just strip and jump in. It's lovely, warm—I promise." He was waist deep in the Yellowstone River. Steam rose around him as if he were the subject of one of his own prize-winning photographs. Alex was tempted to grab his clothes and run—anything to wipe the smug smile off his face.

"Turn around."

Pete obeyed and Alex swiftly disrobed.

She ambled down the ridge and then gingerly dipped a toe in the warm and inviting water. She explored the cushiony riverbed with her feet, taking one step and then another, until she was submerged to her chest.

"Mm. You were right I'm warmer in the water naked than onshore in all my winter clothes."

"Nice? Even Jasmine Anarpour prefers this to the ritzy spas in town," Pete said.

"Then why isn't she here with us?" Alex asked.

"Jasmine? Crowds aren't her scene."

"We are hardly a crowd."

"Anyone more than two is a crowd for her." Pete laughed. "We're just friends," he added.

The warm soft mud squeezed between Alex's toes and

lulled her further into the water until she finally gave way and submerged her whole body.

"Stop!" She heard Pete yell through the thin layer of water above her head. She darted up and out of the water and immediately understood his alarm. The air was like little icepicks needling at her scalp.

"Alex, quick, get out. You cannot expose a wet head in this temperature. You'll get hypothermia."

"Oh..." She was barely able to form words.

"Let's get your clothes on," Pete said calmly.

Alex shook from the cold and humiliation as Pete helped her up the ridge and to her clothes. He patted her down quickly and effectively with a small micro-fiber towel he had in his jacket pocket. When she was dry, he dressed her in his own wool shirt and hat.

"This is warmer." Pete wrapped her in his thick down jacket. It was like wearing a giant sleeping bag that smelled of musty cologne and cigars. The scent of maturity. A tinge of embarrassment shot through her; it was as sharp as her frozen fingertips. Pete dressed quickly and helped her to the car where he nestled her into the passenger seat.

"Heat's coming." Pete said. He slid into the driver's seat and turned on the ignition. "You'll be warm in no time; you're going to be OK," Pete assured her.

He backed the car out of the parking space and turned out of the lot and onto an unfamiliar road that led them out of the park.

When they reached the little town of Gardiner, Pete pulled up to the curb alongside a row of eateries and cafés. He put the car in park, and without cutting the ignition, he got out and bid Alex a hasty good-bye.

"Sorry," he apologized, "I'm late for a meeting." Then he disappeared into the Wonderland Café.

Alex slid over to the driver's seat. What just happened? Pete saved her and then ditched her. A hot chocolate wouldn't have gone amiss.

She had driven less than five minutes when Diana called.

"Come warm up here at Kamran's; you're less than a mile away."

* * *

The paved but snow-covered drive leading up to Kamran Anarpour's cabin was as ceremonious in its length and design as his estate in Bozeman. Only, the cabin was less ostentatious, and there was no one waiting to park her car.

Diana was waiting outside and waved her in. "Kamran, meet Alex; she's one of your fellows." Diana ushered her in.

"Pleased to meet you. Come in." Kamran leaned past Diana to shake Alex's hand. He was a handsome man with long lashes and mesmerizing dark-brown eyes. Kamran must make everyone feel a little bit out-of-breath.

"What cat dragged you down here in this weather?" Kamran asked.

"Diana," Alex said, frowning at Diana.

Kamran laughed and led the way into a large room with a bright orange Calder-like mobile and a blue and orange Mondrian-like carpet.

"I love this rug."

"It's a Gabbeh. Each rug tells the story of a Bakhtiari family; they are the tribe in southern Iran near Shiraz. They dye the rugs with a natural pigment, which is why they look a little faded. The little white dots symbolize flowers, and the brown ones are goats."

"They're lovely." Did Marta know what the dots symbolized? She never mentioned their meaning to Alex. Anthropology was all about interpreting symbols.

"Come sit," Kamran gestured to the sofa in front of the fireplace and excused himself to make coffee.

As soon as he left the room Alex teased Diana about "losing track of time" at his cabin.

"I'm working," Diana protested.

Kamran returned with three foamy cappuccinos. "Blue period." Kamran said, confirming that the small painting that caught Alex's eye was indeed an original Picasso.

"If I lived here, I'd never leave," Alex said, still studying the delicate drawing.

Kamran frowned, "I don't get down here enough. If it weren't for Diana making me a miniature diorama, I would not be here now," he winked at Diana.

"Like a dollhouse?" Alex asked.

"Oh no, much bigger. They don't call them Persian palaces for nothing," Diana laughed awkwardly.

"You find my idea cheesy?" Kamran teased.

"No. Come on, how many people commission a museum artist to make them a full-scale diorama?"

One who can afford to, Alex thought.

"A mini one," Kamran said.

"For that, you should commission Alex."

"Really?" Kamran evidently had not read her fellowship application. Nor had Jasmine mentioned the dollhouse she had all but commissioned.

"She's joking," Alex said.

"You see, this is all Jasmine's taste. It's her domain. Over the years she's become less interested in being in the park," Kamran told Alex. Which might explain why she gave away her rug.

"What I love about Diana's art is her cinematic lighting," Alex changed the subject.

"True. Creating stories from a million different moving images is nothing compared to the detailed story of a single frame, a single moment," Kamran agreed. Alex noted that he knew a lot about photography.

"Where or when have you seen my work?" Diana asked.

"Catalogues," Alex lied, "Of past shows."

"Diana doesn't replicate the light mechanically like a two-bit photographer—she creates it," Kamran asserted.

"My parents were devastated when I turned down film studies at the University of Chicago to come to Montana State. My father stared at me in disbelief, and my mother whimpered, 'Dioramist, is that a career?' 'Who do you think made all those big animal exhibits at the Field's Museum?' I asked her. She had herself to blame. After all, she was the one who dragged us there every weekend. Honestly, what did she expect?" Diana asked.

"It's like the parents who play their children Mozart in the womb but are then disappointed when their kid becomes a musician instead of a lawyer." Kamran said.

Why hadn't he and Jasmine had children?

"Or girls who play with dollhouses and then become dioramists." Alex regretted her joke.

Kamran's phone rang and he turned away to answer it.

"Of course, immediately. No, you're not," he said into his phone. He stood, gave them an apologetic look, and left the room.

"Sorry I left you alone with Pete. We got a little carried away over here." Diana smiled sheepishly.

"Pete was actually nice," Alex said.

"How's your work coming?" Diana changed the subject.

"Not great, honestly. How do you know when you're done with a diorama?"

"With a diorama? You just do." Diana said.

"Oh," Alex replied and took a sip of her coffee.

"Sorry," Diana said and added, "there's never a definitive answer, a sure sign of completion. My advice: if you're still wondering if you're done, then you're not. Something must be nagging at you; you've missed a detail."

"That's the problem. I feel I've missed every detail. How do you complete an incomplete picture?" Alex asked Diana.

"Ask any paleontologist—it's what they do all day: they put together little shards to tell a story."

"Yeah, but what if you don't have any little shards? What if there aren't any objects to place inside?" Alex asked, frustrated. She couldn't help thinking of Joseph Cornell's boxes that were all about the objects inside them.

"A diorama without objects. I'm intrigued. What's the situation?"

"Marta."

"Oh, yes. She's a tough nut to crack. But, then, maybe she wanted to clean up for the interview. She's house-proud when it comes to the museum."

"You mean hide everything? But where? Her place is a tiny studio. Imagine, no junk mail lying around. Not one family photo," Alex complained.

"Weird. She may have arrived here with nothing but the clothes on her back, but a photo doesn't take any space. It's been a year; we pay her well enough; she could have bought new things by now. That is odd. Did she give you a reason?"

Alex was embarrassed for not asking. She did not want to upset Marta or push her away.

"Wasn't up for chatting much, either." Alex admitted that much.

"She's been a little skittish lately. She's usually so friendly," Diana agreed.

"Where's she from anyway?"

"Krakow, maybe? Gdansk?" Diana suggested.

"That's specific enough. I should have taken a photo of her cabin."

"Photography is overrated." Diana insisted, and continued, "Look, Alex, when it comes to censorship, either the subject is the one holding the leaf to his genitals or it's hanging there defying gravity."

"What is that supposed to mean?" Alex chuckled at the vision.

"Models are complicit. They could refuse the fig leaf. You're an anthropologist, and Marta is a free agent; she's complicit in how you frame—" Kamran walked in, and Diana stopped abruptly.

"Sorry to interrupt," Kamran took a sweater that had been discarded casually on the couch. If the disarray of his cabin was anything to go by, Alex must have interrupted something. He pulled the sweater over his head and straightened his shoulders. "Diana. I'm sorry..."

"We need to head back to town?" Diana asked, standing.

"No."

Diana exhaled.

"Not us; *I* am needed. It's a work emergency. Stay. The weather forecast is horrendous."

"Horrendous?" Alex asked, alarmed.

"You're not planning to drive back in tonight's storm?" Diana gave away the fact that she was there to spend the night. "Who needs you on a stormy night? Aren't you the CEO? Can't you refuse? It's almost four o'clock." Diana's desperation was out of character.

"I am sorry; it's personal. I'll be back for a late dinner,"

Kamran promised, taking his coat from the rack. "You'll stay?" Kamran intoned diplomatically, "Join us for dinner." Alex knew this was *tarof*; she had read about it in an anthropology book on the linguistic habits of Iranians. *Tarof* was a ceremonial invitation the recipient knew not to accept. One need not understand the convention of *tarof* to see that Kamran was being polite. He wanted Alex to stay for dinner as badly as Diana wanted Pete to stay for her opening—which is to say, not at all.

Alex thanked him for the invitation and declined. As she reached for her coat at the door, Alex spotted a familiar blue cardigan hanging on the coat rack. Neither Jasmine nor Diana would be caught dead in it. Where had she seen the blue sweater? And then she remembered. The museum kitchen. It was Marta's.

Chapter Twelve

J asmine, decked-out in a long magenta colored puffer jacket was waiting at Alex's door when she arrived home.

"I heard you had a little brush with death?" She handed Alex a small basket. "I was going to leave it."

"Thanks," Alex said, taking the basket and the accompanying card. It was a stunning photograph of a wolf pack dotted across a frozen white landscape and signed by *Pete Holgan*. Alex caught her breath. Did Jasmine know about the hot springs? Had Pete called and told her? She doubted Diana had.

Was Jasmine there in the park—watching? Or was she the person Pete met at the café? Alex shivered.

"You're cold," Jasmine noticed, "I didn't mean to keep you standing at your door. Kamran said you were a bit shaken-up this afternoon after a dip in the hot springs. I happened to be at the honey store when he called, and I thought Manuka might ward off a chill." Jasmine lowered her hood, fluffed her hair, and smiled warmly at Alex.

"Thank you; this is generous."

"Looks like a storm," Jasmine observed the darkening sky.

"Yes," Alex mumbled. "Would you like to come in for coffee?" Her cabin was a mess compared to Jasmine's estate, but hopefully Jasmine would recognize the *tarof*—though Alex was sure Iranians didn't expect Americans to participate in Iranian social graces.

"No, thanks. I should...actually, maybe I will pop in to use your restroom." Jasmine slipped off her felt clogs and stepped inside.

* * *

Jasmine was in and out quickly, politely refusing Alex's offer of coffee. Alex herself decided to forgo the coffee for a nap, wanting nothing more than to drop on the couch and sleep. She was not by nature a napper, and so, after five minutes of lying on the couch and staring at the ceiling, she gave up.

She filled her stainless-steel swan-neck kettle and waited for it to boil. She lined her porcelain Japanese dripper with a paper filter and filled it with fresh ground coffee. She then poured the hot water in a swirling motion and watched the crema rise from the fresh grounds. The strong aroma of freshly brewed coffee revived her.

Alex sat with the hot mug of coffee between her palms,

remembering the warm sensation of Pete's touch as he tenderly dressed her at the hot springs. She shook her head, put down her coffee, and got to work on Marta's Nutshell.

She was missing something important about Marta's life. She stood, went to her large picture window, and gazed out over the field toward Marta's cabin. The sky was an ominous swirl of gray, like the shadows in graphic novels that, according to Artist William Kentridge, alluded to darkness, to violence, without having to show it. What wasn't she seeing? What piece of the picture was she missing among Marta's shadows?

The curtains. She turned and ran down the stairs. It was now or never if she was going to retrieve those lace-curtain swatches Marta had promised her the last time they met. She retrieved her coat and dialed Marta. There was no answer.

Outside, the cold wind bit at Alex's face. Night was approaching faster than it should, obscuring all recognition of the familiar field in the wake of an impending storm.

As she got closer to Marta's, Alex could see smoke dancing in the air above Marta's cabin. Marta's stove fit two logs at a time, which meant that Marta was home, feeding the fire. Why wasn't she answering her phone? Alex sent a text, *In the area. OK if I stop by?*

Her phone beeped back immediately. *I'm out, Marta.*

The phone beeped again, a second reminder of the same text. It was as if Marta was watching her walk closer to her cabin and was warning her to stay away. Alex felt exposed to more than the frigid air. She wondered about the smoke in Marta's chimney. If Marta was out, then who was feeding the fire?

Kit called Bozeman Alex's "exposure therapy." It was a kiddie pool as far as field-sites went. A place where she could ease back into doing research after her debacle with the disappeared filmmaker. *It's the shallow end, Alex; wade in slowly.*

But was it? And was she wading in, or was she already in over her head? Had she spooked Marta? Or was she imagining it? Marta had pulled back. Was history repeating itself? What happened with the filmmaker was unusual. She dialed Kit. No answer.

The soft, silent snow was quickly accumulating into a whiteout. Alex had no choice but to turn back toward home.

* * *

She beat the dark to her door.

In her studio, she excavated a swatch of lace from the bottom of her sewing kit, took out the glue gun, and paused mid-task. She bit her lip, thinking, *Something else is missing.* Sound?

She set down the swatch and glue gun and leaned back against the wall. She remembered a Janet Cardiff show she saw in New York. It was a table-top diorama—a seemingly perfect suburban model of tranquility. Every detail was spot-on right down to the street lighting that illuminated the thin strip of gray sidewalk in front of the brick house. Every door, shutter, and curtain was closed or drawn. There was no way an onlooker could see in. But they could hear. The sound, Cardiff's preferred artistic medium, was designed to mimic the way a neighbor might hear a couple fighting next door. The voices were muffled, but escalating, both in volume and in tension. And then—a single gunshot.

Alex touched her miniature model. A soundscape might add life to the scene. She sat down and took out her iPhone and played back her first interview with Marta.

"Marta Heron agrees to give Alex Klein full permission to record her in any and all conversations for the next two weeks, beginning Wednesday December First." Marta's voice was calm and assertive—friendly. Nothing like the last interview. There was the sound of rustling papers as she handed Marta the *permission to record* forms. Alex learned in a documentary film class to get permission early and then to let the camera roll until the subject forgot it was there. But Marta never stopped glancing at Alex's iPhone. Not for a minute did she forget she was being recorded. Still, Alex had learned a lot about Marta, especially that she loved numbers. Marta was a math person. Alex was not. Alex listened to her recording.

"Anthropology, it says whether a number it is bad or good?" Marta asked.

"What do you mean?" Alex asked.

"Why 13 is bad, but maybe the four is good? Four, it is a perfect square." She remembered Marta's smile, the dreamy look on her face as if she were imagining a perfect square. Alex concentrated hard on Marta's heavily accented English but still could not place her accent.

"I need to say ... something..." Marta was saying on the tape recorder when Alex heard a step on the landing. She fumbled with her iPhone, paused the recording, and listened intently to the silence. Had it been the recording? The wind outside? A city girl was careful not to drown out a warning, but this was Bozeman, one of the safest cities in the country. Regardless, Alex would listen to the rest of the interview in the morning. Now, she would work in vigilant silence.

She took another look at her dollhouse. It had the same sorry façade as the store-bought kit: each part neatly popped from a pre-cut sheet of wood and attached with Elmer's glue. She moved her lamp around the gables, playfully throwing shadows along the walls. She flooded the front door with light. But nothing helped. It remained a cheap imitation of a Nutshell. She was not an architect, nor an artist, but an anthropologist, and, here and now, in her own studio, nothing needed to be exacting and well-measured; she was free to create and to innovate. She had already illustrated a social picture, a life; in this regard, her model was complete. It was good enough. But Alex was tired of settling for good enough. She had learned the rules of anthropology—good enough—and now she wanted to break them. She wanted to make new rules, revolutionize her field, and finally prove herself. She picked up a piece of shingle and the glue-gun and got to work.

Her phone rang, surprising her. It was close to midnight, and she had not taken a break. She used her elbow to slide her phone closer to read the caller ID, hoping it was Marta. It was Diana. Odd. She assumed Diana and Kamran would be well intwined in their romantic interlude. She let it go to voicemail; she couldn't let go of the pieces she was holding together until the glue was dry.

When she was satisfied that it was dry, Alex put down her work and listened to Diana's message: "Call me." She called her back. No answer. She left a voicemail.

She stretched and yawned. She was tired; it was bedtime, but something was bothering her. She picked-up the gallery guide to the Nutshell Murders and thumbed through it until she came to the farmhouse murder. There it was: the pot-belly stove. It was the smoke coming from Marta's cabin earlier that reminded Alex of the farmer's stove that still burned a healthy stack of logs, suggesting that the farmer had not been long dead. Someone, presumably the farmer, had fed the fire. An image, unbidden, came to Alex of Marta asleep on her couch with a little toy dog licking at her draped arm. Marta did not have a dog. Marta did, however, have a similar stove that needed feeding. Which meant that Marta had been at home when Alex called her.

Alex stretched and said, "Hey, Siri, remind me to find a

miniature stove for Marta's model." When Siri agreed, she said, "Hey, Siri, call Diana." It went straight to voicemail. Again.

It was late. Alex placed a bookmark in her gallery guide, glancing again at the murdered farmer and his dog. The dog knew something.

She stood and stretched and nearly fell. She was still weak and dehydrated from the hot spring's fiasco and had forgotten to eat dinner. Her body was hungrier for sleep.

She felt a chill and remembered her bathroom window was stuck cracked open. She forgot to put in a work order. She blocked the crack with a towel and hoped there weren't any peeping students around.

She climbed into bed thinking of a Man Ray poem.

Several small houses
  Discreetly separated by foliage
  And the night—
  Maintaining their several identities
  By light

Which fills the inside of each—
  Not as masses they stand
  But as walls
  Enclosing and excluding
  Like shawls

About little old women—
  What mystery hides within
  What curiosity lurks without
  One the other

Knows nothing about.

She was *the curiosity that lurks without*—a curious outsider trying to solve the mystery of lives closed into Nutshells. Anthropology was like a good mystery, the unraveling of cultural secrets, the possibility of magic, the power of belief and human emotions. Not to mention the beauty of the ritual objects.

Man Ray was a photographer *and* a poet. As an anthropologist, Alex operated in the space between belief and beauty, art, and anthropology. She wanted to be like the surrealists and break out of neat categories and tidy little boxes. Their work was not catalogued into separate cabinets of curiosity by genre. Man Ray's photographs were not mere mechanical reproductions of life, but poetry fixed to paper by the alchemy of time and light. She would have to be patient for a picture of Marta to fully emerge. Anthropology, like photography, relied on time.

Marta's model house was near completion. All that remained were the curtains and the ritual of the final interview. Alex fell to sleep dreaming of Marta's lace curtains—*Like we have at home.*

Field Note

Anthropologists used to show-up in a village or among a tribe and record family trees or genealogies. To what end, you ask? To look at power dynamics, class, and position that the various players held in a society or tribe; to examine the continuity of family, tribe, clan, and village lines. Did all those early anthropology studies reinforce a colonial class system? Either way, whether I do a formal genealogy or not, I still need to pay attention to informal kinship relations. Wasn't it Socrates who said we should judge people by the company they keep? Every anthropologist pays special attention to networks: webs of friendship, familial bonds, social relationships, work hierarchies, and economic relations. Kinship tells us a lot about people's social status and power relations—which drive so much of human life. What's the first step a detective takes in a murder mystery? Finds out who was close to the victim. Note to self: pay close attention to kinship.

Chapter Thirteen

Alex finished her breakfast and still in her pajamas, slipped on her felt clogs and made a run for the mail box. It was empty.

Until the package arrived with her latest object, there was nothing more to do on Marta's model. Alex was not by nature a patient person. She needed to busy herself. She did not want to go for a walk or a hike and risk missing the delivery, so instead she went to the kitchen and dumped the rest of the oats from the cardboard oatmeal drum, fished a soda can from the recycling, rinsed it, and marched up the stairs to her studio.

She set her supplies down on her work table and noticed

that Marta's model house had inched precariously close to the edge of the table. Earthquake? She was after all living inside an inactive volcano, a caldera. She bent down to push the house back but stopped short of touching it. Something else was off.

Before going to bed, she had sat her Marta doll at the kitchen table with a cup of tea. But now the doll was draped over the edge of her couch—Marta's leg dangling like the farmers in Alex's favorite Nutshell. Had she unconsciously replicated the scene from the Nutshell house before bed? The Nutshell catalogue was still open to the page of the Farmer's house. She clearly remembered placing a bookmark and shutting the book, but then it would not be the first time her memory tricked her. Or that she had done something without thinking.

That was the problem with her distracted brain—it was great for multi-tasking, but not so great at remembering the tasks later. *Alex, think*, she pleaded with herself. She was exhausted last night; anything was possible. Her lack of focus was amplified when she was tired. She took a deep breath to calm her thumping heart. This was more than exhaustion; she was frightened. But why would anyone move the doll? Was it a joke? A warning? Did someone know about her past fieldwork? Was it revenge? Impossible. No, she shook her head; this was simply the danger of working too late into the night and skipping dinner.

She bit her lip and reminded herself not to get distracted. She continued to go about her task, first spray painting the oatmeal drum black inside and out, then cutting a little hole into the side and continuing the familiar steps until she had a working pinhole camera.

She took the camera and ran downstairs and outside where she placed it on a stump facing the field. She was busy propping it just right when the postal van pulled up to Old Museum Road.

Finally, her flower. It was the only other object she could think to add to Marta's Nutshell. The last time she had visited Marta she'd looked around and asked, "No plants?" Alex's childhood neighbor, Mrs. Granity, had a story for every single one of her house plants.

"Too much trouble." Marta had answered while inadvertently glancing at the fireplace mantel where a white flower peeked out of a chipped ceramic vase. The stems were long and thorny, and the petals were white, withered, and unfamiliar. Mrs. Granity always said that thorns meant to stay away.

Alex abandoned the pinhole and ran to the door to sign for her package.

The delivery was small and compact, and contained a single tiny box that held, not her special-order miniature house plant, but a prickly cactus.

"Seriously?" Alex threw the box on the table. Between Marta's broken promise to deliver the lace swatches and being sent the wrong flower, her work was going nowhere. At this point, she was obliged to make a model of Jasmine's house. In her grant proposal, she promised an interview and a new house every three weeks. Overly ambitious was an understatement. She needed to sneak into the museum basement and use the art department's coveted 3D printer to make her own replica of Marta's house plant. It was a holiday, and, with any luck, she would have the museum basement to herself. But, first, she needed a pattern and tools from her studio.

* * *

Diana's blue Mini-Cooper was parked outside the museum lot. Had she left the car behind and driven with Kamran to Gardiner? Alex hoped so. She had no desire to run into Diana.

She entered the museum and walked quickly past the staff kitchen toward the back stairs that led down to the Bones Room and the 3D printer.

Alex rarely visited the intimidating labyrinth of labs—a morgue of ancient bones. She paused at the bottom of the stairs where the silence confirmed that she was alone. She moved along the cold hallway so swiftly that the light sensors could barely keep up with her. Alone or not, she did not want to risk someone seeing her. She turned each dark corner like a determined sleepwalker, making her way through night as if it were day.

She paused at the Bones Room. She heard footsteps. They came fast and furiously from around the bend behind her. She darted behind an exhibit poster and held her breath.

Jack Horner passed her and entered the Bones Room.

She breathed a sigh of relief. The only danger might be a silly-schoolgirl reprimand. Jack did not like his fossils, including the replicas, manhandled. But he was not the type to scold.

Diana, for whom Jack would forgive anything, worked from sketches done for her by interns (at her request) who delivered them to her within an hour. She rarely came down to the basement. And yet it was Diana's unmistakable voice Alex heard shout, "Jack!"

"Didn't mean to startle you," Jack apologized.

"Why is this place so darn difficult to navigate? It's freezing, and it has taken me an hour to locate the correct box, let alone the right bones."

"Pre-show jitters," he reassured her.

"What does that mean?"

"You have these sketches already. No need to triple check."

"They never arrived."

"That's odd. I sent them up yesterday."

"With whom?"

"Marta. I left them in her cubby. Anyway, I thought you might be hiding down here."

"Hiding?"

"You have a visitor in the lobby," Jack said.

"Nobody knows I'm here. Besides we're closed. How did they get in?" Diana lowered her voice.

"Special visitor. Special privileges."

"OK Jack, I get it; who is it?" Diana asked. Alex knew exactly who it was, and she was pretty sure Diana did too. She wished for a better hiding spot. It was too late to pop-out and say hello, having effectively eavesdropped on their conversation.

"Our biggest donor ... looking for you," Jack said.

"Really?" Diana feigned surprise.

Kamran's footsteps could be heard in the distance. Diana peeled off her lab coat and threw it on a chair.

Alex inched closer to the Bones Room entrance and slid behind a discarded shelf. She was both better hidden and better able to see inside the room. Kamran's tall, lean shadow came within inches of her hiding spot and Alex's heart skipped a beat. But all of Kamran's attention was on Diana.

"Diana." He kissed her on both cheeks and whispered, "You disappeared."

"And I'm off." Jack left.

"Hardly. *I* waited out the storm. You are the one who disappeared."

"It was no weather to drive in, even with a Mercedes jeep."

"And a phone call?"

"Let's talk outside. Can you steal away for lunch?" He

placed his hand on the small of her back and lightly steered her toward the door.

"Where? There are eyes everywhere." Diana said squirming out of his grasp.

"Is that a problem?"

"Not for me," She answered firmly. "Of course not. I thought—you know—Jasmine?"

"I meet many women for work. Why should this be any different?"

"Absolutely. Assuming then that you are here to donate the diorama budget?" Diana said.

"Not until you finish my commission," Kamran's tone was affable. "We left other things unfinished. How about a quick bite at Feed? Somewhere we can talk without being overheard," Kamran suggested.

Alex's heart skipped another beat. Had he seen her?

"Here's our dilemma...," Kamran continued.

"The dilemma is you disappeared and left me alone in a storm," Diana interrupted.

"Exactly, a storm. I couldn't exactly turn around."

"The electricity was cut off," Diana's voice rose.

"I'm sorry you were uncomfortable." Kamran soothed like a hotel manager who would not concede to failure. "The generator took over immediately, no? The steak was cooked, the Napa Merlot was decanted and waiting."

"As if you planned your departure. You never called."

"There was no cell reception."

"I would have called your home line, but, well, I didn't want Jasmine..."

"You're more concerned with my wife than I am, Diana. It was a horrendous drive, as you can imagine. Nowhere to pull-over, no reception. I arrived home dead exhausted. Jasmine handed me a glass of water, and I passed out on the couch."

"You know, I've lost my appetite. I need to get back to work. You could have called in the morning."

"This is me calling. I just woke up."

"Look, Kamran, let's move on."

"Where's Marta?" Kamran asked. "I could use a cup of coffee."

"I don't know, she's usually here by now. She knows I am working overtime on an opening. She said she would come in."

"She was supposed to work for us today as well. When she didn't show-up, I figured she'd be here. Listen, it's about the crittercam," Kamran lowered his voice.

"Not here," Diana said.

"I told you, let's go to Feed," Kamran insisted.

Diana shook her head.

"Fine, I came to let you know that you should tell the police the truth if they ask," Kamran said.

"Ask what?"

"Where I was last evening."

And where was that? thought Alex.

"The police?" Diana asked.

"Don't feel obligated to protect me or to lie for Jasmine's sake. It's OK to tell the truth."

"The truth?" Diana frowned.

"That we were together. At the cabin." Kamran took her hand and Diana pulled it back.

"It was reported stolen. The camera."

"Stolen?" Diana rushed toward the door.

"Don't bother, it's here. I checked before I came down."

"I'm confused. You need an alibi for a camera that may have been stolen, but wasn't?" Diana placed a hand on the table to steady herself and sent a tray of shards flying with a crash. "Jack will have my head." She bent to clean the mess and ignored Kamran who was kneeling beside her. "How did the police get the idea it was stolen if it's still here?" she asked.

"Marta. She reported it stolen. I assumed it was while we were in Gardiner."

Marta was in the museum last night. No wonder Alex couldn't find her. Who would pretend to steal a camera? Did Kamran drive to Bozeman to steal the camera? To what end?

"You OK, Diana?" He moved in closer to help her with the shards. "May I?"

"You need gloves. There's a pair on the table." Diana pointed.

Alex sighed; she was in for a long afternoon. She wiggled into a more comfortable position, took out her phone and silently tapped out her field notes.

Field Note

Anthro 101

Kit calls my project the Bozeman Bones. Why do we anthropologists look down on each other's subfields? We have four fields in anthropology, and it's a constant fight over resources and funding. Every boundary we put up in the name of a disciplinary method limits what science can discover or do to change the world. I want to make the world a better place. A more open place. And this won't happen with more fences and gates.

Whiner told me in no uncertain terms that an archeologist cannot do what we social anthropologists do, because they aren't trained to. And, yet the number of journalists and essayists who claim to be doing "ethnography" without a Ph.D. is astounding. And guess who gets read? That's right—not professor Whiner, but the journalists. Their output is more user-friendly, i.e., readable. Now, I admit, as a person with dyslexia I prefer a narrative that paints a picture, tells a story, but I'm not the only one. We researchers are limiting ourselves by the strait jackets we create in terms of what is or is not an acceptable form to output our research.

Paleontology is classified as biological or evolutionary anthropology—the study of species how they have evolved over time. Like archeology, the paleontologists use remains from the past to create a picture. Though we are talking 'way, 'way in the past. Archeology looks at a particular moment in time. What I do isn't so different from an archeologist who digs up physical evidence from the past to recreate what life may have been like in historic societies. I'm digging up the dirt on people's lives and recreating it in 3D.

For the record: I will be doing structured interviews, informal interviews, and participant observation to re-create Marta's daily life and story in the form of an ethnographic dollhouse.

Right now, I'm doing participant observation: deep hanging out. I've been following Marta around in her daily life.

Whom does she talk to? Not many people, and all are "hi-bye" interactions.

What does she do: cleans at the museum and shops for groceries. Anthropologists don't merely tag along; we partici-pate. I carried her groceries. I dusted the dinos.

*Cool title—Dusting the Dinos: A year in the life of a Bozeman immigrant. Or, if I'm being honest: *A life in one page.* I get ahead of myself. Always ahead or behind.

Following someone around all day—is that participant observation or plain old-fashioned nosiness? It's so intrusive.

Whiner never warned me that I'd feel guilty doing field-work. Anthropology is a form of surveillance. Even so, can we be certain private moments reveal who a person really is? Isn't identity different in different contexts? Don't we all perform our identity depending on where we are and with whom we are interacting? Following Marta around in her bubble of silence revealed nothing new about her. Would it have been easier if Marta led a louder life? Silence is intimate—it whispers *Keep out*. Honestly, what is the difference between participant observation and spying on someone? Zora Neale Hurston called it poking and prying with purpose. It comes down to not just purpose but permission. Good thing I am making a dollhouse and not writing a text, because, frankly, Marta had no words.

Feeling deflated, need coffee.

**Find signed release form from Marta. Already misplaced it. ADHD sucks.

*Must make a Marta file.

OK, the participant observation yielded nothing. So, I tried an informal, unstructured interview, where the conversation just flows. We did this over tea. Like unstructured interviews, they can be done any time we hang-out—like at the grocery store, where I said, "Hey, you buy a lot of olives and Feta cheese; are you on a Mediterranean diet?"

No answer. What a surprise. Is it me, or is it her? Is it a game? Everything is about power and where it is located. How power is obtained, structured, and retained is tantamount to understanding human societies—from friendships and marriages to office environments and governments.

For now, power is silence, and it's located in Marta's court.

Chapter Fourteen

Alex craved intense endorphin-releasing—cathartic, physical movement—after crouching behind the museum shelf all morning. She sprang out of the museum exit the minute Diana and Kamran left and ran as fast as she could. She had bolted in the wrong direction and was on the path straight toward the creepy Tinsley House.

Alex could hear the hens clucking away in the nearby enclosure as she passed. Feeding them was one of Marta's odd jobs. Was clucking a sound of satisfaction, or were they hungry? Had Marta fed them this morning? Next to the coop was a collection of carriages and plows gone to rust and a small cabin with a slate roof. The plaque read "smoking shed."

Alex walked swiftly past the large, dilapidated barn. Why had the museum let it go to rot? It was potentially both a great storage place and a serious liability. It was battened down for the winter but surely full of bats and rats and anything else that might slip through.

The Tinsley complex was nestled in a grove of tall pine trees. The grove was already dark and lent a film of gloom to the overcast day. The wintry woods smelled of frozen, wet earth and smoke, as if someone was burning leaves in the field. Alex and Marta were the sole inhabitants for miles, and neither of their stoves would emit smoke this far out, which meant there was a fire in the Tinsley House.

Alex sped-up. The smell of smoke got stronger the closer she came to the old house. Alex stopped and caught her breath when she saw the smoke rising from the chimney. Only Marta was allowed in there during the winter. Was Marta in there cleaning? Or was someone squatting? Alex walked up to the front entrance, expecting to see lights in the windows. She remembered her Lyft driver telling her that everything was authentic, right down to a lack of electricity. Would candlelight or a Gaslamp be obvious through a window? Aside from the smoke, the house was utterly still and completely dark. Was someone sitting in there in the dark? If not, then someone had left behind a still-smoldering fire. Alex took out her phone to call the fire department or the police, but instead texted Will. He was a ranger; he would know what to do. In the meantime, she would put out what little fire was left before it did any damage.

There were no footprints on the porch, which was not surprising given the light snowfall earlier. Whoever had been here was either still inside or had left hours ago. Alex tapped lightly on the door and turned the knob. The door opened easily.

"Hello?" she called out. She took a short, sharp breath of cold air. There was no response. She moved inside where the smoke was stronger. An antique wood house like this could go up in flames in seconds.

* * *

Despite the strong stench of smoke, there was no sign of a fire or a fireplace anywhere. Alex called out again and got no response. She fumbled for her phone and slid on the flashlight. She moved the light around the room, half-expecting someone or something to jump out at her.

She inspected the kitchen first, as it was the most likely place for a fire. A McGuffey's reader was laid open on the kitchen table. Poor kids—even a hundred years ago, children were forced to learn to read the hard way. A gas lamp was cold to the touch, and the round, knotted rug looked like it had not been stepped on in years. The adjoining room was a cozy alcove large enough for a small woman to sit at the antique Singer sewing table, a wicker sewing box at her feet. Alex sat among the antique props like a doll in a life-sized dollhouse—was she being played?

In the next room an old-fashioned pram and a set of silver rattles were neatly displayed under a sign for "leisure activities." There was a baby's crib, a large empty trunk, and a row of carved wooden ducks with wheels and a pot-belly stove that was cold to the touch. There was no fireplace. The smoke was not coming from anywhere downstairs. Alex had no choice but to climb the narrow banister-less staircase and look upstairs for the still-burning fire. She held her phone out with one hand

and used the other to brace herself against the wall, as she inched-up the sliver of stairs.

The upstairs was musty, but warm, which meant the fire was in one of the three closed bedrooms. Alex chose the middle door.

A warm yellow glow lit the room where a single log still burned in a cushion of ashes in the shallow fireplace. Alex took a bucket of sand, conveniently placed by the fire, and tossed it on the log. She fingered the brass poker. Should she take it for protection? She left it and exited the room.

Halfway down the staircase, Alex turned back. She had a strong urge to go back and check the remaining rooms.

First, she peeked in the smaller room, where there was nothing more than a pair of empty toddler-sized cots and children's toys. The last bedroom was larger and slightly better lit than the other rooms. Someone had opened the curtains. Alex glanced at the lumpy four-poster bed and in the receding light of day could make out an arm dangling from under the colorful quilt.

Alex screamed, which did nothing to wake the sleeping body. She approached the bed, and cautiously pulled back the quilt, to find Marta, splayed-out in the exact position Alex had found her Marta doll that morning.

"Marta?" Alex felt for a pulse. Marta's expression was pained, and her pulse was weak but present. Her arm was dangling uncomfortably off the side of the bed. Was she drunk? Alex sniffed at her face but did not smell any alcohol. She fumbled for her phone and dialed 911.

* * *

"Yes, of course I tried to wake her. She's unconscious. No, no vomit. No blood. Yes, I'm sure. She's not asleep. Yes, I tried waking her. I don't know." Alex answered the paramedics' infuriating questions. "Come quick!"

Alex wanted to run as fast and as far as she could from this place. The intruder might still be near, and she had no intention of letting the EMT find two bodies when they arrived. Given the location, they would be a while. Alex decided to meet them at the road.

The main road was slippery and barely paved.

"Finally!" Alex ran toward the National Parks Jeep as it came into view.

Will pulled up alongside her and rolled-down his window.

"Where's the fire? I don't see any smoke."

Alex remembered a line from a Miss Marple mystery she had recently watched: Everybody watching the smoke, nobody seeing the fire. *Where* was *the fire?* Alex thought.

"You look like you've seen a ghost. Get in, you'll freeze out here." Will opened the passenger door.

"No," Alex pointed toward the house. "Marta," she muttered, "She needs help, I called an ambulance. We will have to walk."

The ambulance had found another path and was already at the Tinsley house when they arrived.

"Hey, Scotty. Is she OK?" Will asked. The police officer had short blond hair and a round Norman Rockwell face.

"You get a distress call?" Scotty asked.

Alex walked up the stairs toward the front door of the house.

"Ma'am, you can't go in there," Scotty stopped her. He took a roll of police tape out of his jacket pocket.

"I need to see..." Alex said. "I need to show Will."

Scotty shook his head. "You need to stay behind the police tape." Scotty pulled the tape around the door. "She the one who called this is in?" Scotty asked Will.

"I'm right here; you can ask me. And, yes, I did." Alex informed him.

"I got this, Scotty," Will said.

"I ..." Alex pulled her scarf tighter around her neck, "Is... is she OK?"

"We think so." Scotty offered.

"Think?" Will asked.

"Vitals are good. Bump on her head, but not too bad. Odd thing is, she's not waking up." Scotty shouted above the wailing sirens of the EMT's departure. "What were you doing at the Tinsley House?" Scotty asked Alex.

"It's complicated. There's more." Alex was shivering.

"Is there somewhere warmer we could go?" Will asked.

"Yeah, the station," Scotty said.

Chapter Fifteen

Making coffee was usually a meditative practice for Alex. Today, however the ritual only lent more time to contemplate Marta and the oddly short interview with Scotty at the station. She gave her statement, and he sent her home without further questions.

She had tried to call Kit, and sent several texts, but she had received no reply.

Why would Kit have her phone off? Alex wondered.

She sipped her coffee and watched from the Loft's big bay window as the sun slipped behind the mountains. When the caffeine had kicked-in and calmed her mind, she set down the cup, ready to delve into Jasmine's interior.

Just yesterday she had built the armature of Jasmine's model and neatly placed it to dry on her worktable—and now it was gone. Alex looked around, confused. Was she losing her mind? It would not be the first or last time Alex had misplaced work—but a dollhouse? This she could not blame on her ADHD. She clearly remembered seeing it on her worktable before leaving for the museum. Alex's heart raced, every instinct in her body told her to examine Marta's house. Bracing herself, she went to the dollhouse and peered inside. Her Marta doll was still draped over the edge of the miniature couch—but now with a pool of shiny blood circling her bashed-in head like a halo. Alex's heart thumped wildly against her chest. She put her finger on the red paint. It was still tacky, wet.

She raced down the stairs, found her phone, and dialed Will.

Minutes later, Will arrived.

"That was fast; were you waiting around the corner?" Alex asked, opening the door before he had a chance to knock.

"And you? Were you standing here waiting for me?"

"Yup."

Will removed his shoes and followed Alex up to her loft.

"The dollhouse," Alex said beaming the light of her iPhone flashlight into the model of Marta's life in Bozeman.

Will peered at the miniature Marta, head bashed in, and suspended from her couch. He frowned, "Bad playdate?" When Alex did not laugh, he asked more soberly, "Was this how you found her at the Tinsley House?"

"Yes. I mean... not bleeding. And look..." Alex pointed carefully to a miniature piece of flint floating in the little red puddle of blood. "And her face..."

"They disfigured her face."

"Who would do this?" Alex whimpered.

"Probably the same person who left her for dead at the Tinsley House."

Alex gasped. "It's less glossy," she noticed.

"Glossy?" Will crouched down and craned his neck to get a better look. He examined the scene for an uncomfortably long time.

"It was wet." Alex noted the time on the clock and added, "It was wet when I called you. And now. Now," she stammered, "Is it dry?"

"Not sure, don't want to touch it."

"Nail polish shimmers, and then dulls when it dries. But I don't smell acetone. Paint? Real blood?"

"Could give us an idea of time if, as you say, it dried between when you found it and now." Will looked up at her.

"I touched it," Alex admitted. Her touch left a perfect print of her finger. "Whoever assaulted Marta was in here. She wasn't randomly attacked while she was cleaning the Tinsley House." Alex hugged herself. "In here with me. Her assault was planned and deliberate."

"This isn't play." Will agreed.

"No, it's not. It's a murder scene." Alex stared at the scene through a blur of tears.

"Murder? Marta?" Will was concerned.

"Look," Alex pointed at the model, but Will kept his eyes on her.

"I mean, I don't know." Alex said.

"Why call it murder then?" Will's gaze was unnerving.

Alex took a deep breath and said, "The Nutshells." She paused before elaborating, "The aura of the original leaves a trace." Marx and his stupid ideas about the animation of objects. Philosophy gets in the way of reality. How could anyone call this a coincidence?

"I get it." Will took pictures with his phone. "The murder aura was not lost in translation." Will sent a text, which got an immediate reply. He said, "Police are sending a forensics team over. So, you were saying something about aura?"

"I was innovating ethnography, not encouraging murder," Alex stammered.

"Should hope not, but isn't it a little superstitious to believe you brought this on with your model?" Will studied her.

"Superstition is an anthropologist's bread and butter. It's like I created a voodoo doll. Oh, my God," Alex cried as Will helped her to the couch.

"Sit."

"Objects have power," she continued.

"Remind me not to get on your bad side," Will joked. He was trying to lighten the mood, but his relaxed attitude was making her more nervous. She pointed at the bloody Marta doll, "Messing with the doll first is magic, voodoo."

"How so?"

"You do something to the voodoo doll, and it manifests in the real person."

"Like bashing in Marta's head and splaying her out on a couch? I'd say this looks more like a warning, or like someone is trying to implicate you," said Will.

Was there a connection to the filmmaker and her failed fieldwork? Either she had terrible luck, or someone was out to get her.

"Unless it happened before she was attacked? When was the last time you worked on this?" Will stood. Alex could not remember. Everything was such a blur since Marta's attack. She barely remembered starting Jasmine's model.

"Time is not my strong suit. Besides, would someone who committed a brutal attack then have the self-composure to sneak in here and recreate this scene, in such an exacting, and clean, manner? Nothing got dirty. Do you have any idea the challenge? Dollhouses are not easy. You need slim fingers and a good grip. And nerves of steel to do it under those circumstances." Alex was losing her nerve. She took a breath. "Like a surgeon."

"Where are your supplies?" Will's composure was as impressive as it was unsettling. Alex pointed to a tray by the window.

"Without touching anything, can you tell if anything has been moved?"

Alex was embarrassed by the disorganized mess. She had a habit of hyper-focusing on things until she was beyond tired. The H in her ADHD. And last night was no exception. She had been too tired to bother with dirty paintbrushes. She shook her head no, in answer to Will's question.

"So, if the person didn't use your supplies, we can assume they brought their own? Which points to premeditation— prepared, planned."

Alex looked at Will in disbelief.

"How many people know that murder scenes influenced your project?" He asked.

"My friend Kit." Alex started wearily. "And you." Tears welled-up in her eyes, "I feel responsible." She swallowed hard.

"That's the problem with superstition," Will said gently.

Alex did not tell him that it was more than that.

"The point is this is *not* how I arranged it."

"I should hope not. Because that would make you either a murderer or a fortuneteller."

"She's still alive," Alex pointed out.

"In which case it would make you an attempted murderer or a lousy fortuneteller."

"With a paleolithic tool?" Alex reached for the piece of flint, and Will slapped her hand away, "No!" Alex drew back.

"Sorry," Will apologized. "Need to keep the evidence sterile." Will had quick reflexes.

"Glessner had a real eye for detail," Alex reminded him.

"You're saying whoever did this has an eye for detail?"

"Yes. And they did a better job. I was having a hard time finding things to put in the house. Whoever did this embellished it."

"Such as?"

"The cross above her couch. The person—the attacker—" Alex shuddered, "added that cross."

"It's unusual looking."

"Greek or Russian orthodox. I don't remember a cross, or any sort of religious artifacts, in Marta's cabin. Anthropologists are trained to study detail, to look for signs of religious belief, for any belief. I wouldn't have missed something so obvious."

Will glanced at his watch. "It's getting late. This needs to be dusted for fingerprints, though they won't find any. Anyone who is this detail-oriented would know to use gloves. OK, now, how many people knew about your project? Who's seen it? Who had access? Somebody knew you were up to this."

"Anyone on the museum board would have read my application. Diana helped me find the miniature pieces. Jack was on the committee. And they might have mentioned it to others. Maybe Kamran knew? It's his money ... and Jasmine ... I was making a model of her life. Everyone knew."

Will's look told her she was in as much danger of being the next victim as she was at risk of being the prime suspect. A tear rolled down Alex's cheek. Will produced a clean cotton handkerchief from his pocket, and was about to dab her cheek, but handed it to her instead.

"How many of these do you own?" Alex smiled for the first time since he had arrived at her door.

"As many as it takes."

"Am I in danger?" Should she mention the creaking sounds the other night? Someone had been watching her, waiting.

"We need a motive. Did Marta have any close friends or family?"

"I have no clue," Alex admitted sheepishly.

"Don't anthropologists sit around villages and take genealogies?"

"Yeah, back in the 1950's."

"What concerns me is the attacker intended to kill her. If this was done last night—then they hoped she'd be dead by the time you found it. By the time we found her. There's something I don't like..." Will said pensively.

"Aside from the fact that someone broke into my house. Or tried to kill Marta? You seem to know a lot about crime for a park ranger."

Will ignored her comment.

"I walked across the field to Marta's the night before she was attacked. I sensed something was wrong." She paused; could she trust Will?

"What time was that?" Will asked.

Alex showed Will the text she had sent Marta.

"4:45 pm. This is helpful," Will said and dialed Scotty. He briefed him about the text, and everything Alex had told him. "When's forensics showing up? I'll ask her now." Will hung up and turned to Alex, "Where were you when you texted her?"

"I was standing outside her cabin. Her lights were off. I thought it odd that there was smoke coming from the chimney. I almost knocked on the door."

"What stopped you?"

"Intuition. Though fear is more like it."

Alex was desperate to speak with Kit. Will had too many questions about human behavior for a man and who worked with animals. If work with animals was indeed what he truly did. She was not at all sure what his job was.

"Tea?" Alex offered.

"Tea sounds great." Will smiled.

Alex took him to the kitchen and put the kettle on. She stared out the window and across the field to where she could barely make out the oncoming police lights.

"Could it be real blood?" Alex asked.

"Don't know. Need to ask Forensics. They should be here soon. In the meantime, Alex, I need you to remember. Aside from the obvious additional details left here by the intruder: the piece of flint, the cross—" Will paused to sip his tea, decided it was too hot, and set it down.

"Someone was in here the night before Marta disappeared. The doll was moved." Alex blurted out.

"Moved?"

Alex explained.

"Was it a warning? Was someone trying to scare you off? Did Marta tell you something she should not have?"

"She hardly said anything of import. That was the problem. It was a spectacular ethnographic failure. I learned nothing," Alex put her head in her hands. *This can't be happening, not again.*

"Is anything missing?" Will was practical.

"Missing?" It was a question she hadn't asked herself. All the details seemed the same—or were they? Was it the power of Will's suggestion, or was something missing?

"Something is off. It's been nagging at me since I first saw it," Alex agreed.

"Concentrate," Will voiced a directive she had been receiving her whole life. If only she could. She took a deep breath and steadied her mind. She sensed a detail screaming for her attention from the quiet stiff calm of her desecrated dollhouse—her accidental Nutshell.

Field Note

Did someone deface my house to take back the narrative? Well, it wasn't Marta because the whole point of the project was to allow her to control the narrative, to add to it, to embellish it. In short, she declined that offer with her silence.

But someone else felt the need to make a point. To add to my narrative, to the story. Someone added that cross. A cross is never just a cross. It's a fetish object that contains the power of religion, ritual, and belief. It's sacred to someone—but who? Was Marta religious?

Chapter Sixteen

The forensics team, two men and a woman, followed
by Will's police-friend Scotty, arrived in full protective gear.

"Hey, Scotty." Will led the team toward the loft.

"Not you." Scotty stopped Alex at the foot of the stairs.

"Don't they need a warrant?" she addressed Will.

"Is there something you don't want us to see?" Scotty asked.

"No, just making sure."

"Sure of what? That we're real professionals, and not rent-
a-cops?"

"Coffee?" Alex regretted getting off on the wrong foot with him.

"Not a social visit." Scotty motioned for Will.

Alex sat on the couch and meditated on Will's question: "What's missing?" What am I not seeing? What should be there? By the same token, what things should not be there? Marta's sweater at Kamran's house. A crittercam in Diana's diorama. A tea-timer on Jasmine's tray—time is cultural. Each beat, each action a person takes—the rhythm of their movement, the length of their stride as they move down the street, the choice to pause and gift a double-cheeked kiss or rush off with a quick hello—is all cultural.

What was missing? What was outside the frame? Was she being framed? She stared at the dark walls and waited for Scotty to finally call her up to the loft.

* * *

"Did someone send it to you as a threat?" Scotty asked, pointing at Marta's model house. Alex glanced around as if the culprit might still be there.

"No. I made it. It's Marta."

"Why?" Scotty studied Alex.

"Why the house?" Alex clarified, "Why Marta?"

"For or of Marta?"

"It's anthropology," Alex said, as if that would explain any of this.

"Right. So?" Scotty asked, and Alex explained.

Scotty's walkie talkie crackled.

"It was the hospital." Scotty reported, "Marta's stable, but in a coma; they're not sure why. They pumped her stomach; no other injuries..." Scotty glanced at Alex, and then wrote something down on a pad. "So, you saw smoke coming from the Tinsley House?" Scotty asked, looking up at her.

"Yes." Alex answered without elaborating.

"Hmm," Scotty said and made another note.

"You saw my model house; someone wants her dead," Alex insisted.

"That's a big leap from prank to murder. Lucky you saw the smoke," Scotty remarked. "You're quite an artist," he added.

"Anthropologist." Alex corrected him.

"So, they have no clue what happened?" Will deflected Scotty's attention away from Alex.

"Whacked upside the head is my guess. But no bump and no weapon."

"Probably a rock." Alex suggested.

Scotty looked at her, but addressed Will, "Now how would she know that?"

"Sarge," an officer called over, "need you here."

"Hang on." Scotty answered curtly. "How did you know that?" Scotty asked Alex.

"Didn't you see the little rock by the doll's head?"

"No." Scotty admitted. "I'm listening," he added. "Tell me exactly what you saw."

Alex saw Marta in the Tinsley House, splayed out on the bed, her toe grazing a sign: *Do Not Sit.*

Field Note

Screen memories: Sigmund Freud believed repressed memories surface as perfect film recordings. A memory appears exactly as it happened—flashing before us like a film.

Psychologist Elizabeth Loftus refutes this. In high-adrenaline moments, people rarely remember things like the color of a car that hit them, or the correct time on a clock on the wall as someone beat them. Our experiences are funneled through feelings, thoughts, smells, touch, activity...we will never see a past scene as if we are a camera set to record.

Chapter Seventeen

It seemed strange that life should go on while Marta fought for hers in the hospital. But go on it did. Alex believed that, to change her mood, she would need to move her body. And her current mood, a mixture of exhaustion and fear, needed changing.

The Sourdough Trailhead was teeming with dog walkers, kids, and cross-country skiers enjoying the fresh snow from the previous day's storm. Alex joined the masses on the public trail, imagining safety in numbers, and taking comfort in the thumping pulse of life moving on, as it did after every day, good or bad. She was determined not to keep recounting what had happened, but she could not unsee Marta, passed out on the lumpy bed in the Tinsley House.

As Alex meandered up the path, she was forced to occasionally jump out of the way of a faster skier, or a group of hikers. A couple of times, the same skier who had a minute before been ahead of her, was then behind her. Was she being followed? Or was it the way the trail split for cross-country skiers? There was no reason anyone would be following her, and certainly not on skis. *Safety in numbers,* Alex intoned. It was Kit's idea for her to get back out into the world. Either Kit had downplayed her concern when Alex relayed what had happened, or she simply did not see a connection between Marta's doll being moved in the doll-house and Marta's attack.

"It's a coincidence," Kit said too quickly.

Midway up the trail, a friendly off-leash miniature white doodle stopped to sniff Alex. The dog would have been almost camouflaged by the snow, had it not been for her caramel markings and pink collar. Where was her owner, Alex wondered, when a figure emerged from around the bend. The skier approached, and Alex recognized Jasmine Anarpour's face beautifully framed by her magenta goose-down ski hood.

"Jasmine." Her greeting came out more like a statement.

"Alex. No skis?" Jasmine smiled stiffly.

"Not my sport."

"I've made quite a sport of it today—- better get a move on before my sweat freezes." Jasmine shivered for effect.

"Of course," Alex stepped aside to let her pass. As she did, she called out to her, "Jasmine?"

Jasmine made a sharp half-turn, cutting the snow like an Olympian. "Yes?"

"You heard about Marta?"

"Marta?" Jasmine pulled up her ski poles impatiently.

"She was attacked. She's in a coma. Thought you should know, since she works for you."

"Poor thing," she said evenly.

"Actually—" Alex paused to read an incoming text from Will, "—she's awake!"

Jasmine's face turned as pale as her ski suit. She turned swiftly and skied off, leaving her dog to politely wag a proper goodbye before bouncing along after her. A minute later, the skier in the dark ski suit who had been treading in and out of Alex the whole way up the trail flew down the hill after Jasmine.

Alex's curiosity got the better of her. She ran down the trail after Jasmine and the skier, losing them immediately amid a pack of snowshoers.

Alex arrived at the parking lot as Jasmine was pulling out. Without equipment to disengage, she jumped into her car and followed Jasmine along the icy two-lane country road.

"This is ridiculous." Alex slowed to make a U-turn but changed her mind when she saw Jasmine pull-over to the side of the road, park, and leave the car. Alex parked across the way in a bundle of hay bales that clumped together like survivors of a storm. From her glove compartment, she unearthed the binoculars Will had lent her to observe wildlife and focused them on a fuzzy Jasmine.

She watched her step out of her car, look both ways, and then cross the road and disappear into the side of the hill.

Alex waited for Jasmine to return and drive away before she attempted to retrace her steps up the footpath. She opened her maps app to drop a pin and save the location in case she needed to come back. As she did, she saw that the little mound was called Sugar Pine Hill.

* * *

Jasmine's prints dead-ended before the summit. Strange. The view was the same as it had been all the way up the hill. There was nothing special about the spot. Alex turned to leave and dropped her keys. "Darn," she muttered and bent down to retrieve them, when she saw them: tiny, delicate, white flowers camouflaged by the snow and ice. The same flowers that Marta had in her cabin. And the same ones that Alex had failed to procure by post or by printing at the museum the day she found Marta at the Tinsley House. Alex bent down and gently pulled a single white flower from the frozen ground.

Field Note

Since a cross is never just a cross, was placing the cross in the dollhouse defacement, or secondary production?

According to French sociologist Michel De Certeau, colonial subjects re-purposed colonial products forced upon them by their oppressors. Whether it was uniforms or household items, they would give them a new unintended use. In short, they would make the object their own. This was a political as much as a practical act. It was a form of agency (being in control of your own life and representation). Like using the Berlin wall to write messages to loved ones...that's secondary production. Spray painting it with obscenities, that's deface-ment. But then what is or is not defacement is subjective, even contextual.

Jasmine told me that, in Iran, where there is a strong Islamic code of behavior in the streets, boys and girls cannot hang out together, so they use state-sanctioned and mandatory mourning processions to meet-up. Rather than mourning a martyr, they flirt and exchange numbers. Secondary production is more than using things in a new way, it's about taking back power, and this includes the ways in which we use public space.

Funny—if Banksy had defaced my dollhouse, it would be worth millions. His destruction adds value. See again the idea of spirit, the commodity fetish and cultural capital. Banksy's spirit is pricey.

Anthropologists don't just make art; we don't just describe daily life either; we dissect it, we criticize it, we take it apart to see how it works. But we rarely put it back together the way we found it. We rewrite and re-imagine it—and create a third meaning. Nothing's ever depicted the same as how we found it. Did I destroy something of Marta's life? Is this my fault?

I feel taken apart. It's hard not to see the dollhouse as an extension of myself. It's hard not to feel that I have been assaulted.

Chapter Eighteen

Bozeman's best artist, mother nature, was hard at work on a tapestry of purple mountains that met a fiery sunset—a tableau reflected in the lobby windows of the Museum of The Rockies, where Alex skidded in, late.

A young curator with an iPad called out, "Over here." The party could already be heard in the distance, and Alex was in no mood to be social. She quickly changed from her boots to her flats as the woman checked her in.

"You're the new fellow? Welcome." She secured a VIP band around Alex's wrist. "Go left to the end of the hall and then..."

"Lost?"

Alex startled.

"Don't you look the treat," Diana said, approaching Alex from the direction of the kitchen. "Channeling Audrey Hepburn, despite the cold?" (Alex was freezing in her black capris and flats—grateful for her cashmere sweater. She had not packed party clothes.) "I'm thrilled you came; I can't imagine how rattled you must be," Diana continued.

"Putting it mildly." Scotty had instructed her to stay vague about the details if anyone asked her about finding Marta.

"Follow me. Let's distract you, at least for tonight," Diana took Alex's arm and led her into the Wolf Exhibit.

"Wow." Alex adjusted her glasses and regarded the large and loud crowd.

"Didn't know we had this many people in Bozeman, did you?" Diana laughed.

Alex pointed to the buzz of activity in the far corner of the Dino Hall. "Drinks?" She was parched

"Yes, head over to the Maiasaura and turn right. You're in for a surprise. It's my best work. But now I need to run and check on things."

* * *

If the museum was royalty, Jack Horner would be king.

"Our deus ex machina," Alex heard Jack tell his crowd of admirers gathered by his Maiasaura discovery. His discovery in northern Montana was one of those "average-day" legends—when a paleontologist casually spots a bone sticking out of the side of a hill while eating a peanut-butter sandwich. This bone was much easier to spot than to uncover, as it was lodged below the edge of a cliff with a substantial drop. As luck would have it, a mathematics graduate student who was volunteering at the dig happened to be an expert climber.

Jack caught her eye, and Alex asked, "Have you read that Scooby Doo story about a dog who steals a bone out of a dinosaur exhibit before the museum's grand opening and buries it in the museum yard?"

"Missed that one." Jack smiled.

Alex turned a beet red. What possessed her to re-tell such a silly story to a famous professor?

"Didn't read as a child. Dyslexic," Jack added casually.

"Me, too!" No wonder she felt so comfortable with Jack.

"That explains your creativity. I loved your project proposal the minute I read it," Jack complimented her.

"You read my proposal?"

"Very out-of-the-box."

"Even though I'm putting people in boxes?" Alex chuckled.

"And there's the dyslexia sense of humor," Jack smiled at her warmly. Alex felt like the dog who had found her bone in the least likely place.

"There are good attributes?" Alex was surprised.

"Are you kidding? Haven't you read *The Dyslexic Advantage* or *Thinking like Einstein*?"

A waitress passed with a tray of appetizers.

"Marta?" Jack looked at her, confused.

"She's in the hospital—coma," Alex said carefully.

"That bad? Didn't realize."

"Appetizer?" The waitress asked impatiently. They took a satay stick each, and she hurried away.

"Tough job, stepping into Marta's shoes at the last minute. This is not an easy crowd. Marta knows everyone—knows how to handle everyone. Especially after the champagne starts flowing. Poor Marta." Jack shook his head.

"Isn't the Tinsley House usually closed this time of year?" Alex asked.

"She cleans it once a month."

"Apparently nothing was taken?"

"That's odd. Are you sure?"

"Third-hand information," Alex said tentatively.

"This never happens in Bozeman," Jack sighed heavily.

"So people keep telling me."

"I assure you. Horrible what happened."

"She was my first volunteer." Alex looked wistful.

"Why her?" Jack rubbed his beard, "She strikes me as a private person. Did her job and went home. Didn't mingle much. And we know Diana likes the museum staff to mingle. Odd choice for your first volunteer."

"Diana strong-armed her," Alex half-joked. "She came to clean my cabin the day I arrived. Maybe it was impulsive of me. Not my usual modus anthropologus."

"We are an impulsive bunch. So, no coercing?"

"I may have bought her a hot chocolate the next day."

"From the little French place in the Baxter Hotel? No wonder she agreed." Jack smiled.

"Are you saying you'll be my next subject if I buy you a hot chocolate?" Alex asked playfully.

The lights flickered; the show was about to begin.

"Will the Wolf Project stop the poachers? I doubt they frequent museums." Alex's question was lost under the crackle of the microphone as the MC for the evening cleared his throat.

"That's my cue," Jack said and disappeared into the crowd.

If the MC's eager grasp on the microphone was anything to judge by, they were in for a long night of speeches.

He began by holding up a flint tool. Alex's heart raced.

While one paleo tool looked like another, the flint tool the MC held up bore a striking resemblance to the one left in Alex's model of Marta's life.

"Andy!? Where is Andy?" asked the MC.

A burly man with wild curly gray hair that would have looked more appropriate on a local hunter than the museum's head artist joined the MC on stage and took a bow.

"No one re-creates more authentic-looking and precise paleolithic tools for our museum outreach program than this man. You could probably kill someone with this hand-axe." He paused for effect; no one laughed, and so he continued: "Andy would have nowhere to place his tools if it weren't for this powerhouse woman." A cadre of loud students roared and repeated, "Place his tool!"

Alex prayed for brevity—paleo poetry would have been better than the MC's bumbling jokes. Her prayer was answered.

"I give you—Diana of the Diorama!"

Diana, petite but foreboding in a little black dress, her hair in her usual chic chignon at the nape of her neck, strode onto the stage as if she were in London or Paris.

"It's my great pleasure..." Diana started.

"Her great pleasure!" the students roared.

"...to introduce this year's museum interns and fellows," Diana continued.

Finally, the welcome charade was over, and they were granted a brief intermission, courtesy of the Anarpours, who had yet to arrive. A surprisingly good university quartet was quickly drowned out by the clamor of the crowd. Alex was searching for the quickest route to the bar when Pete Holgan appeared and handed her a glass of fizzy apple juice.

"Pete to the rescue again," she smiled and gratefully accepted the delicate glass, "Was I eyeing the bar that obviously?" She took a sip of the cold, sugary bubbles and sighed with pleasure.

"Deus ex machina, bubbles from the Gods," Pete laughed.

"Or from the goddess Diana's geyser. She re-created Punch Bowl Spring," a student said.

"Are you sure it's not the Devils Punch Bowl?" Pete joked.

Alex noticed Pete's graying hair for the first time.

"What is it?" Pete asked and brushed his hand through his hair.

"Nothing," Alex was embarrassed to be caught staring. His bio in the Museum catalogue mentioned he had been a photographer his entire career, and that his career began in 2004. Unless he was graying prematurely, he must have had an alternate career before becoming a photographer.

"It has two names," the student brought the conversation back to Diana's geyser.

"It's all about how you see it," Pete suggested.

"Actually, it has three names," said another student who joined in. "H.B. Calfee, a photographer from the 1800s called it the Fairy Well—an enchanted place of less menacing magic."

"Like Baudelaire," Alex added, absently.

"Huh?" the students asked in unison.

"Projecting dreams, rather than recording reality. Don't all photographers frame the world as they see it? The neorealists did. They claimed not to film what exists but what has the possibility to exist," Alex said, looking at Pete.

"You mean they staged things?" the intern asked.

"Staged?" Pete took affront.

"Instead of documenting reality through a recording, they recorded to re-create reality. They wanted a new vision for the future. Who wouldn't after living through World War II?" asked Alex, tired and ready to go home.

"Didn't they simply let the camera roll?" Pete was unimpressed.

"No. And that's the point," Alex said, sipping her Martinelli's.

"Openings are such a bore," Pete said dismissively.

And yet here you are. She was still hurt he had ditched her in Gardiner.

"So, how's the project going?" Alex asked, impatient for the show to proceed so they could dig into the gourmet catering Diana had promised.

"The Nat Geo one?"

Alex nodded. She had no idea Pete was working on more than one project.

"The alpha female of the Yellowstone Pack," Alex answered.

"Ahh, the rare white who was shot by a poacher right outside the park some years back. Yes, it's the anniversary of her death. She's the star of tonight's big exhibit. I'm doing a story on the survivors," Pete said. His laser-blue eyes scanned the room.

"Didn't they determine it was a natural death?" Alex asked.

"What—with a bullet in her hind? I doubt it. Either way, the rest of the Lamar Pack is still in danger of extinction. The park needs to raise funds for the wolf-conservation project."

"I hear there's a lot of controversy there." Alex said. She noticed the student and intern leave, less interested in this topic.

"Cattle farmers did not want the wolves back. Between their pranks and the poachers, it's been hard to keep up the numbers." Pete swiveled on his heels and pointed toward the back wall. "That photograph is one I did of her three years ago when I was here on assignment. This is the sequel," he said, pleased with himself.

"Same wolf in the Nat Geo shot?"

"Yes, with her pack."

"It's sublime," Alex conceded.

"Right place at the right time, with the right equipment, and a steady hand. My parents would have preferred I was a surgeon," Pete said, holding out a shaky hand. Alex smiled politely and asked, "Will they catch him?"

"Catch who?" Pete was distracted by something at the far end of the hall.

"The poacher."

"You assume a male?"

"Yes."

"You're probably right. And, no, I don't think they will catch him. They never do, which is why they keep getting away with it."

"With murder?" Alex asked.

"Yes. Precisely. The wolves were all but extinct a decade ago. It's a precarious situation. It's important to keep putting the beauty of this incredible species into the public's face. Beauty is the best form of advocacy," Pete said. He was gazing at the back of the hall toward the kitchen where Marta's replacement was standing with her empty tray.

"Beauty. Survival of the fittest?" Alex asked.

"Not in the animal world; poachers go after beauty." Pete touched Alex's cheek. She backed away, spilling her drink.

"Easy." He swayed; Alex reached to steady him. He seemed drunk. He scanned the room as if in search of someone, spotted whoever it was and took off.

"Odd," she muttered. "Rude." Alex watched him get swallowed by the crowd.

Will appeared and handed her a monogramed handkerchief.

"How did you know? I was hoping Marta's replacement

would come by with napkins." Alex set down her sticky glass and took the kerchief. "Do you have them dry-cleaned or do you wash and iron them yourself? Surely no one uses starch anymore."

Will laughed.

"Looking for your stray? He took off that way," Alex pointed in the direction Pete had gone.

"Hardly. Pete Holgan is the last person I want to follow around."

"Following me then?" Alex asked.

His reply was lost to the crackling microphone—the MC had re-appeared at his perch.

"Silence, gather, silence! Diana? Diana?!" He surveyed the shoulder-to-shoulder crowd, "Oh, Diana?

"Now, before she comes up on the stage, I'm going to embarrass her a little with the story of her arrival. We have an anthropologist in our midst today, and I hear they are big on arrival stories," the MC squinted in Alex's direction.

"What does that mean?" Will asked Alex.

"Ah, the arrival of the anthropologist among the 'savages.'"

"You have one for Bozeman?"

"Yeah, Diana taking me to the Back Barn," Alex said. Will laughed.

"It was in the Dino Room that fate smiled on Diana—" the MC started.

Diana rushed onto the stage and reached for the microphone.

"The rest is history. Ladies and gentlemen, I give you once again Diana of the Diorama, who will lead us down a path to a world of wonder and delight."

Diana smiled tightly and took the microphone. She caught her breath and said, "You all know how hard we, the museum, and the wolf conservationists have worked to rebuild the

Yellowstone pack. After years of near extinction, the wolves have returned to Yellowstone!"

There was wild applause.

"To," Diana cut into the applause, "To find a new generation of enemies. It is our job as stewards of this beautiful place to preserve what we have tirelessly rebuilt. Tonight, the museum is pleased to introduce our new Wolf Exhibit, generously funded by the Jasmine and Kamran Anarpour Foundation." Diana gestured for Kamran to join her on stage. He bowed but stayed put.

"I am also pleased to announce that the tireless Peter Holgan, whose beautiful photography is at the center of this exhibit, is here with us this evening." Diana paused, and, when it was clear Pete was nowhere to be found, she continued. "He will be signing copies of his latest book, *Freeze Frame: Yellowstone in Winter*, at the back table after the unveiling." She handed the microphone back to the MC.

"Without further ado, let us unveil Diana's world of the wolf!" He swept his hand toward the velvet-roped platform where Diana's Diorama was covered by a satin curtain.

"*Voilà!*" He said, but nothing happened. "*Voilà!*" He repeated.

Someone missed their cue.

"Lights! Curtain!" he yelled furiously. The lights dimmed at his command, and the hall fell into darkness. The curtain dropped from the diorama and a spotlight lit a red taxidermized fox that played in a snowbank below two tall pine trees—a snow owl in one, an osprey in the other. The light moved, illuminating a path of paw prints along the course of a thin stream. Finally, the spotlight found what it was seeking, and blazed a brilliant beam on the Lamar alpha female, standing sentinel atop a clear, clean, pristine mound of (fiberglass) snow. The wolf gazed out in the distance, oblivious of Pete Holgan, who lay motionless like carrion at her feet, his wide eyes staring up into the face of his bestial assailant.

"Pete?!" Diana screamed and charged toward her diorama. She tripped on a wire, and a loud bang erupted from her tree-stump crittercam—inches from Pete's head. Had the snow been real, it would have been saturated with Pete's blood. But everything inside the dark, quiet diorama was already fixed perfectly in place—save for Pete's blood, dripping down the Formica snow and splattered across the soft white fur of the stoic wolf.

The Devil's Punchbowl fizzed and hissed in the brief hush of disbelief. The MC fumbled for the diorama lights and accidentally shut off all the lights in the auditorium. Pandemonium ensued as people rushed toward the only exit.

"No one move!" someone demanded, too late. "Jack, the doors!"

"Call 911!" Diana screamed.

Finally, the MC managed to turn on the house lights.

"It's too late, Diana." Will held Pete's wrist in his hand. "It's too late," he repeated. "And—" He said no more.

"The police are on their way," Jack announced calmly from where he ministered to an extremely pale-looking Diana.

Chapter Nineteen

"Shot at close range" was the buzz in the cafeteria where Alex would have preferred to have stayed, drinking watery coffee among the comfort of a crowd —albeit a crowd of possible murder suspects—than at home alone. But the police took their statements with speed and sent everyone home, where Alex was faced with the dread of walking into her cold empty cabin.

She dialed Kit, again, and hung-up without leaving a message. Where was Kit?

She texted Kit, *CALL ME.*

Freezing, and with no better plan, she inserted her key into the door and turned it. She gathered her courage and stepped inside. She sensed a presence. She glanced around the room and saw that her computer was still sitting on the coffee table. If there had been a break-in, they'd left and did not take the most valuable thing she owned.

This did not reassure Alex.

Marta's assailant took none of the valuable antiques from the Tinsley House. In New York City, crimes were anonymous, unseen, and marked by a faraway siren. In sleepy Bozeman, a man who had intimately brushed her cheek was murdered shortly after. In New York, she was in a big building surrounded by other tenants who would hear her if she screamed. Here, she was surrounded by acres of uncultivated land and a single neighbor who was laid-up in a hospital bed, recovering from an assault.

Alex called Diana.

"She pulled the trigger," Will said, answering Diana's phone. "She took a Tylenol PM and went straight to bed. Will you be OK?" Will asked.

"Yes," Alex lied. She did not want to be alone. She thought of Diana, who would forever relive the visceral tug of wire against her leg that killed Pete.

Alex pulled down all the blinds and turned on all the lights. She checked every window and door. All the while, she imagined breath on the back of her neck. It became heavier with every step—closing in on her with each minute that passed. Pete joked that her the cabin was haunted, and now who knew where his ghost would choose to drift?

She changed into sweats and pulled on a bright chartreuse sweater. *At least they'll see me coming against the snow when I flee.* It was too early for bed. She could drive to a local motel and put it on her credit card. Professor Lilian would say, *No hasty decisions. A Samurai sits with her sword and waits.* Alex had neither a Samurai's nerves of steel nor their swords.

* * *

"Where have you been?" Alex demanded, when Kit finally called.

"My grandmother's eightieth. I told you I was driving her to Martha's Vineyard. You know how Thea feels about mobile phones. She made me turn it off and dump it in her big old church bag. What's going on? Did something happen with the ranger? Is he making the moves?" Kit teased.

"Pete's dead."

Alex filled Kit in on the past 24 hours, including her missing model house and the defacement of the Marta model.

"Alex, come home," Kit responded.

"I am not sure I'm allowed to. I might be a suspect or a witness or something." *Home where?* When Cora died, Professor Lilian became her guardian. She took Alex to Oxford where Lilian was a visiting professor and where Alex, to her own surprise, ended-up as an undergraduate. The tutorial system was perfect for a student like Alex, who learned better in small groups. Lilian passed away during Alex's last year at Oxford, leaving Alex effectively alone in the world and without an inheritance. Alex went straight to Columbia for graduate school, by which point she had lived half of her life in university housing. Without her Columbia scholarship, she was effectively homeless.

She fought back tears, set her imaginary Samurai sword aside, and admitted, "I'm scared."

"Alex, come home," Kit repeated. Kit was her home, her family.

"Look, I'm going to call—" Kit started, but Alex abruptly said, "Shh."

"Alex?"

"Someone knocked...What door doesn't have a peephole?" She crouched down and crawled to the living room window and peeked outside. "It's a National Parks Jeep."

"Let him in, Alex."

"Kit, I don't know who to trust. I feel as unhinged as my dollhouse."

"Pray to Cardia."

"Who?"

"The Goddess of hinges," Kit said seriously.

"Love you." Alex smiled.

"Call me if he leaves. And text me if he's staying."

"Staying?"

"What gentleman wouldn't? On the couch, of course."

* * *

Alex answered the door as Will turned to leave.

"Wait," she sounded desperate.

Will turned back. "Thought I'd stop in and see how you are," he said.

Alex was about to give her knee-jerk "I'm OK" when tears welled-up.

"Not great," she answered honestly. Will handed her a handkerchief, and she smiled.

"Have you eaten?" he asked.

She shook her head.

"Neither have I. I stopped by the Co-op. I have groceries in the Jeep. We could cook dinner?" he offered tentatively.

Alex blinked back the tears and noticed that Will was still dressed in the navy suit he wore to the opening. "Sounds great.

Though you might be a bit overdressed." Alex smiled. "Come in."

They took his groceries to the kitchen.

"Cake-pop?" Will handed her a bouquet of freshly baked cake-pops.

"What are we cooking?" Alex asked. Will was preoccupied by a slew of incoming texts.

"Right, sorry." Will set down his phone, opened the grocery bag and pulled out the ingredients one by one. "Cauliflower steak, sautéed portobello mushrooms, and a Risotto." He laid everything out on the counter at the ready.

"Vegetarian?"

"Since I was five."

"Hippy parents?" Alex finished off her second cake-pop.

"Hardly," Will laughed, "My waspy parents eat a burrito? Now, that would be something. No, I've been into animals since kindergarten. I can't love them and eat them at the same time."

"I wonder how many murderers are vegetarian?" Alex picked up the cauliflower and held it out, "Yorick's skull," she joked.

"A fan of Hamlet? I don't consider people who eat meat murderers. Murder is a deeply neurotic, emotional instinct. Unless it is premeditated, it rarely has anything to do with ethics."

"So, the premeditated ones are ethical?" Alex asked.

"Like the activist who kills the abortionist. It's murder, but it stems from a personal, if not paradoxical, ethics."

"Paradoxical for sure: thou shalt not kill," Alex declared.

"Eye for an eye?" Will suggested.

"Do you look down on meat eaters?" Alex squinted at him.

"No."

"Was Pete's murder premeditated?"

"All signs point to yes."

"So that eliminates a serial killer?" Alex suggested.

"How so?"

"Don't they usually fly by the seat of their pants?" Alex asked.

"Interesting way to put it," Will said.

"Do you think your buddy Scotty is capable of solving this?"

"Not sure; he may need a little help." Will was pensive. "He's been a good friend."

Will told Alex about the first time he met Scotty. It was at the edge of the Yellowstone River where Scotty was knee-deep in the water with his fishing pole and his thoughts.

"It was his day off, and all he wanted and expected was to be alone. But, when I appeared, he simply nodded and pointed to a spare fishing rod. 'Help yourself.'" Will smiled at the memory, "I was glad to be spared the usual surprise that I am a Ranger."

Alex blushed; she was guilty of the same surprise.

"Instead, Scotty said, 'Got some bait right over there.' He pointed to a rock where his gear was laid out as tidily as a surgeon's tray: a neatly wrapped sandwich in wax paper, car keys, sunscreen, fishing tackle, and bait. I took the rod up and managed to get it into the river without completely knotting the line. We spent the rest of the afternoon in silent companionship, waiting for a bite. By dusk, neither of us had caught a thing, and Scotty suggested dinner at the Back Barn. It's been an easy friendship. Scotty is hardy and kind and allows me to be myself," Will concluded.

· · ·

After dinner, Alex asked Will to help her fix her bathroom window. He tried moving it up and down, but it would not budge.

"If I can't move it no one can," Will said.

"OK, Superman."

"A kitten couldn't crawl through here," he assured her.

"Thanks." She was unconvinced.

"Anyway, it's getting late, I should..."

"We should start a fire. It's getting cold," Alex said. She turned to look at him and he lightly brushed a piece of hair from her face. It reminded her of Pete. She turned away.

"You're shivering, let's go sit by a warm fire."

They were sitting companionably in front of the fire that Will had started when he broke the silence and said, "There's something else; I wanted to wait until you had some food in you. Scotty wants to see you first thing."

"Me?" Alex asked.

"This is confidential. Pete was not killed by a bullet. That was not blood we saw."

"What?"

"Like everything else in the diorama, his murder was staged."

"Obviously," Alex said.

"I mean, it was a paint gun. He was already dead. The gun was all show." Will paused and then added, "The paint...it matches the sample from your model of Marta's house."

Alex's heart raced and her eyes teared.

"I..."

"It's OK. You don't have to speak..."

"But surely ... I mean, do they think I did it? Or is someone after me and Pete, and Marta? So, he is dead? But how?"

"Yes. That's all I know. We'll learn more tomorrow."

"I need water." Alex said, standing.

"I'll go," Will stood.

"No, I need..." she needed space. She needed to cry privately.

Alex poured herself a glass of water and stared out the kitchen window and across the field, past Marta's cabin, where police tape flapped in the breeze.

Paint? There had to be a connection between Marta's attack and Pete's murder. And, so far, she seemed to be it.

A coyote howled in the distance, and Alex mourned the innocent house cat that would get it tonight.

Field Note

Plato thought poetry was deceptive because it was beautiful. And beauty lured people away from truth. People tend to distrust beautiful documentaries. Grit makes something seem more real. Is beauty deceptive? Does my dollhouse have to be beautiful to be ethnographic, to represent life?

The phrase "If it bleeds, it leads" keeps popping into my head. The more traumatic, destructive, or gory the photo or the headline, the more newspapers it sells. That's pretty much why any given war is front-page news. Does that make photography complicit in war? Look at what happened in Vietnam. Had a Western photographer not shown up for the execution, would the execution have happened? Eddie Adams won a Pulitzer Prize for photographing the execution of a Viet Cong—he captured the moment the bullet entered the man's head. The executioner waited for the photographers to appear before shooting the prisoner. Again, had Adams not shown up for the execution, would the execution have happened? If a tree falls in a forest and no one photographs it...

So much to think about.

Anything to avoid thoughts of Pete. I can't believe he's dead. He is no longer subject but object. He is now the central theme in a photograph of his own death taken by a pathologist, a detective. Only, his photo will be evidence, and not a memento mori.

Chapter Twenty

The lights dimmed behind them as they made their way through the vacant museum.

Scotty had questioned Alex about the paint at the station and then asked Will to meet him at the museum to look at the crime scene.

"Tell me again what she's doing here?" he asked pointedly.

Will had invited Alex to come along. He knew she was afraid. That she was innocent.

"I'm staying with her until it's safe," Will answered.

"What's up with these lights going on and off?" Scotty narrowed his eyes.

"Keeping the lights on a timer conserves energy." Alex explained.

"A sensor triggers them when someone walks in, and they go out when the warm body leaves," Alex continued. At what point had Pete's body gone cold? Alex shivered.

"And why are we going to the basement?" Scotty asked.

"You want to find Jack, you got to find the bones," Alex answered. She led them into the Bone Room. The ugly metal shelving reached like never-ending tendrils to the top of the unusually high ceilings. Coupled by the institutional brown linoleum floors, the dark, creepy room became a claustrophobic cavern.

"Where do we sit?" Scotty asked.

"It's a lab, not a drawing room," Will answered.

"Each shelf contains a single body part, every column a single animal, and every wall a single archeological site," Alex explained.

Scotty banged around the room like an elephant in a China store—fingering specimen splinters from tiny glass vials, moving femurs, and displacing discs.

"What are these, anyway?" Scotty asked holding up a puzzle piece of vertebrae ready to be played with by one of the museum's many paleontologists.

"He's not here," Alex said quickly, turning to leave before Scotty did any more damage to Jack's lab.

"We just arrived, and you want to leave?" Scotty said.

During the day, the booming excitement of intern gossip bounced off the metal cabinets as a hive of co-eds meticulously tagged every shard. By evening the interns left and took with them all the reassuring sounds of life. And without Jack there was an off-limits vibe. A vibe Alex's anthropological training urged her to obey. It was as if the spirits of the specimens were guarding their secrets until Jack arrived.

"Joseph Campbell said of voodoo ceremonies, 'The spirits arrive when the anthropologist departs.'"

"So, depart." Scotty said, annoyed.

"Scotty," Will implored him.

"Don't anthropologists have a history of pillaging?" Scotty asked. "Was all this pillaged?" Scotty was smarter than Alex gave him credit for.

"You hear about Penn?" Alex asked.

"No, what happened?" asked Will.

"The Anthropology Museum's forensics department was using human remains from the Move Movement bombing—children no less—to teach their lab classes."

"What?" Scotty asked.

"A Black-liberation movement," Will explained. "The police bombed their headquarters. Let's be grateful these are animal bones."

"My friend was a summer intern there. She said the museum tried to repatriate ritual objects to their original owners—you know, like canoes, totems, masks, and... bones."

"Oh, so now they're the good guys?" Scotty asked.

"Hardly. They pulled all these objects from the exhibits and readied them for the big day when the museum officials would hand them over to the tribal elders. The repatriation ceremony basically was the janitor wheeling in one object after another for the medicine man to cleanse, bless, and welcome home. The ceremony was ending when an innocuous piece was rolled out for the medicine man's final examination. Get this: he took one look at it and said, '*Dark magic.*' He refused to touch it, to cleanse it, or to take it home."

Will whistled.

"Nobody moved. Not a single twitch. You could hear a pin drop. Finally, the director of the museum asked the janitor to wheel it back to its cabinet. The janitor took one look at him and said, 'No way,'" Alex told them.

"Shoot," Scotty said, looking around. He pulled his wool scarf more tightly around his neck.

"Wondering which objects contain dark magic?" Alex asked him.

"This might be an ideal temperature for bones, but not for human flesh," he said.

"Bone-chilling." Will joked.

"Is that right?" Jack asked, walking in and taming the energy of the restless spirits. "Fossils are fine at temperatures between 60-80 degrees Fahrenheit, but this fossil thinks better in the cold. What's up, boys? This is the wrong time and place for Scrabble night."

"A little bone bingo." Will did not seem the type to joke when he was nervous.

"We could use help around here sorting shards." Jack patted Scotty on the back.

"Too busy. The FBI is taking over Pete's investigation, as if that would stop me. With Marta's assault the same week, we can't be sure a crazed killer isn't on the loose here in Bozeman. I'm staying on the case. So, tell me about the crittercam. The mechanics? Who had access, and all that?"

"Diana is the person to ask." Jack buried his hands in his pockets.

"Not returning my calls."

"Hmm," Jack was worried, "That's not like Diana. She was doing much better when I checked on her yesterday. Listen, folks, no offense intended to Bozeman here, but Pete was part of a much larger world of international intrigue. He was based in Washington, DC. I'm sure that whoever pulled the trigger, and pulled is the operative word here, was not from Pete's life in Bozeman."

Alex texted Kit. *Call me; need you to check something at Nat Geo.*

"Well, the trigger that killed him was pulled here in Bozeman," Scotty said—a point no one could argue.

"Go on," Jack rubbed his beard.

"We know the crittercam was outfitted with a gun triggered by a trip wire." Scotty pulled back on an imaginary rope for effect. "But how exactly? I bet the FBI already knows. Can you believe it?" Scotty paced as he spoke. "How can they expect our help if they won't give us any information?"

"Because they don't expect our help." Jack pointed out the obvious.

"Oh, come on, Jack; you love solving a good puzzle," Will said.

"As much as you do, my friend. This one is more up your alley."

"How so?"

"It sounds like a metaphor."

"Yes," Alex agreed. "The night I met Pete at the Back Barn, he told us a cozy fireside story about the villager who goes off to shoot a tiger. When he corners the animal, he shoots him with a camera."

"Ah. Shoots. See, metaphor," Jack added.

"His weapon of choice is a camera." Alex agreed.

"There's something to this interchange of a camera and a gun," Will suggested.

"Shoot to kill," Scotty said.

"Shoot being the operative word," Will agreed.

"Which is why everyone says it's a poacher," Scotty noted.

"But you don't agree?" Jack asked.

"Those men kill animals. They're hunters, not murderers." Scotty insisted.

"I'd venture that they are one and the same. Depends on who you're talking to," Will said.

"Hey, Will, I'm not saying they aren't criminals and in the wrong, but it isn't murder. Having had the undeserved pleasure of meeting a few of these fools, I am unconvinced that they would go that far."

"Really? Have you seen *Gorillas in the Mist?*" asked Alex.

"That's in..."

"Don't say it Scotty. If you say Africa is different, and that we aren't capable of that here ...," Alex started.

"I wasn't going to say that. I was going to say that was in a high-stakes trade, real mafiosos."

"And wolves aren't?" Alex asked.

"Not to that degree. That's serious money in Africa. Anyway," Scotty took out a pad and a pen; he was getting down to business. "For starters, who all had access to the diorama between the time we last saw Pete alive and when he died?" Scotty read his question from his notepad.

"Anyone at the opening."

"Seriously? Jack, how does that narrow things down? You sure? I was counting on you."

"This might help—the crittercam had a trip wire that needed to be set up before the party. The killer would have needed time, light, and privacy. Not to mention access. None of which was available during the party," Jack explained.

"Timeframe?" Scotty asked the next question from his notepad.

"Any time after Diana was done tinkering with it. Had she done any last-minute adjustments, she'd have been the one with a bullet through her head," Jack answered solemnly.

"A paintball bullet," Will clarified.

"Now you're saying she may have been the intended victim?" Scotty was wide-eyed.

"I'm not saying anything. I'm telling you what I know," Jack answered.

"And I know this: the crittercam was a contentious addition to the diorama as far as Pete was concerned," Alex told them without thinking.

"Really? So..." Scotty started when Jack put his hand up to stop him.

"Let Diana tell you," Jack told him. "Her story; not ours to tell."

Alex breathed a sigh of relief; she did not want to admit that she heard Diana fight with Pete while hidden behind a crate in the diorama.

"Besides, Diana couldn't have been the intended victim because the person who would want revenge on Diana was already dead," Will pointed out.

"OK, what else?" Scotty made another note.

"Look folks, I'm not a mechanic, but I played with these things as a kid—someone disconnected the wire. Maybe it happened after it shot Pete. It wasn't connected when the police showed up," Jack told them.

"Could it have come undone?" Will asked.

Jack shrugged.

"What else?" Scotty asked, poised to take notes.

"Mechanically, the trip wire is an easy set-up. But had to be done when no one was watching. My bet is on off-hours. However, the killer would have to be there at the time the wire was tripped, right after the lights came on, to ensure that Pete, and no one else, got shot," Jack explained.

"Maybe he wasn't the intended victim?" Alex suggested again.

"Who else?" Scotty asked, annoyed.

"Marta, for starters. Someone wants her dead. Wouldn't

she be the one to dust and clean before a big opening?" Alex asked. Jack nodded in agreement.

"Diana let Marta clean the Diorama? Yeah, right," Scotty chuckled and bit his pen.

"Actually," Jack contradicted him, "Marta was the only one she allowed to clean it."

"Who would know this?" asked Will.

"Any one of us who works here would know Marta cleans right before a big show," Jack answered.

"But surely not when she is laid up in a hospital," Scotty protested.

"Maybe they expected her back. Maybe they hoped to scare her off?" Alex suggested.

"With a paint gun?"

"Or they scared her off and incapacitated her to be sure that Pete, and only Pete, would be in there. Which means they would have to know that Diana would not allow anyone but Marta in. And know how hard it is to get a replacement cleaner in 24 hours," Jack noted.

"But you all managed," Scotty noted.

Jack was pensive as he said, "Yes, in time for the opening event, but not before."

"The killer hit Marta upside the head to get her out of the way so she wouldn't catch them rigging the camera?" Scotty summed up.

"Or she staged her own assault to get us off her track. She has keys to my cabin." Alex told them. "No, seriously, this whole ruse needs more prep. This was not a last-minute rig," Alex concluded.

"No way; too much could go wrong. They could have killed the wrong person." Will agreed.

"Who says they didn't?" The men looked at Alex.

"But it *feels* correct." Jack said, stroking his beard, "When

I'm putting together a scenario with nothing but shards, I need to sense the story: was this a herd run off a cliff? Did they die of malnutrition? What signs am I looking for? Broken bones, calcification? Anyway, Pete was a natural addition to the diorama scene; he belonged there. You said so yourself, Alex," Jack explained.

"Did Diana plan for him to be in there at the opening?" Scotty asked.

"No way." Alex regretted this admission. How could she admit to hiding behind a crate? Spying on Diana?

"Either his big ego took over, or he was purposefully getting her goat," Scotty said.

"Or he was lured in there," Will suggested.

"Hard to say, tracks and prints don't register on Formica," Scotty said.

"Well, he certainly stole the show," Alex concluded.

"Not the best last act," Jack added solemnly.

"Poor guy," Scotty paused for a moment of respectful silence before adding, "It had to be someone who knew he was staying for the opening. And someone who didn't like him."

"You think?" Will said.

"Oh, it was more than dislike. This killer wanted to kill and humiliate him at the same time. Otherwise, why risk getting caught in such a public place?" Alex asked.

"True. If they knew this much about his schedule, they'd know how to find him alone. This couldn't possibly have been their best option," Jack agreed.

"Unless it was." Will suggested.

"What do you mean?" Scotty turned to look at him.

"Someone for whom this would be the best opportunity," Will explained.

"Diana's too obvious a suspect. If anything, it looks like

she's being set up. Besides, I've known her since she was a student; she wouldn't hurt a fly," Jack said.

"But she sure can scare one," Scotty gave a low-whistle, and Alex laughed.

"Yes, she can." Jack agreed and added, "I'm off."

Jack left, taking the warmth with him.

"We need to talk to Diana." Scotty slipped his little pad in his coat pocket. "But first let's go look at the kitchen," Scotty said, eager to leave the Bone Room.

"The kitchen?" Alex inquired.

"The killer might have been hiding out in there," Scotty explained. "There's a passage from the kitchen to the exhibition hall," he said, looking at Alex. This was news to her.

Will reached for Alex's hand as they left the Bone Room.

* * *

"Used pod. Still hot." Scotty was inspecting the coffeemaker as Alex and Will joined him in the kitchen. He tossed the used pod in the trash and placed a new one in the machine. "Someone's around; voices down, OK?"

"OK, Sherlock." Will winked at Alex. "I'll take one too if you're buying," Will pointed at the coffee machine. "Want one?" he asked Alex.

Scotty popped another pod in the machine and handed the freshly brewed cup to Alex who thanked him, grateful to have something warm in her cold hands.

"Marta's domain, huh?" Scotty walked around picking-up knives and opening drawers like a TV detective.

"He's a good guy," Will whispered to Alex as they both watched Scotty's one-handed search with amusement.

"We're missing something," Will said when Scotty was done with his surveillance.

"No kidding. Better put: we have nothing. Let's go; it's getting late." Scotty took one last exasperated scan of the room when something caught his eye.

"Wait," he said, walking over to the far corner of the kitchen, where he bent down and gingerly retrieved a perfectly ironed and starched white handkerchief with the initials HWD.

Field Note

Here's another little secret: Anthropologists abridge culture. An ethnography is never the full story. We are expected to do several things in our ethnographies: describe what we have observed and then critique the data. Critique does not mean to criticize but to observe and report with a critical eye. We dissect meaning, actions, rituals, beliefs, and explain why something is the way it is. Take for example the international ritual or craze of seeking-out little yellow characters that don't exist. *Pokemon GO*: the largest treasure hunt in history. What are the economic, social, and cultural incentives to playing Pokemon GO? What are the risks? Is there a negative or positive view of people who play? How does it interfere in daily life (stopping traffic, falling off a mountain, losing a whole day to a fruitless search)? What are the benefits? Teens get fresh air.

We judge the rituals we observe all the time, though we would never admit it. We anthropologists are "open-minded," but we draw conclusions. Many of us come to our research area with preconceived notions and stereotypes—what we call prior field experience. The very choice of a field area already means there is a sense of something...interest, curiosity, fear, loathing ...something that makes the eight-year endeavor of a PhD worth our while. We choose something that is meaningful and interesting to us for deep personal reasons that we may not unearth until we are in the field.

The kernel remains and becomes the subjective frame we have already placed on our research. We try to stay cognizant of this; but it's hard to step outside of one's own subjective frame.

What's a subjective frame, you ask? It's basically everything that makes you: your upbringing, your religious beliefs, your political and cultural beliefs, your sex and your gender, the environment in which you grew up, the people around you, and your life experiences. All of this affects how you interpret the world, and, in turn, how you, as a social scientist, study, interpret, and represent it for others. We see the world through our own subjectivity. There's a lot that goes into the cultural frame, and more still that goes into the subjective frame and, especially, a photographic frame. Take something like framing a film scene: even documentary cannot fully represent reality because we are still framing and cordoning-off a limited view.

Take Margaret Mead. She thought if she used a tripod and aimed the camera at a ritual or a scene of daily life then she could replicate it exactly as it was playing out before she set-up the tripod and started recording. It's called "reproducing a 'pre-filmic reality.'" It's the idea that the camera is a fly on the wall capturing life as it is. But that is just not the case. When a camera arrives on the scene, people become self-conscious; they hide what they are doing, perform for the camera, or freeze-up. The camera rarely captures events as they would have been without the camera—the pre-filmic. And it would be unethical to use a hidden camera. So there you have it, the camera muddies the petri dish, so to speak. The anthropologist is entangled in the footage. An anthropologist can't take her subjectivity out of the frame. It begins with something as simple as deciding where to place the tripod, where to aim the camera. *Where to place the crittercam.* So, when you place a tripod, you frame an area. That, my friend, is a subjective frame. The documentary is a subjective representation of reality because, whatever we do, we are still framing a subjective view—our view. Every time we aim a camera or set down a tripod, we make a subjective decision about what to show at the cost of letting something else slip outside the frame. What's lurking at the edges of the frame, present but unseen? Like a classroom. If I aim my camera at one end of the classroom at a clump of men, inevitably sitting together, it will look like only men take visual anthropology; whereas, if I move my camera to another corner of the classroom and keep only the women in the frame, it will look like visual anthropology is only popular among women. It's all about the frame. Photography is subjective. It is framed.

Anthropologists are so obsessed with representing what's there...but what's missing?

What did Marta take out of the frame? What did she hide before I appeared?

Who is HWD? Is Will being framed?

Chapter Twenty-One

Shadows crept alongside Will's White Tesla as he maneuvered it expertly over the snow and ice, down the barely open park road. Alex stared out the window at the dark clouds and worried about the impending storm. The park tour was meant to be a diversion from all the recent stress, and not additional stress. Alex would make a great risk assessor. She knew where all the exits in a cinema were located before she took her seat; on airplanes, she counted the rows to the exit in case she would have to feel her way to safety during a night-time emergency landing. And now, as she re-assessed the situation, she wished she had checked for walky-talkies, a hand-cranked radio, or any other Ranger-type accoutrements in the car. A car she guessed did not belong to the National Park Service. Not that she would know what gear to look for. An icepick could come in handy, for example, or could prove a threat. She hoped that whatever they might need was packed away in the trunk, and nothing more. She would not insult Will's intelligence by asking if he was prepared for what she thought was going to be a little jaunt into the park, and not a fifty-mile trek. Could the car go 100 miles on one charge? If they got caught in a storm, fifty miles was a lot to fight their way back through. She sank back into the luxuriously heated seats, looked up at the darkening sky through the sunroof, and worried.

Will slowed as they came up behind a line of cars at the embankment.

"Miles of empty road and now a traffic jam?"

The small crowd of mostly men stood alongside their cars pointing expensive long-range lenses at a rocky outcropping above the bend in the road. Will parked and got out of the Tesla, followed by Alex who quickly changed her mind. One inhalation of burning cold air, and she was back in the vehicle.

"Wait," Will called her back, "Alex, look up!"

Above her, a mother ram and her baby waited to cross the road. Alex was furious at the photographers for intimidating and cornering a mother and baby at a dangerous outcrop. Would Will reprimand them? He was neither wearing his ranger uniform nor in an official car.

"Get in," he said.

"Is it legal for them to get in the way of the animals?" Alex asked, wishing there were car doors to slam as she waited for the Tesla's wings to fold her in.

"The law exists to mediate the natural world and humans. The entire point of a national park is to garner an appreciation of the animals, and, to do this, we need to allow people to watch. This mother is used to it. She wasn't showing any signs of distress. They will take their photos and move on," Will promised as he drove away.

"How can you be so sure?" Alex was baffled and angry. If she were a ranger, she would be back there handing out citations.

"I can't be sure." Will answered. "Of course, the professionals will stay here all afternoon. If they're still here on our way back, I'll book 'em," he promised with flare.

"Funny," Alex said. "Photography is its own system of poaching, isn't it?" she asked, thinking of Pete Holgan's story of a villager and the tiger.

"Yeah, you're right." Will's eyes scanned the road as he drove, "The alpha was spotted this morning at Nymph Lake." They were on a mission.

Dark clouds floated in hurriedly above them, as if running late for a funeral. A busy reception at a heavenly ritual. Alex bit her nails and incessantly checked her phone for reception. They had lost all the cell signal a mile into the park, and there was no sign of regaining it. *Trust Will*, she repeated the mantra in her head. *Trust Will. Trust Will.*

"You must be used to these storms?" Alex asked casually. Will smiled and turned on the car stereo. Jazz unnerved her. Just as her unruly mind caught a musical phrase to follow, the syncopation would slip into something else. The constant change of tempo and rhythm, the up and down of the sound, made it impossible for her to focus on whether they were safe. She needed to concentrate, to ask questions; this is how she dealt with anxiety, by becoming a geyser of bubbling questions, like how much experience did Will have driving in storms? Did he know how to build an emergency shelter? Had he packed blankets and flares? Was there extra water?

The more anxious she became, the more obsessive her thinking, and the more questions she would need answered to feel calm again. It was about creating the illusion of control. All she wanted was for him to tell her they would be OK. Would he lie to soothe her? Or would he respect her intelligence and tell her the truth? She did not plan on finding out by offending his intelligence at the expense of her own comfort and asking if they were going to be OK—not yet, anyway. Will's was a natural intelligence that both impressed and intimidated her. Slower minds frustrated him. She saw how hard he worked not to show it: his impatient body language during Scotty's investigation, his heavy sigh during an inane conversation at the Back Barn. In this, he was a lot like Kit. Smart women were practiced at hiding their intelligence. For women, it was a survival tactic; in a man, humility—a privilege rarely afforded to smart women. She found Will's humility, his need to put others at ease, both endearing and incredibly attractive.

"I want to show you something," Will said, and pulled into a snowbank.

"Come," Will said, jumping out of the car. Alex reluctantly followed him up a steep and icy trail that plateaued at a snow-covered meadow.

"Look," Will pointed in the distance at a large pool of boiling water—an Azur mirage produced by steam and heat that burned through the snow. It was circled by a snow-covered boardwalk. A sign read "Punch Bowl Spring."

"Come." Will led Alex closer to the fumarole. It was all sparkle and color, like an art project thrown on the ground by a precocious toddler. She peered over the edge into the saddest, most beautiful pool of water. It did not take long before the beauty of the place gave way to the smell. The hot mist on her face, the rancid smell of rotten eggs and the memory of Pete's blood dripping toward Diana's fizzy creation made her queasy.

"Devil's Punch Bowl." Alex swayed. Will took her elbow.

"What's in a name?" Will asked.

"So much." She relayed her last conversation with Pete and the young intern who told them about the nineteenth-century photographer and the many names of this one fumarole. Had Will overheard them?

Alex moved in closer despite herself and took a final look, as if the spitting pool of steam was trying to tell her something.

"You'll boil to death if you fall in," Will said ominously.

"Good to know. Is that your job? To keep people from falling?"

"One of them." Will took her hand. "Today is the perfect day for crystal dust."

"What's that?"

As if on cue, hundreds and hundreds of twinkling little stars appeared out of nowhere.

"An alchemy between the thermal boiling hell below us, and the freezing heavenly cold above us. When they meet, their molecules collide and form a crystal dust."

As the dust swirled around them, Will leaned in and kissed her on the forehead. For a split second she thought she was hallucinating.

"The alchemy of two extremes," she said, keeping as still as possible lest movement disturb the unruly molecules to move toward a different chemical reaction.

"My eyes..." Alex blinked.

"It's the sulphur; let's go." Will led her away.

"Will, wait."

"Yes?" He turned back to her.

"If you had to choose any geyser to describe me, what would it be?"

"Teakettle Spring," he answered without hesitation.

"Teakettle?"

"Teakettle is an active Geyser that never erupts but is audible from the trail."

"So, I'm vocal, but muted?"

"You're friendly and approachable. Now, let's go; the storm's looking bad."

* * *

Even after the effect of the sulphur faded, the world still seemed blurry. Something had changed.

"You're quiet," Will remarked, keeping his eyes on the road, "You still back there with mama ram?"

"The sheer audacity of those photographers intimidating that poor mama ram and her baby for a photo."

"Don't worry, we'll get them on the way back."

"Does the storm really look that bad?"

"I hope not." Was not the answer Alex wanted to hear.

"What if it is?"

"Then we drive through it. There isn't anywhere to shelter in the winter. Don't worry; I know this road like the back of my hand. I could drive it in the dead of night during a new moon."

Alex remembered how bright the full moon was the night before Marta was attacked—how it lit up the entire field between their cabins and illuminated the smoke gently undulating from Marta's cabin. If Marta was at the museum reporting the camera missing, as Kamran claimed to Diana, then who had been feeding log after log to the fire in her cabin? She wished that she had peeked inside the cabin—why hadn't she?

"The curtains!" Alex exclaimed.

"Huh?"

"Marta's. I knew I was forgetting something important."

"And?" Will encouraged her.

219

"You asked if anything was missing. Little swatches of lace material for her curtains. They were sitting on the table right next to my model house, cut and hemmed, and ready to be glued in. Whoever defaced my model took the little lace swatches."

"Really? Are you sure?"

"How could I have forgotten?" Alex hit her forehead.

"Because somebody wanted you to."

"It's creepy, being outwitted by a murderer." Alex shivered.

"Don't worry; criminals make stupid mistakes." Will assured her.

"The curtains were her most intimate object."

"Really? How do you know they weren't hand-me-downs?"

"Instinct and stereotype—not something anthropologists are supposed to do, of course. Slavic accents, lace curtains. Reminded me of Brighton Beach. All the apartments have lace curtains. Herring, beets, vodka, and lace curtains."

"Don't forget the sour-cherry jam," Will added.

"You've been?"

"Just for a day, to get Piroshky."

"You're making me hungry."

"Shall we have lunch?" Will asked.

"What's open?" Alex gestured at the great expanse of snow.

"The picnic basket I brought in the back." Will was pleased with himself.

He pulled over onto an embankment and retrieved a large wicker basket from the back. It contained two thermoses of hot chocolate, baguettes, mango chutney, a creamy tofu spread, and roasted vegetables.

"Hmmm, is the cocoa from the bank?" Alex asked as she sipped the hot chocolate.

"That was dessert! The bank?" Will asked.

"You know the super-expensive chocolate Shoppe in the

lobby of the turn-of-the century bank? A sign, by the way, that the Anarpour's are not the only wealth in town."

"Good guess. Yes, the Baxter. I'm a sucker for their chili chocolate." Will said blushing.

"I met Marta there my second day in Bozeman, by chance."

"In the chocolate shoppe?" Will sounded surprised.

"I was treating myself."

"I'm surprised Marta was there. I would think it's above her means," Will explained.

"I wanted to sit and journal somewhere opulent. I miss New York cafés. There was a Dean and Deluca Café in Washington Square with the black-and-white checkered floors and a big brass espresso machine. It had high ceilings and a large picture window that looked right out onto the square. You could people-watch for hours if you were lucky enough to score a window table. The Baxter's lobby is like a cave in comparison."

"Because it's a nineteenth-century hotel lobby. They needed to protect their guests from outlaws."

"Outlaws? Under an art deco dome? Anyway, that's where I was when Marta walked by." Alex paused, "There is something sad and depraved about her battered leather jacket."

"The brown one with the Dracula collar circa East Berlin?" Will joked.

"Yeah, but she's no hipster. She doesn't strike me as having the means to update her wardrobe. I offered her a hot chocolate."

"And she accepted?"

"You sound surprised?" Alex said.

"Well?" Will answered through a mouthful of food.

"I couldn't place her accent, and it's something I'm categorically good at."

"Balkans? Russia? Ukraine?" Will suggested.

"Turkish is as close as I got."

"Middle East?" Will was surprised.

"No, Turkish is Altaic, it's a relative of Korean."

"Wow, who knew?"

"She spoke so little. And when she did speak, she muttered as if she was trying to hide her accent. She came through a second country; her accent is not clean. But her command of English is better than she lets on. She seemed in a hurry but pretended not to be."

"Wow, that's a lot of observations!" Will sounded impressed.

"She sat on the edge of the seat, drowning in her jacket."

"Didn't plan on staying?" Will surmised.

"No, she looked like a student forced to sit in front of the principal. I got her a hot chocolate and explained my project. The whole time I was half-expecting her to run."

"But she stayed," Will observed.

"Well, wouldn't you for the cocoa?

"'Sipping chocolate,'" he corrected her.

"What's the difference?"

"Powder versus real chocolate. What was your impression?" Will sounded serious again.

"Intense. She's intense. But my first *true* impression of her was ..."

"True impression?" Will asked. "What's that?"

"Yes, you know, when someone unintentionally lets down their guard. When the mask slips for a moment. That's when people reveal themselves to you."

"OK?"

"Ever catch someone looking at you without knowing they're being watched?"

"I guess."

"My reading specialist in third grade was all sugar and

spice. Called me *Honey* and sprinkled 'good girl' like sugar. And then, on one particularly difficult day, when I was struggling to sound out a word, I saw it: the unmasked, caught-out face of unadulterated disappointment. She gasped when our eyes met. She quickly smiled, but it was too late. I understood right then and there that *Honey* was codeword for failure."

"I'm sorry," Will leaned over and placed his hand on Alex's. Her whole body lit up in response.

"Being bad at decoding letters made me stronger at decoding people. Marta was weird at our last visit. At one point, she dozed off, and I startled her. She stared back at me as if trying to decide whether I was going to pull a gun on her."

"Were you?" Will took a bite of his sandwich.

"Ha-ha. It wasn't fear but more like anxiety, with a passing flare of anger. She was both nervous and angry."

"Really? Maybe you inconvenienced her?"

"It was primal. She was vigilant. At one point she finally relaxed a bit back into her chair. She was like a drowning person giving into the current. I can't explain it any better. It was such a victory. One for the anthropologist. It was *that* loaded. All of it."

"Could she have lived through a war?" Will wondered aloud.

"She's too young to have lived through the Balkans. Chechnya? Ukraine is too recent; she was here last year."

"Maybe she's meek."

"Being meek and being scared are not the same thing. She was scared."

"Did she say anything at all significant?"

"There was something weird. When I first told her my project is on transplants to Bozeman, she immediately jumped to the conclusion that I was studying medical transplants."

"That's odd."

"When I saw her at the Baxter, she said I look like a friend of hers." *Maybe she hated her friend?* thought Alex.

"So how do the curtains fit in?" Will asked.

"They reminded her of home. I asked her to elaborate, and she ignored me. I thought it would be a nice ethnographic touch to take Marta with me to choose the lace for the curtains. You know, hoping it might kindle a conversation about lace and home. The house mimicking life and vice versa. It wasn't as enlightening as I had hoped. The local craft store carried one type of lace. There was nothing to choose from, to mull over, and converse about. We spent less than five minutes in there. I bought the swatches, and we parted ways in the parking lot, which is when she promised to find me a better match as soon as that afternoon. I couldn't remember any lace curtains in her bedroom."

"And?"

Alex realized she was never shown a bedroom. She assumed it was a studio cabin, but then where did Marta sleep? On her couch? On the rug? What an oversight. She did not mention the bedroom to Will; she did not want to reveal her incompetence.

"Why take the curtains?" Will asked.

"Maybe the assailant was afraid that we would find out where she's from?"

"How so?" Will asked.

"The curtains are distinctly from somewhere unique. I was obsessed with them."

"OK, Margaret Mead. Did someone from her past return to kill her?" Will asked.

"I don't know. Perhaps. Is Mead the only anthropologist you know?"

"The rest are men. So, you asked Marta to pick-out the curtains? That's brilliant."

Brilliant—Alex's heart skipped a beat, and she was no longer afraid of the storm.

"Do you know if the police have anything yet?" Alex turned to look out the window. Compliments made her uncomfortable.

"I haven't heard, but it's worth a call to Scotty."

"I should have photographed her cabin." Alex said. Once the police tape and *Do Not Enter* sign were affixed to the door, it was too late. Scotty was not going to do Alex any favors. "I know better than to rely on memory. I'm an anthropologist, not a literary theorist."

"What's the difference?"

"Literary theorists are utterly gaga over Sigmund Freud's ridiculous idea of screen memories. As if humans are cameras recording memories exactly as they happened, and then can recall them precisely, as if bringing up a film on a screen," Alex explained, "Regardless of the most precise lens, photography is still edited by emotion."

"Like when a human aims the shot instead of using a crittercam to record whatever happens to walk by?"

"Exactly. Ever seen *War Photographer?*"

"No."

"There's a great scene when the photographer, James Natchwey, asks his editor to make a picture darker before publishing it. It was of a bombed-out village somewhere in the Balkans. Nachtwey saw everything darker than the F-stop on his camera registered."

"The what?"

"The light reader. Freud's views predated an exacting photographic science. Freud was thirty-two by the time Kodak invented the first film camera, and yet a screen image is the metaphor he chose."

"Interesting," Will mulled this over. "We need to look at

your Marta model again. Maybe it will reveal the intruder's emotions?"

"My guess is anger. You have that level of access? Scotty confiscated it," Alex reminded him.

"Bozeman's a small town."

"And why take my other model? It was barely an armature." Alex flushed; she'd failed to mention it before. He might become suspicious of her.

"Whose house was it of?"

"Jasmine."

"Jasmine?" Will sounded both impressed and surprised, "When did you and Jasmine have a heart-to-heart?"

"Over tea."

"How did that come about?" Will turned to look at her.

"On demand. I mean by invitation. I was lured into the den of an alpha wolf. We met in the honey store."

"And the rest is history?" Will's laugh sounded forced.

"She all but ambushed me and accused me of generalizing Bozeman by basing it on one economic class. I was so flustered, and ashamed, I agreed to interview her pronto."

"She has that effect on people," Will said.

"Some people," Alex breathed out.

"Her bark is worse than her bite."

"You're right." Alex said and added, "She seemed lonely."

"She's a smart woman, an engineer who should be doing more than shopping and skiing."

"She told me about a young Afghan girl, the janitor's daughter, who lived in the basement of her building in Tehran. Life was hell back home in Kabul. Not that it was any better in Iran. Jasmine explained how Afghans are undocumented in Iran, unsupported socially, politically, economically. They build the roads, clean the hospitals, dump the trash, pump the oil. They were doctors back home, engineers, artists, and writers. Imagine, educated people's children not allowed to go to school in Tehran? Jasmine read to her every day. Having someone read to you every day is the greatest gift in the world," said Alex.

"We should head back. We're too late to catch her," Will said.

"Catch who?" Alex looked around, confused.

"The wolf. If she's smart, she's already gone back to her den. That storm is definitely looking bad."

Field Note

Would Pete have made a stronger impact had he photographed a dead wolf?

The Victorians took photographs of their dead lovers, husbands, and babies. Photography critic Roland Barthes pondered a photo of his deceased mother and wondered if this photo had always presented the possibility of her death. The camera clicks, a moment passes, and the photograph is already history: an archive of a moment that has disappeared, that is gone, over, done—dead, never to be again. The photograph of the now deceased is proof they once lived—of life.

Maybe that is why it is so painful to look at my childhood pictures?

And Marta? Has she buried the proof of a dead life? A dead relative? Or, does she feel, like Barthes, that to look at a photograph of her mother (Marta had a mother) would be too painful? Is Marta being brutally honest by not keeping any photographs of people, places, and things she may not have known, of a past she was not privy to? Was she adopted? Was I?

I've been rereading Barthes' meditation on photography, *Camera Lucida*, hoping it will provide an insight about why Marta lives without a single photo—if that is the case. Perhaps she's keeping them from me.

Barthes says privacy is a space where one is not an image. The Geneva Conventions protect the privacy of a citizen from becoming an image in war, especially after they die. It's crazy that we need protection from becoming an image. But only in war, and only as a dead body are we granted this right. Only when we become a body without agency, without a voice, without the ability to protect itself from the gaze of a camera. In death we are protected, but in life everyone is turning everyone else into an image or an icon or—as Andy Warhol showed—an advertisement. If only he could see social media.

Barthes refuses to show us his mother's photograph because it would not mean anything to us. It cannot wound and hurt us, the way it does him. We have no personal connection. For us, the photograph is merely historic. It depicts a particular style of clothing, a historic moment, but nothing more. It's what Sontag calls an *objet trouvé*, a gift from the past. Photographs are most powerful when they move us personally; otherwise, they're only information.

Can photographs of violence, war photographs like Eddie Adam's of the Viet Cong general (if that's what he was—jury never came in) hurt and move us if we don't have a personal connection to the person, place, or event? Virginia Woolf and Susan Sontag thought not. They believed that, the more we show violence, the less we care.

Barthes leaves us with this question: can a person's likeness relay the truth of their identity? If I had Marta's photograph, would it tell me more about who she really is? Is this what she fears? Is this what I desire? And why does she not have a single family photograph?

Walter Benjamin—there is a loss of uniqueness, of individuality in accepting a copy for the original.

Barthes—a photograph, even staged, cannot lie.

Is this true? Which is it?

Chapter Twenty-Two

Will waved tentatively to Alex from the other side of the kitchen window. His breath fogged the air as he spoke on his phone. What was so urgent, and so private, for him to run out into the freezing cold without his jacket? Alex poured herself a cup of coffee and opened her laptop.

There were two emails from Columbia. One was from a committee member who wanted to know what a dinosaur museum had to do with anything: *Send your literature review now!* And the other was from the registrar's office with an unexpected invoice for

$5,000 in non-resident registration fees, *Which you are to pay, stat, to maintain your status in the program.* So much for savings, let alone accruing interest. At this rate, she would never get a leg-up on her debt. Her lacking lit review concerned her more.

She opened her Bozeman notes and typed: *Bozeman Field work Proposal: If the job of the anthropologist is to make the strange familiar, and the familiar strange, then...* What? Alex wasn't sure. *Anthropology is Murder,* she typed, and then deleted it when she saw Will walk back inside.

"Ready to head into town?" he asked her without sitting.

"Aren't we in town?" Alex laughed. Will had spent the night on her couch. By the time he'd driven her home from the park, it was too late and the weather too inclement to drive back.

"Main Street," he answered.

"Sure." What could he need in town?

* * *

Town, Alex soon surmised, was the police station; a building that looked uncannily like her two-story middle school. They walked inside and were directed to an office at the end of a long, dark hallway with a row of empty benches.

"No one to book?" Alex joked.

"Wait here," Will pointed to a bench just outside Scotty's office, which he then entered, leaving the door ajar.

Scotty had not noticed Alex in the hallway; he was too busy making a dramatic gesture, holding up a handkerchief.

"Explain," Scotty demanded, turning to sit at his desk, his back to the door.

"This one you can figure out on your own," Will laughed uneasily.

"Not funny, Will. I waited to show you in private, did not want to embarrass you in front of your lady friend."

Lady friend—Alex stifled a giggle.

"Have I been called in for questioning? It's a handkerchief, obviously." Will sounded annoyed.

"It's *your* handkerchief. Any idea how it found its way into the museum kitchen?"

"I obviously lent it to someone who dropped it there," Will said, matter of fact.

"You don't remember to whom you lent an expensive, dry-cleaned kerchief? Do you pass these things out like Kleenex?" Scotty asked. Alex already had three she kept as souvenirs of her encounters with Will. He never asked for them back, though the etiquette would be to dry-clean and return them— it's what Kit would have done.

"Yes, I pass them out like Kleenex. What do you want me to say?" Will laughed.

"Does nobody in this town respect that I am a detective? This is serious. I'm letting a lot slip here."

"Like what?" Will asked.

"Your alibi for the night before Marta was attacked, for instance."

"She was attacked during the day," Will pointed out.

"We're open to the possibility that she was at the Tinsley House overnight. Alex said she wasn't home the night before, and she may have stumbled on a thief at the museum that night. Lots happened that we cannot ignore."

"We? I was home alone," Will answered.

"Miles from any neighbors who could vouch for you. You didn't order take-out," Scotty wiped his brow. "I'm trying to help you."

"By suggesting that I eat processed foods so that I have an alibi in the event someone I know gets hit on the head with a paleolithic stone tool? Or offed in a museum diorama?" Will raised his voice.

"OK, pipe-down. I brought you in to show you this letter. Seems your lady friend..."

"Oh, don't start."

"Marta received a threat." Scotty told Will. "It's misspelled," he added gravely.

"So?" Will said.

"Someone placed the letter on Marta's hospital food tray. It's a threat."

"What does it say?" Will asked.

"'Go home, immigrant dirt.' Only it's *Go home imigrant drit* —there's no comma, the 'r' in dirt is reversed, and 'immigrant' has only one 'm.'" Scotty handed the Ziplock bag with the letter to Will to examine.

"So that means that our suspect isn't a spelling-bee winner. So what? Frankly, it looks like someone reversed the letter purposely; it's unnatural." Will was losing patience. He handed the letter back.

Alex inched closer to the door.

"Our forensic handwriting specialist says that it's a typical trait of a dyslexic," Scotty informed him. "Isn't Alex dyslexic? It's in her fellow's description," Scotty continued delicately.

"Yes, but that doesn't make her a murderer."

"Did you know there is a school-to-prison pipeline of dyslexics?" Scotty was still unaware that Alex was sitting on the other side of the open door.

"Yeah, because they don't get the interventions they need," Will said tightly.

"The prisons are *full* of them."

"Well, no wonder, when they're this quick to be accused.

You can't progress in this society past third grade if you can't read. Besides, what other proof does Forensics have? Spelling prowess? I'm a terrible speller, and I have a Ph.D."

"In math."

That was news to Alex. Math?

"Jack has dyslexia. Have you questioned him?" Will asked.

"Jack is not a murderer."

"That's my point. Neither is Alex. I don't like what you're insinuating, Scotty. And since when have you had a forensic handwriting specialist?"

"Mrs. Grady, the Special Ed teacher was most helpful."

"I bet she was," Will said, his anger building.

"You should know that I'm bringing her in."

"Who, Mrs. Grady?" Will asked. "You don't have a shred of evidence. Have you any idea how much trouble you will be in for discriminating against a person with a documented disability? Not to mention false arrest. You have no evidence against her," Will said tightly.

Alex stood. She wanted to charge in and let Scotty know about the hours she spent with an OT working on her dysgraphia. She stopped reversing letters by sixth grade. Besides, not every mirror writer has dyslexia. Or did they? She was fuming.

"I've seen her finances: she's broke; she won't be able to afford a lawyer," Scotty told him.

Alex backed away, embarrassed and, for the first time, afraid.

"I can, and I will get her the best lawyer, Scotty."

"What about the dollhouse?" Scotty reminded Will.

"What about it? That is not evidence against her. It's a legitimate anthropology project."

"A dollhouse?" Scotty scoffed. "It's a legitimate excuse to interrogate Marta and case her place."

"To what end? She didn't even know her before she got here. Are you now going to tell me her fingerprints are all over it?" Will was angry. "So are you bringing in Jack -- if dyslexics are your suspects..."

"Jack has an ironclad alibi for the time of Marta's alleged attack."

"Which is?" Will asked, though he did not believe for a moment that Jack hurt Marta.

"He was in the Bones Room, on a fossil job, confirmed by security cameras. Pretty boring footage."

"Are you sure it wasn't spliced and run on a loop?" Will asked. He had learned enough from Alex about editing film in the past week.

"Who can tell after hours and hours of looking at the same fossil." Scotty tried to lighten the situation.

"Alex could. She's a visual anthropologist."

"Yeah, she seems to know a lot. You seem to know Alex a lot."

"Not in the biblical sense if that's what you're asking." Will lowered his voice.

"I..." Scotty studied his feet.

"Just saving you the circuitous questioning. Hope you're more direct with your other suspects; otherwise, we're going to get nowhere with this case. Look, Scotty, I'm leaving, and I don't want to hear any more about this."

"Be careful, Will. She's turned your head, and not in the right direction."

Field Note

Stories create a moral order. They tell of origins; they provide belief systems; and they transport us to places we've never been before. They can give us an experience we hope to never have. Greek tragic actors take us to places too painful to experience so we can experience the gift of catharsis: the release, relief that comes with having lived through a difficulty without leaving our seats. Kind of like armchair anthropologists.

According to Edward Said, in the mid-eighteenth century, stories were written and told to control and to colonize people (discourse—remember Foucault). Telling our own stories, taking them back, gives us power and a sense of control—agency. Like a bedtime story told to a child in which stories of the child's day are relayed and reworked into the safety of fiction where no one is called out or judged for bad choices, where decisions can be reversed, and heroes made.

My mom created an archetype of me, a girl named Al with heightened talents. She lived in a castle and practiced magic. Cora knew her eight-year-old daughter was dealing with one disappointment after another in school and needed magic. If only at night. Al dealt with all sorts of things in our bedtime stories: acceptance (of who she was), jealousy (about who she wasn't and preferred to be), and defeat. She was empowered.

As a child, I read with my ears: audiobooks. Fiction engaged all my senses; it made my heart beat faster; it made me swoon and hide under my covers. It gave me a sense of place that differed from my own. These elements are integral to ethnographic reality, but so many ethnographies fail to utilize the elements of fiction to create a more real picture. The irony is that fiction is closer to reality than hard, cold facts. And, without a visual picture, it's hard for someone like me to engage the text. It doesn't have to be a graphic novel to be visual. I need to be able to see a word. Words like "the" or "at" are so difficult for me. I cannot see "the" ... but I can see "cat," and so I will remember what C A T looks like in my mind (even if the C is reversed by my standards): gray and fluffy, with a pink nose.

Fiction is an invitation to imagine—to imagine oneself in someone else's shoes. It transports us, and places us in worlds we could never enter on our own. Just like anthropology. It makes the strange familiar and the familiar strange for the armchair traveler.

Before we had anthropologists, we had novelists.

C.S. Lewis says, "Always the real world is the bank on which the poet draws his cheques."

Funny to think he believed in an objective world of reality. I'm sure it's out there, but, the minute we look, it disappears. And when we anthropologists go a step further to translate and then to write up an explanation of this "objective world" through our subjective positions, we may be factual but not honest about all the ways in which we are creating meaning, fiction, or—god forbid—fantasy.

Chapter Twenty-Three

Will came out of Scotty's office and held his finger to his mouth to indicate silence until they were out of the police station.

"We'll talk when we get there," Will said, leading Alex out of the station and along the cobble-stone strip of downtown to the nearby Bear Bones Café.

Alex and Will slipped into a booth by the large picture window where they could watch the tourists and townsfolk milling about like Parisian *flaneurs*.

Will took a miniature whiteboard from his backpack and placed it on their table.

"You don't think I'm guilty, do you?" Alex asked weakly.

"No, of course not, which is why we need to solve this before Scotty gets any more crazy ideas," he said, and dug around in his bag for the expo markers and handed one to Alex.

"We are going to solve this with a whiteboard?" Alex smiled.

"Ever seen congresswoman Katie Porter with her white-board? It's impressive." Will scooted in closer so they could share the whiteboard. She could feel his breath on her neck as he spoke, "Let's at least try." He uncapped the dry-erase marker, ready to make the first mark.

"A professor's best friend." Alex said and took the cap off her own marker.

"Jack says there's no way Marta's been whacked with a paleolithic stone tool. Not one is missing," Will said.

"Why then leave a miniature paleolithic weapon in my model?"

"Maybe someone's trying to frame Andy?" Will sounded doubtful.

"Andy? The museum prop-artist? Isn't he, like, eighty?" Alex exaggerated, then said, "Someone's thrown a red herring in our path."

"Our path?" Will raised an eyebrow.

"Who else is going to solve this? Certainly not Scotty."

"He's OK," Will said.

"He's decided I'm a suspect." Alex said without meeting Will's eyes—her heart raced.

"We're all suspects," Will said bluntly.

"Except Marta. Unless she left the hospital, killed Pete, and then slipped back into bed without anyone noticing. Possible? Her assault could be a ruse."

"Her weak vitals are not. She was still in the hospital last I checked," Will pointed out.

"What if she had a connection to Pete? Did she know him?" Alex asked.

"Not sure. She feared someone. Think there's a connection?"

"Come on, don't you? Or do things like this happen regularly in Bozeman?"

"No, they don't," Will said definitively.

"Well, then, you don't need an anthropologist to point out the obvious," Alex said.

"Maybe it was someone close to Marta?"

"The poet."

"And the motive?"

"Jilted lover," Alex offered.

"Hardly. She didn't give him the time of day."

"How do you know these things?" she asked.

"I was with Marta a few nights before she was assaulted," Will finally admitted.

Alex nearly said, *I know.* Instead, she asked, "Doing what?" She remembered Marta's call to Will at the Back Barn, and his Jeep parked near her cabin. "Rangers pay emergency calls to humans in the middle of the night?" Alex prodded.

"We don't limit our clientele to squirrels and wolves," Will said without looking up.

"What was the emergency with Marta?" Alex peeked at Will's doodle—it was a squirrel.

"It was private. I promised not to say anything to anyone."

"What are you—a priest?"

"No, I'm honoring a trust. This isn't a murder investigation; she's not dead," Will pointed out.

"But Pete is. Aren't we solving this together?" Alex asked, taking the marker from his hand, and forcing him to look at her. She could sense the tension in his grip.

"If you're asking if Marta and I were romantically involved, the answer is no."

"Not that it's any of my business," Alex said, embarrassed. "I mean, I was doing a life history, you know, as an anthropologist. It's all information." Alex blushed.

"Right. A genealogy, was it?" Will produced a wry smile.

"Touché. We need objectivity in this investigation. Perhaps an outsider's perspective."

"Like an anthropologist from New York? Need more coffee?" Will offered.

She wished he had not said *need*. Words mattered. And she preferred *want* to *need*. The irony was her overstimulated mind needed a stimulant to calm her, especially now. It was one more misunderstood paradox of ADHD. Wanting and needing were not the same, and she was loath to cross the line. She didn't need Will, for example, but she wanted him.

Will signaled for the waiter, who appeared with a pot of coffee.

"Hey, I see you survived the hot springs." The waiter said to Alex. Will's interest was piqued.

"I was the guy pulling into the lot as you all were leaving," he explained and left.

"I was supposed to meet Diana; she didn't show, but Pete did..." Alex told Will about the fiasco.

"Really? You realize you may have been the last person to see Pete before the day of the opening? In effect, the last-known person to have contact with him alone before he was killed?"

"That sounds ominous."

"What kind of mood was he in?" Will asked.

Alex blushed; the word amorous on the tip of her tongue. "Calm," she said instead, looking down at the whiteboard. "Not especially worried." Alex could feel Will's eyes on her. He could read right through her.

"Nothing happened. He drove the car straight to the Wonderland Café, ushered me back into the driver's seat as fast as he could, slammed the door for good measure, and was off. He did not want me following him into the café."

"Did you want to?" Will asked tentatively.

"Follow him in?" Alex asked.

"Kamran and Diana were at Wonderland Café just before Pete arrived. Together," Will said.

"You seem to know a lot about everyone's movements that day." Hadn't Scotty mentioned Will's lack of an alibi for the night of Marta's disappearance? But then he did live alone.

"Diana and Kamran? Explains why she stood me up at the hot springs, and why she didn't return my calls until I was already on the road back to Bozeman. They must have just returned from the café when she called. She invited me to stop by Kamran's cabin."

"To establish their alibis? Busy at work on the diorama, were they?" Will asked.

"Yeah." Will knew more than he let on. But, then, he *did* have a direct line to Scotty.

"Tell me more about Pete. Scotty says he was photographing raptors in the Tetons."

"Diana is a raptor of sorts," Alex said and added, "Odd; he didn't have his equipment with him. Maybe someone brought it to him at the Wonderland?"

"Same person who took him to the Tetons?" Will suggested and then added delicately, "She had a nightmare."

"Diana?" Alex studied him.

"Marta. That's why she called me that night. It scared her."

"So, if I have a nightmare, I can call a ranger?" Alex nudged him gently.

"She was clairvoyant. It terrified her. She said she needed

protection," Will shredded his napkin as he spoke, which may have explained his need for cloth ones.

"Why didn't you tell Scotty or get her protection?" Alex tried not to sound critical.

"I left him a message. I planned to come into town myself, but the storm was coming, and I didn't get out of the park in time."

"Did Marta tell you what the nightmare was about? A premonition about the future? Or a bad dream of the past?"

"If it was a premonition, it was super accurate; she said she was in danger. I got the impression someone from her past showed-up. She wouldn't elaborate. She didn't fully trust me. She wanted protection, no questions asked," Will said.

"As if naming the person might discredit her?"

"Nightmares can be foggy," Will explained.

"No kidding. So can premonitions. Are we overlooking a foreign element? Or maybe you're close to the person who assaulted her, and she wasn't sure if she could fully trust you?" Alex suggested.

"I'm not close to too many people." Will admitted, "And the ones I choose to be close to wouldn't try to kill someone."

"We are missing something. The cross added to my model cabin is an important hint." Alex drew a cross on the whiteboard.

"There isn't a single Orthodox church within a 100-mile radius. No one has seen a cross like that. And all the Polish workers left at the end of the summer."

"Besides, they're Catholic. It was not a Catholic cross. What about a tourist?" Alex suggested.

"No clue."

"Let's go back to the people she may have spoken with," Alex said.

"Do any of the fellows have an Eastern Orthodox connection?" Will asked.

"There are two of us. Me and the paleo poet. And I've never been to Eastern Europe or Russia."

"And the poet? What's his name?"

"David."

"He said something interesting in his interview to the police," Will told her.

"Scotty sure shares a lot with you." Alex offered him an opening to tell her about his meeting with Scotty.

"Look, Scotty's a good guy as far as police go, but neither he nor his teammates are, shall we say, equipped for this kind of investigation." Whereas Will was used to being the smartest person in the room, Alex reminded herself.

"No kidding. He's wiped you off the suspect list *and* asked for your help?" Alex was amazed.

"*You* trust me, and you've known me less than a month," Will smiled at her.

"Who says I trust you?"

"Would you have let me sleep in your house if you didn't? You're not stupid."

"I wasn't expecting you to stay the night. For all you know, I was up all night waiting behind my door with a kitchen knife."

"You weren't."

"How do you know?"

"Because I carried you to bed. And I checked on you through the night. You were sound asleep."

Alex took a large gulp of coffee and scalded her tongue. "We have to solve this," she said. "I feel responsible. I interviewed her, found out nothing about her, and now..."

"And she came to me for help and I let her down," Will admitted.

"And why desecrate *my* model house? Was it a message? A threat?"

"Like, 'Go home, anthropologist; stop digging around.'" Will gave her a quizzical look.

"Social-cultural anthropologists don't dig."

"I meant into her past—into her life." As if that reminded him of something, Will abruptly changed the subject. "Right. By the way," Will reached into his bag and pulled out a small brown paper package. "For you." He handed it to her.

"What's this?"

"Open it."

Alex unwrapped the package, secretly hoping it was something delicate and beautiful—romantic—and not something practical like a headlamp or an icepick. Would he trust her with an icepick? To her delight, under layers of pink tissue was a miniature tea set, the kind one would put in a dollhouse.

"In case you want to make me a Nutshell."

"Make a Nutshell of your life?" Alex laughed, "Now, why would I want to do that?" She smiled at the beautiful miniature tea set. "Where did you get this?"

"It came with the original set. A bespoke edition for daughters of ladies who lunch. Don't girls like mimicking their moms?"

"Entitled ones with matching teacups." Alex immediately regretted her comment.

"What about entitled adults with matching teacups?" Will smiled slightly.

"I'm sorry; I've hurt your feelings," Alex said.

"Not at all." Will took a bite of his pumpkin scone and changed the subject, "So, going back to the interview—the poet told Scotty that Marta walks past the Bear Bones Café where he writes every day. Every single day. But not the day before Marta was found."

"Weird. Wait, that's the day of our last interview," Alex said.

"The one that went south? It was also the night she called me."

"She was acting strange. Do you trust the poet?"

"He seemed genuinely upset."

"How many times has an unrequited love killed the object of his affection and later regretted it?"

"No idea. Why would I have?" Will asked.

"Rhetorical question, Will. Requited or not, it's not visible to the naked eye," Alex said.

"What isn't?" asked Will.

"Love," Alex answered, and gazed out the window.

Field Note

Maya Deren was a dancer, a filmmaker, and—to Margaret Mead's horror—an amateur ethnographer. Mead despised Deren's move into her academic territory without a Ph.D., her documentary territory without a tripod, and into her marriage without a second thought. Deren, who practiced and studied voodoo in Haiti, believed that the best way to learn about rituals was to practice them. This may have extended to her need to sleep with the two most important men writing on culture and ritual in the sixties, Joseph Campbell and Mead's husband, Gregory Bateson.

Joseph Campbell, referring to anthropologists who were trying to understand a person in a trance state, said: "The spirits depart when the anthropologist arrives." Perhaps that's why Deren had better luck than Mead. Perhaps spirits can only be experienced by the believer. They do not make themselves available for the anthropologist. There is a spirit lurking around Marta's house that hides every time I show up.

Chapter Twenty-Four

Alex spent every day of elementary school learning reading rules others took for granted and could deploy naturally. As a result, she hated rules, and, when she encountered one, her impulse was to break it. She took a quick look around the darkening field and slipped under the police tape guarding Marta's cabin. There was nothing she could do about her footprints in the fresh snow, except to be as quick as she could before she got caught breaking in, which could end in losing Will's trust or, worse, landing in jail.

While there had been little in the way of material culture or personal possessions in Marta's cabin, Alex had missed something important and was determined to find it. And no way would she let a deranged killer frame her for Pete's murder or Marta's attack.

She took another furtive look around and then slipped her key into Marta's lock. Scotty said it was a universal skeleton key for both museum properties. Which meant that Diana, Marta, and, as Scotty put it, "Too many to count" had access to both her and Marta's cabins. Alex held onto the key after they changed her lock, and now it clicked and turned effortlessly to open Marta's door.

She pushed the door open, and slowly stepped inside. Marta's cabin smelled of orange blossoms and bergamot and was as tidy and sparse as the last time Alex visited. Possibly cleaner. It was hard to tell in the low light, and Alex did not want to risk turning on the single floor lamp. So she paused a moment for her eyes to adjust to the light and slowly made her way to the mantel to check for dust. It was spotless. *Surely a little dust would have collected by now*, thought Alex. There was something else that seemed odd. Alex looked around the low-lit room and then back at the dustless mantel. The flowers. Not only were they gone, but so was the vase. Had they died in Marta's absence and been tossed? By whom?

And that's when it came to her: that was what was missing from her Nutshell. The flowers—the intruder had removed them from her model of Marta's cabin. But why?

Alex scanned the room slowly, trying to sense what she missed before. She walked around and examined every surface, every drawer: Nothing.

She was frustrated and already late to meet Will. But, before she left, she needed to relieve her bladder and ducked into what she thought was the bathroom, but found instead a small bedroom with a single twin frame and a small bedside table on which was the snow globe Alex had given Marta. Alex smiled; this gift had meant something to Marta. She picked it up and shook it, leaving her prints in the fine film of dust.

Alex could not help thinking of the Nutshells. The dust was a detail that Glessner Lee would have been sure to add to her rendition of the snow globe had she been the one modeling Marta's cabin. Next to the snow globe was a well-worn book of Rumi's poems. A personal item! Alex gingerly opened the book. It was a bilingual edition with the Arabic text on one page and the English on the other. Why Arabic? Was it on sale? It looked used. Marta's dad had taught poetry; maybe he insisted she own an original version? Rumi was supposedly the most popular poet in the world and the most quoted. She would take it with her and leaf through it later. There could be important annotations, bookmarks, stashed letters, or pictures—clues about Marta's life. She found a lace swatch tucked inside as a bookmark.

She left the book on the nightstand and went to the adjacent bathroom. No wonder she assumed the bedroom was a bathroom as it was only accessible through the same door.

Alex had just unzipped her jeans when she heard what she was sure was the front door. She froze. Someone had stepped inside the cabin. She zipped her pants. Where to hide in the tiny bathroom? Marta's slim claw-footed tub was her only option. She pulled back the plastic curtains and carefully, quietly lowered herself into the cold ceramic tub.

She held her breath and her bladder for an eternity, listening, straining to hear anything. But whoever had come in had either left or was also silently waiting for Alex to make her next move. She waited. Had anyone even entered the cabin? Had she imagined it? Or had someone merely opened the door to slip something in? Her painfully full bladder gave her no choice but to move. She rolled over onto her right hip and felt the sciatic twinge her yoga teacher called "dissertation writer's delight." Lying there, immobilized, brought unbidden images of Marta on the bed at the Tinsley House and Pete Holgan on the floor of the diorama. She held her breath and waited, but she never heard another sound.

Finally, she lifted herself uncomfortably from the tub and stood while the blood rushed back into her hands and feet. She stepped into the bedroom and put her ear to the door. Silence. Could she trust it? Wait. Had she even closed the door? She turned the doorknob slowly and stepped out into the dark living room and looked out the window, expecting to see fresh footprints on the canvas of snow. Not a single pair save her own. The absence of footprints was more terrifying than evidence to the contrary. Had she imagined it? She could not waste any more time at the cabin. The remaining light was quickly fading, and she had promised Will to be at his cabin by dark. She turned to leave and remembered the book.

Rumi was no longer on the nightstand. Alex's heart raced. Was her brain playing tricks on her? No, someone had been there and had taken the book. And left without a trace?

She went back outside and looked again. Nothing. But then, as she made her way away from the cabin, she saw them, running away from Marta's door and parallel to her own path, thin, faint lines in the snow—skis.

She reached the end of the field and jumped into her car. As she warmed the engine, she asked herself, *What is the cultural significance of Rumi?*

She was late, and knew she should turn right toward Yellowstone Park, but instead she turned left and drove into town.

The door chime sounded as Alex walked into the Fireside Reader, Bozeman's favorite bookseller.

"We're closing," the proprietor informed her.

"I'm looking for a book of Rumi poetry," she said breathlessly. Chances were, if Marta bought the book in Bozeman, the store might carry the same edition.

"You're in luck; we have one left. It's popular around here."

"Oh, really?" Alex feigned ignorance. "I'm new to Rumi. Do you have a bilingual Arabic one?"

"Arabic? He was a Persian poet—born in Balkh, which is in Afghanistan, but buried in Konya, which is now Turkey." Alex should have known better. The text was Persian, almost the same alphabet as Arabic.

"He was translated into every imaginable language, maybe even Elvish—most widely read poet in the world."

"Why so popular?" Alex asked.

The man glanced at his watch and answered, "He espoused a direct relationship with God. Pretty heretical religious view at the time. People like being in charge, no middleman. He used dance to encounter God."

Who dances in Bozeman?

"Rumi believed in relinquishing the ego..." he continued.

Well, that narrowed down the list of possible readers in the museum crowd to basically Marta, Jack, and the paleo poet. Everyone else had a healthy ego.

"I'm curious; what's the demographic of Rumi readers in this part of town?" In other words, why steal a book that can be bought anywhere?

"Demographic?" The man continued to count his cash.

"Who reads Rumi?"

"Who doesn't?" the owner replied.

"Right. I am a fellow at the museum. I saw a copy in the

museum break room, must've been one of the workers..." she trailed off hoping he'd bite.

"Wouldn't be surprised," he commented.

"You wouldn't happen to have one of the original Persian, would you?"

"Do you speak Persian?"

"No. Hostess gift. I am invited to the Anarpours'," Alex was a terrible liar. "For dinner." She bit her lip.

"Oh, you can bet they will have gorgeous editions themselves. I'd take a bottle of wine if I were you."

"In that case, may I see the English edition? I would love to delve into this poetry everyone's reading."

"Of course." He took Alex to the Bookshelf marked *New Age*.

"Are most of Rumi's readers interested in the New Age angle?"

"Hmmm," he said and handed Alex the last copy. She was disappointed to see it was not the same one Marta had.

"Oh, I nearly forgot. Do you know Marta, the museum worker? She helped me when I first moved in, and she's laid-up in the hospital. Do you have any idea what she likes to read? Thought I'd take her something."

"Oh yes, the Polish girl. Explains why she hasn't been in to pay for or collect her book. She ordered this a while back," he placed a large volume titled *The Philosophy of Math* on the counter: $75, Alex noted. No wonder she had not picked-it up.

"Great idea," Alex said and reluctantly reached for her credit card.

Field Note

A scene set for murder.

Kit teases me about playing Miss Marple; little does she know that I have much more in common with Miss Marple than I do with Margaret Mead. Agatha Christie is prominently listed among the famous people with dyslexia, despite the fact she could read without difficulty, and most likely taught herself. Dyslexia is not just a reading disorder, or what Jack told me the British called "word-blindness." It's a neuro-difference marked by more than trouble with decoding. My guess is that Christie had "stealth dyslexia," which, according to the *Yale Center for Dyslexia and Creativity*, is often missed, as most testers diagnosing dyslexia will first look at reading ability rather than examine the neurological superpowers that come with dyslexia. Christie's dyslexia is evident not in a low Lexile level but in her dyslexic powers. Many of which she gifted to Ms. Marple, who did not solve crimes like Poirot did, with his little gray cells, but by using what Dyslexia experts Brock and Fernette Eide call the MIND strengths. M: material reasoning; I, interconnectedness; N: narrative reasoning; and D: dynamic reasoning.

In Miss Marple, Christie exposes her own prowess.

I like to say, *I'm not nosy, I'm an anthropologist.* Miss Marple is an unapologetically nosy amateur anthropologist. And, as an older woman, she fades right into the background where she can engage in participant observation and acutely observe the world around her. It turns out people with dyslexia learn best by observing. We are not book learners but experiential learners. And Marple is better at doing the anthropological part of detection (out in the world, making large connections, and observing the big picture) than sitting in an office sifting through clues.

She listens to people's stories and encourages them to keep talking, inadvertently interviewing them, all the while muttering, "Oh, dear." This is a disadvantage to a murderer who may reveal something that they do not realize they are revealing. As she says, "I don't comment; I inquire." She comes off as a nonjudgmental older aunt who encourages a person to spill all sorts of confidential information. What's more she remembers all these seemingly random encounters and comments. Sometimes a case hinges on a throwaway comment deemed innocuous that later becomes a vital and ultimately incriminating clue. She is a collector of emotional artifacts, and personal histories, which she often uses to crack a case.

Like many people with dyslexia, she learns more by chance experience than through memorization. In *Three Blind Mice*, she says: "Living in a village as I do, one gets to know so much about human nature." Especially if one has, as Marple does, the dyslexia gift of diffuse attention: an ability to hear a nearby conversation while engaging in one's own conversation.

She has the dyslexic superpower of declarative memory: conscious memory of facts about the world through episodic experiences and interactions, which is often remembered visually and cinematically.

She uses relationships and interconnected reasoning to solve cases. She notices similarities in human nature based on experience that she uses to creatively construct mental models of past and future time—sounds just like a paleontologist I know!

Many dyslexics learn best through storytelling. Which is why, when I finally start teaching, it will be through stories.

Dyslexic thinkers with N strengths are conceptual thinkers, good at understanding and seeing systems and relationships, which is why we make good anthropologists. Miss Marple weaves kinship relations in her head so accurately that she can predict an affair that leads to the killing of a husband, a child who is illegitimate, a sister who is really a fiancée. Marple often explains her reasoning or conclusions through analogies and stories. "This reminds me of my uncle Henry," she tells a politely nodding, but ultimately uninterested audience in *Three Blind Mice*. "I know how your uncle was; he was like my uncle... a bachelor fond of jokes...methodical, suffered an early disappointment." Her first clue is never obvious and always begins with human nature and psychology.

Jane Marple excels in detecting patterns and visualizing complex events. In short, she's a whiz at dynamic reasoning, which allows her to use experience to predict or simulate the future. "You never knew Archibald Spate or his habit of fidgeting with his cufflinks, when he was nervous, just like Archibald." In many Agatha Christie books, the detective predicts the next move of the murderer in order to capture them. Sometimes there is the parlor-room reveal, but often there is the trap, and the trap can only be set once the detective correctly predicts the next move of the murderer. Marple does this by reconstructing the unwitnessed past, by putting together all the clues (including crime-scene findings, investigative interviews, research into people of interest and their pasts and their connections) to predict what happened and what will happen. Marple does all of this with ease and often beats the detective to the punch. She makes a leap of faith and is often right. Dyslexic thinkers often skip the middle of a process by jumping from point A to point D and maybe back to B before getting to F. Dyslexic scientists are valuable precisely for their non-linear thinking, and the ease with which they make creative leaps: jumping to conclusions is often necessary to solve a problem. It's a big "no-no" in academia, but not in the real world. It's a good thing that Albert Einstein, another famous dyslexic, had no problems jumping to conclusions.

Detectives use dynamic reasoning by taking fragments of experience based on physical evidence and stories (interviews) to reconstruct the unwitnessed past and solve a crime. What Frances Glessner Lee did was help them do it better, by placing all the information in a visual world that could be easily manipulated. Maybe she was dyslexic, because her M strength or 3-D spatial, material reasoning is strongly at play with dynamic reasoning...who else would come-up with such a brilliant way to solve mysteries? She made it possible for detectives to visualize the murder in 3D, which is what a dyslexic detective can do in her head without needing to use a physical model. With the nutshells, Glessner Lee provided the detectives a way to do what she did naturally. It's like reverse assistive technology...we dyslexics need dictation software and scanning pens to read sometimes the same way a non-dyslexic detective needs the 3D model to see the scene of the crime!

People take us dyslexics for granted. We are the dark horses, the ones no one expects to come out on top. Miss Marple encourages this by being hard on herself when she doesn't get an answer immediately; she says, "I feel so helpless, frustrated, so slow." Because she is so fast that when she doesn't get something immediately it frustrates her. Slow is a word too often attributed to people with dyslexia. The truth is that our neuro neighborhood is 'way more dense and more complicated to walk through. I'm pretty sure that, if I pull off a good ethnography, the only person at Columbia who will not be surprised will be Kit.

Chapter Twenty-Five

Alex was surprised to find that Will's cabin was as sleek and contemporary as any she had seen in the new Millionaires Mile, as she jokingly called it. It was less a cabin and more of a lodge. Perhaps the rangers lived together?

Will waved to Alex as she parked and stepped out of the car.

"Dumping the trash. Suspicious," Alex joked.

"You caught me red-handed. Last-minute cleaning."

"Bags?" Will asked Alex. She pointed to her toolbox.

"Love a woman who gives more space to her tools than her clothing." He smiled approvingly.

"Thought I might work a bit. Make a place to house my new tea set," she explained. "Lots of material here," she added, noting the size of Will's cabin.

"Can I help?" Will reached for her bags.

"Can you carve?"

"I meant the bags, silly."

They entered the cabin through the side entrance or what Will called the Boot Room, which served as an intermediary space to remove shoes and acclimate before heading into the main room. Alex took her boots off and followed Will inside.

"Oh, yes!" Alex paused after her first step into the main living room to take in the heat from the radiant floors. "Ahh, this feels great. Do all the Rangers have such nice digs?" She wondered if he had a side hustle. Poach—Alex banished the thought. Will loved the wolves; he would never...

"No need to stand in place; the whole floor is heated." Will turned and reached for her hand playfully. She allowed him to pull her, sliding along the floor in her wool socks like a giddy child. "I can feel them!"

"Feel what?"

"My toes! They froze in the field."

"Field?"

"When I stopped home to get clothes," she lied. "By the way, the kiosk was closed. Was I meant to pay an entrance fee?"

Will ignored her question, and instead turned her attention to the rest of the park entrance. "It's a triumphal arc. Rusticated. President Theodore Roosevelt wanted a gate with gravitas and to frame this sublime landscape with something as sturdy and grand as the park itself."

"Sturdy and grand," Alex teased, emboldened by Will's sudden shyness.

"Roosevelt laid the cornerstone in 1903. Yellowstone is the first national park, 'for the benefit and pleasure of the people,'" Will added proudly.

"Yellowstone is my first national park."

"Really?"

"I've never owned a car," Alex explained.

"What about your friends?"

"None of them was interested in camping out of the city. I want to visit every park in the order that they were opened," Alex declared.

"Great idea."

"Come with me," she suggested. Before he could answer, she turned to a framed silver-tone photo and asked, "Is that a real Walker Evans?" Alex recognized a classic Evans subway portrait. This one was of a street child, head held high, ears perked and alert, observing city life from his perch in a moving sardine can. "Evans concealed a camera under his overcoat to catch people unaware. Have you read, *Now Let Us Praise Famous Men* by James Agee?" Alex asked, "The best anthropology is done by non-anthropologists."

"Yes," Will said, "It's a story of sharecroppers in the south."

"Evans did the photography," Alex said, realizing he must know this if he owned an original Evans. "Perfect blend of visual and textual ethnography."

"Did you grow up in New York City?" Will deflected her question about the photograph's provenance.

"Brooklyn," she said.

Will ushered her toward the fireplace, and a sleek gray couch.

His cabin, unlike Marta's was well curated and revealing. Every single item was carefully procured with purpose and provided Alex with a detailed map of Will. One he was not ready to expose if his last-minute cleaning was any indication. Alex pointed to a pinewood derby car peeking out from under the couch.

"Boy scouts?" she asked.

"Yes, my one week of being a typical child." Will laughed, and Alex did not pry. More shall be revealed; there was time. Anthropology was all about time. Journalists were on a deadline of days, whereas an anthropologist had months if not years. And this, in her opinion, was why anthropology was more valuable.

"Have you been to New York?"

"Yes, as a tourist." Will answered casually. "Amazing architecture. You were lucky to grow-up there."

"It wasn't the safest city when I was growing up. Of course, I could never afford to live in my childhood neighborhood now. It has been completely gentrified by independently wealthy trust-funders who 'write.' There's a hip coffee roaster across the street from a park where a man was shot one afternoon as I was walking home from school. Drugs. Lots of hanging sneakers, super Brooklyn. Subway's pretty much the same. Cleaner."

"I love the subway, the museums, the opera. The opera of daily life," Will said wistfully.

"Opera of daily life ...cool."

"People-watching."

"Ever thought of moving there?" Alex tried to sound casual.

"No way. The city was torture on my nervous system. The lights, the sound, the speed of cars, of people, of words. I didn't sleep for a week. No, New York will never be more than a place I pass through."

"Right," Alex said, trying not to sound disappointed. "Love your floor lamps," she offered. IKEA to the casual observer, but anyone who had seen the real thing, as Alex had, would recognize the original Frank Gehry lights. *Expensive.*

Kit found Alex's ability to read people unnerving. Years of being underestimated and belittled by teachers in public school taught her to dumb down. She was used to being underestimated and used it to her advantage with Scotty. But Will saw through her. She eyed a *Mensa Magazine.*

"Paid for by my father. I never read it." He casually tossed the magazine into the recycling bin. Will was far from eager to slip under her microscope and, like any good genius, was obstinately his own therapist. He would eventually learn that childhood wounds had no place in the present. Alex had paid someone good money to tell her that.

"Will, stop cleaning; this place is spick and span." Did her Nutshell project bring out one's inner neat freak, or did they all have something to hide?

"Wait here; I'll be right back."

Alex thought of Will's question about her desecrated Nutshell: *Is anything missing?* What was missing here? For starters, there was no park-ranger paraphernalia. But, then, what did she expect to see in a Ranger's cabin? A gun. She shivered.

Will appeared and said, "Lie down on the couch."

Alex obeyed and he pressed a remote. The room fell dark and Alex screamed.

"Sorry," Will fumbled with the remote. "Was dimming the lights to show you—"

"The diorama." Alex lied to appease him. "It reminded me..." It was less the diorama that came to Alex's mind in the dark than Marta, splayed out across the lumpy bed. It was less the dark that terrified her than laying down in the dark. She sat up and pulled her legs into her chest.

Will brought her a glass of water. "How about a sipping chocolate?"

"Lovely, yes, please." She crossed her legs under her and covered herself with a Tartan blanket that was neatly folded at the end of the couch.

Outside, the white snowbanks receded into the dark like an Agnes Martin painting—white on white. She'd forgotten to call Kit. It was too late now, well past midnight on the East Coast.

Park is fab at night, will call in AM. XOXO Alex texted Kit, turned her phone to vibrate mode, and slipped it away.

Will returned to the room with two mugs.

"When you're done with that, I want to show you something."

"In the dark?"

"In the dark. Here, put your head on my lap. I'll protect you," Will promised.

"Whatever from?"

"The dark."

Alex laid her head on his lap and Will pressed the remote, extinguishing the delicately lit scene, inside and out.

"Look-up," he whispered, as if darkness naturally accompanied silence.

Above her, a skylight opened to a twinkling night sky and a shooting star. She wished for Marta to wake-up; for Pete's killer to be found and couldn't help adding: *Please don't let it be Will.*

"Sublime."

"It takes 1,000 years for the light to reach us from a single star."

"If each star is a message from 1,000 years ago, I wonder what they're saying, and if we would understand any of it now."

"Given our current treatment of the planet, there may not

be humans 1,000 years from now to hear the messages being sent tonight."

Will turned on the lights. Alex blinked.

"It's like being in a big bright fishbowl. Don't you feel watched?"

"By the animals?" Will joked. "Like the tables are turned, and we're the diorama."

Will pressed the remote again and blinds fell over every glass panel save the glass ceiling. The effect was unnerving— now she was locked in. No neighbors or stray tourists would see if...Alex did not finish her thought.

"Bats and owls are all that can see us," Will said. He stood and walked over to the fireplace and lit it. The large stone fireplace opened to both the dining room and living room, fluidly dividing the large open space into two quadrants. One side had the polish and comfort of an Oxford club, with large leather mustache chairs and a gorgeous Persian rug with a tree-of-life motif. The other side was a sleek mid-century modern dining room, with a long wood table that was elegantly set for dinner.

"Come, let's eat."

* * *

After dinner, they returned to the living room where Will set out tea in a beautiful turquoise pot covered in a red coral pattern that matched the one he had gifted her in miniature.

"Honey-pops?" Alex observed.

"For your tea. You can swirl them in there; it's less sticky and easier to serve. Dessert is awaiting us in the kitchen, after the evening's entertainment." He smiled at her, pleased. He was a good host. Why had he slept on her lumpy couch instead of bringing her here?

"Where did you grow up?"

Will took a hesitant sip of tea and said, "I skipped high-school and went right to college."

"So, you didn't grow-up?" Alex teased.

"I was thirteen."

"You began college at thirteen?"

"My parents waited a couple of years; they homeschooled me."

"At what age were they hoping to send you off to college? And what college takes a 13-year-old?" Alex wanted to know.

"Caltech. That's where I met Kamran."

"You're friends?" Alex did not hide her surprise.

"He was my physics TA. Mine and Jasmine's."

"Really?" Alex paused to take this in. "How long have you guys all lived together in this incestuous little village? Margaret Mead would have a field day here."

"Why?" Will asked.

"Her fieldwork was on adolescent sexuality."

"Kamran and I were both engineers with other passions. His was art, and mine was animals. We had in common an utter lack of passion for what we were studying in a place where everyone was obsessed with what they were working on."

"And Jasmine's?"

"She claims not to have any passion." They both laughed. Will continued, "I'm joking. She was always into photography."

"Really? Why didn't you follow your passion?"

"When my father discovered that his only child was a math genius, my career became more important than the prestigious legal career he had been building for twenty years. My only way out of his grasp was to hurl myself in the direction he was pushing me. Caltech was my escape."

For the first time, Alex had no desire to be a genius or to

271

have a father. Cora was always telling her neither was necessary. *You're smart enough*, she would say and then add, *you're just fine without a dad*. Cora neither entertained stand-ins nor questions when it came to Alex's paternity. Only once did Alex suspect that a real, living and breathing person, and not a made-up story or random sperm donor was involved in her conception.

She was waiting for the Subway on the Atlantic Avenue platform when she caught Cora locked in a stare-down with a man waiting on the opposite platform. Only, it was Alex who the man was staring at. The train pulled in and took him away before she could discern whether they shared any traits or determine what ethnicity she might be. Cora did not divulge a single detail. And, for years, Alex enjoyed her ambiguous ethnicity. She was often asked if she was Latina, Jewish, Middle Eastern, Italian. It made things more fun in a field like anthropology where everyone was obsessed with everyone else's subject position, their gender, their race. There was something beautiful about not being defined and being utterly anti-Aristotelian, even if it was by force more than choice.

"Damn train," Alex yelled at the retreating train. There was a very large part of her that wanted to know everything.

"On time for once." Cora was relieved.

Kit suggested that Alex do a DNA test. But, if Alex was not brave enough to fight Cora to know her father's identity and her own genetic history when the woman was alive, then she certainly was not going to defy her mother in death. Cora had her reasons, and Alex had to trust that. Simply put, it was too late. Besides, who is to say he or any of his genetic pool are on file? She regretted not being bolder at the time.

"So why anthropology?" Will asked.

Because I am obsessed with identity, with finding my ancestors. She thought of the imposing volcanic-rock sculptures that guarded the entrance to the Margaret Mead Hall at the American Museum of Natural History. They stood like silent Sphinxes waiting for an answer that Alex could not provide. A young curator, an anthropology graduate student interning at the Museum, remarked casually, "They are deifications of long-gone ancestors." She voiced what Alex believed to be true, that her ancestors' spirits lingered there, waiting for Alex to discover what her mother never showed her.

"Anthropology?" Will repeated.

"Because I'm indecisive. Or that's what I thought anyway, until Jack started telling me more about dyslexia. I've never been able to choose a subject, a field of study. It turns out that non-linear thinkers are inherently interdisciplinary. And anthropology is the ultimate field for people who want to study everything." Alex paused, shame rising in her like acid reflux, "I'm not exactly a natural. I messed-up," she admitted. "I was doing summer fieldwork on women filmmakers at a film festival, and I put someone in danger by asking the wrong questions."

"Wrong questions?"

"Political questions. I..." Alex swallowed hard, "I filmed her interview, and..." Alex paused. "And, when she went home, she was arrested."

"That's quite a leap. Are you sure it wasn't a coincidence?"

"I'm an anthropologist; I should have known better," she admitted to Will without divulging the full story.

"I'm not a political scientist, but aren't you being a little harsh on yourself?"

"I was responsible."

"Says who?"

"The Iranian film collective. She was from Iran. Please don't tell Jasmine. I'm really ... I ditched my research project—too dangerous."

"Is that how Bozeman became the lucky object of your scientific gaze?"

"Yes, and look at how safe that's turned-out." Alex changed the subject. "Had your dad not been in the picture, what would you have studied?"

"Zoology or biology. I thought college would be this great escape. But my father had other plans. My choice was limited to Mathematics at MIT or Caltech. Both offered me a full ride for a Ph.D. I was seventeen, still a minor, still my father's son." Will gazed at the fire, "A gift does not necessarily come with a passion."

"I assumed that whatever a genius excels in is their passion. Like Einstein," Alex said.

"Not always. You know he was terrible at math."

"Wow, really? Zoology sounds cool," Alex said encouragingly.

"I'm developing a more humane system to tag and trace animals. The tags we currently use are the equivalent of a prisoner's ankle bracelet. And to get the tag in place, the animal needs to be captured and sedated. I'm working on a laser gun that can shoot a chip into the epidermis from as far away as 50 feet."

"What then?"

"Then we can use a combination of laser-optics and satellite technology to trace them."

"Like a forehead thermometer?"

"Yeah, actually," Will studied Alex, intrigued. "That's not a bad idea. I'm still trying to figure it out. But it would be much better if we didn't have to trap and sedate."

"Are all park rangers zoologists?" She wondered again about how he afforded this cabin and how useful it would be to poachers to tag animals.

"Park rangers do all kinds of jobs: wildlife-interpretation

programs for the public, marine biology. We have biologists recording climate change, looking at the night sky. Depends on the park. Yellowstone has a volcanologist, being a caldera and all."

"Any chance of an eruption?"

"Sure," Will said and, seeing her worried expression, quickly added, "Probability low."

"Tell that to Iceland, the Congo, or Tonga. How long have you been an animal lover?"

"Since my first stuffed animal. When my mother asked me to tidy my vast collection, my response was to classify them by genus." Will's cheeks flushed.

Alex wanted to either kiss him or pinch his cheeks. "Where are they now?" Alex asked, looking around for his stuffed-animal stash.

"Hibernating," Will laughed.

"So, was it the lonely childhood that made you a loner?"

"Who said I'm a loner?" Will reached out to take her hand.

Alex's heart fluttered, "It's not easy to be different."

"Different?" Will withdrew his hand.

"You're unlike anyone I know." She smiled at him.

"I was until I told you about Caltech."

"Not true. How many people quote Yeats as they're changing a lock?"

"Did I?" He smiled.

"*Caught, In the cold snows of a dream.*" Alex started the poem.

"*The best lack all conviction, while the worst...*"

"*Are full of passionate intensity,*" she finished. "Any chance of lowering the lights and watching the stars again?"

Will dimmed the lights and Alex impulsively leaned over and kissed him, her body vibrating like a wildly out-of-control telegraph line.

"Is that your phone?" Will asked.

It was indeed her phone vibrating deep down in her pocket. She cursed as she leaned back and pulled it out to see who was calling.

"Kit. I'll call her back later." But the moment had passed. Will was already standing and asking her if she'd like dessert.

"I made flourless chocolate cakes that will collapse if we don't eat them soon."

He tossed the red Tartan wool blanket over her and left for the kitchen.

"And...now for our evening entertainment—Agatha Christie." He returned with two flourless chocolate cakes and a book.

"Ah, that's where you picked up your detective skills. *You* read cozies."

Field Note

Panoptic: seeing all around, everywhere, in every direction. Panopticon—a circular prison that allowed a full watch of the prisoners. Seeing isn't just believing; seeing is power.

Those observed are ... objects, targets, imprisoned, in danger. Afraid.

I feel watched. But by whom?

Chapter Twenty Six

A lex was dreaming of the Pitt Rivers Museum in Oxford when she woke with a start. She lay in Will's guest bed and listened to the silence. Why had she dreamt of that dusty, crowded space? Of England?

During her school years in Oxford, Alex spent rainy afternoons at the Pitt Rivers Museum shining a flashlight into the cabinets of curiosity that were crushed into the small space in the back of the Natural History Museum. It had more of an antique-shop vibe than museum. The cabinets were an addiction. A breathless rush of anticipation accompanied every tug of a small drawer: would she disturb a sleeping jinn who had lain in wait for centuries to wake and take revenge on the colonial pillagers that had locked it up? She discovered shell necklaces from the Trobriand Islands, Tarot cards from Milan, voodoo dolls from Haiti—their magic bottled and waiting to be released on the next voyeur.

In her dream, the flashlight was twice its real size. Heavier and ominous—a weapon that could kill with a single whack to the head. In her dream, she pulled the Death card from the Tarot deck: a menacing skeleton warning her to shut the drawer before the magic came after the curious. Was it a warning that she was in over-her-head in Bozeman? Should she shut whatever metaphoric drawer she had accidentally opened?

Her phone vibrated and she rolled over to reach for it, too late. There were four missed calls from Kit. She squinted at the voicemail transcription and swore.

* * *

Alex parked curbside at Bozeman's small airport. Kit would be easy to find in the sea of flannel and jeans that rushed past Alex's car. Bozeman was predominantly white, a check on the con side of the pro-con list that Alex had going in her head, should she find a reason to stay. Even during the height of ski season, the passengers transiting the airport were mostly white. Alex had never skied, but she had seen the price of lift tickets—skiing was a wealthy person's sport.

"Kit!" Alex yelled to Kit who stood out in her sleek twill blazer and knee-high suede boots, looking every bit the professional Smithsonian fellow.

"You're late." Kit shook her head, accentuating her new short, chic curly bob.

"Time is a cultural construct," Alex said as she got out of the car to go hug her friend.

"Yes, constructed from a numeric system that we all agree on," Kit said and squeezed her hard.

"Late is relative."

"To what?" Kit threw her bag in the back and climbed into the passenger seat.

"I'm an explorer bunny; we exist in a different time system," Alex said, sitting.

"A what?" asked Kit.

"It's not that my mind gets off-track; it's that my mind is never on a single track."

"True story," Kit laughed. "And this is new information because?"

"I heard a cool podcast about complementary cognition ... this archeologist, Helen Taylor, was saying that explorer bunnies roam more broadly in the world but also in their imaginations, right?"

"Um, OK. Do go on." Kit buckled her seatbelt and turned to give Alex her full attention.

"So, the explorer discovers resources like water and food, ideas—think of us as a divining tool mapping out all the different places to mine for resources." Alex brushed hair from her eyes.

"Uh-huh," Kit laughed. "Alex you can barely keep track of your keys."

"Funny," Alex huffed. "My problem is not memory."

Kit gave Alex a sideways glance. "Really?"

"It's about focus—and you're distracting me," Alex complained.

"So, what keeps the bunnies on task?" Kit teased.

"Not their working memory, that's a little..." Alex started.

"Faulty?"

"Wired differently," she insisted. "In the end, the explorer bunnies map the forest for the exploiter bunnies who go in and figure-out how to get the resources out of the ground or to distribute them; they do all the detail work. It's kind of like us: I love going out into the field without a game plan and figuring things out as I explore, whereas you're brilliant at sitting down and working out the details and writing it all up after the research is done. Once I've figured out the mystery, the puzzle, the answer—I'm not all that interested in the details, and I'm *definitely* not into the writing. I'm already moving on to the next problem or exploration." Alex's enthusiasm waned as she concluded, "Which is why I'll never finish a Ph.D. As a team, we would excel; it's too bad we can't work that way in school. It's silly that we are forced to work alone—that, instead of working together as complements to each other, we academics are always in competition with each other. From kindergarten on, our whole school system is predicated on this competition."

"Well, I'm here to join forces. To help," Kit announced.

"Help? Wasn't expecting you until winter break." Alex got in and started the engine.

"I couldn't leave you alone in this murderous town. We need to solve this craziness so you can get on with your field-work. Besides, looks like winter is already here. I needed to hear your voice. You, missy, kept promising to call with your one-liner texts. What if someone stole your phone and was impersonating you while you were tied-up in a cabin—or worse? I called last night to tell you I was on my way. When you didn't respond—well, you can imagine. Seriously Alex, I was a wee bit worried."

"Damn reception." Alex blushed. Kit's call had interrupted her almost kiss.

Had Kit really been that worried, she would have called the police. Kit was the practical one. But then here she was. Did she really think Alex was in danger?

Alex leaned over and gave her best friend another squeeze.

Kit's musty Coco Chanel perfume produced a pang of home-sickness—for Kit, and the city. It also created a pang of guilt: Alex was a little disappointed that Kit arrived as things were heating-up with Will.

"Oh, my God, look at the snow! Can't wait to go skiing."

"Skiing?" Was the last thing on Alex's mind.

"Will's friend Scotty usually works ski patrol this time of year. But, well, with the murder and all..." As if on cue a police car pulled up in front of them and Scotty jumped out and ran toward the airport entrance.

"Scotty?" Alex exclaimed.

"You're friends with a cop?"

"Will is. Police aren't really cops here; they're more like mailmen with guns."

"Doesn't everyone have a gun here?" Kit assumed.

"Probably. Buckle-up." Alex said.

"Friends with guns. What has happened to you, Alex?"

"It's a small town; everyone's friends or frenemies." Alex pulled away from the curb. A large group of co-eds were piling into an SUV ahead of her. Alex honked to no avail.

"I'd say frenemies, given that one of your new buddies was done in by a near and dear."

"You think he was killed by a friend?" Alex asked.

"How would I know? I just got here."

"And... you already have a theory." Alex adjusted her glasses and glared at the driver ahead.

"Somehow it strikes me as an act of passion," Kit said.

"Hmm..." Alex replied.

"Well, then who?" Kit looked at Alex.

"The original idea was a poacher, but that didn't pan out for whatever reason."

"Poacher?" Kit asked.

"Pete was photographing the wolves."

"What's the new lead?" Kit asked.

"I'm guessing someone close to him, but not necessarily a close friend."

"Like the anthropologist who went skinny-dipping with him?"

Alex didn't laugh. "Hardly. Like I said, everyone knows everyone. Suspect list is long." Alex left out the fact that she was now Scotty's prime suspect.

"This is getting interesting. For the price of a plane ticket, I'm getting one of those *How to Host a Murder* experiences. Beginning with Colombo on the plane."

"Who?"

"The suit your cop friend is picking up," Kit pointed to Scotty who was walking out of the airport with an official-looking visitor. "He does look right out of Colombo." They both laughed.

Finally, the SUV ahead of them moved on.

"I saw him on the flight. He was reviewing documents and typing furiously on his laptop. His seat was in the bulkhead by the toilet."

"Didn't catch a glimpse of his work, by any chance?"

"Don't think I didn't try. He hugged that laptop close whenever someone passed."

Alex missed the freeway entrance.

"Every single time. Without fail," Alex pounded her palm on the steering wheel and signaled to turn. "Now, I have to drive in circles before I find someone to follow out of this endless loop."

"Like Mr. Bean in his green mini going around the same traffic circle over and over again." Kit laughed. "Alex with a car. Oh, Lord."

"Weird, right? All those years riding the subway. I haven't driven a car since..." Alex paused and sent Cora a mental thank you. "Wasn't sure I'd still know how to drive."

"Do you?" Kit joked.

"Funny." Alex missed the entrance again.

"You seem happy ... at home, in the field, and with a love interest to boot."

"Oh, please don't say anything to anyone. It's a little crush."

"And you don't suspect him?" Kit asked in a hushed voice.

"Of murder?!"

"No, silly! Of having reciprocal feelings?"

"No!" Alex exclaimed.

"The lady doth protest too much."

"I doubt I'm his type. It's winter—no opportunity to see how un-outdoorsy I am," Alex said.

"That's not true. You walk through central park every weekend."

"To get to the Met," Alex said.

"That's 'way outdoorsy for a New Yorker."

"Speaking of museums," Alex relayed her Pitt Rivers Museum dream. "What does it mean?"

"That you're afraid of turning into a museum anthropologist."

"Not funny."

"You're putting too much stock into dreams. They're neurological misfires. You are working in a museum with material culture, objects—seems normal to dream about them, no?"

"Normal? The death card? Come on. We are supposed to be interpreters of symbols. Remember the anthropologist who was looking at how people dreamed in a dictatorship? She used the example of Turkey, where everybody was dreaming about Kamal Atatürk, not as a man but as his angry bust."

"Angry bust?" Kit asked.

"Sculpture. The sculptures of Atatürk were all over Turkey, and so they naturally slipped into people's dreams."

"Of course we pay attention to dreams. They are part of the cultural landscape and reveal how people feel unconsciously—especially about what makes them most anxious. But at the same time, we can't put that much stock in them. And besides, we are looking at *other* people's dreams, the people on the ground, not at our own dreams." Kit already sounded like a professor.

"What happened to the subjective turn in anthropology? We aren't supposed to be above or below our subjects, but right there with them." Alex reminded her.

"You mean go native?" Kit giggled.

"Whatever." Alex was not in the mood for a theoretical argument. "Just saying, my dream meant something. It's important. And I need to pay attention to it."

"I'm not saying not to. I'm just saying don't give it too much credence."

"Solving a murder relies on well-behaved objects staying in place. Clues, waiting to be found. If someone messes with objects, like I did in my dream at the Pitt Rivers Museum, then it's like I have messed with the clues. Did I open the wrong drawer?" Alex asked pensively.

"Now you're reading 'way too much into this. Tell me more about these nature photographers?" Kit changed the subject.

"Looking for a date?"

"Not if they're getting offed."

Alex did not laugh.

"Sorry. Bad joke. I came to take you away from all this. Thought you might like a respite from murder."

"Where to?"

"Drumroll, please: a cross-country ski tour of Yellowstone. Early Merry Christmas."

"Yellowstone, huh? Good place to go hunting for a nature photographer. It's their feeding ground. Thought we weren't exchanging gifts?"

"Hostess gift. It includes a room at a motel, in a town called Gardiner."

"Will lives near there."

"Really? Perchance Mr. Darcy will have us for dinner?"

"As the matter of fact, we're invited tonight."

"*How to Host a Murder*," Kit chortled.

Field Note

My methodology preference? Fly on the wall. You must be outgoing and sure of yourself and willing to talk to people to be a "social" anthropologist. No pun intended. I like to chat. Archeology demands 'way too much detail and patience. Fellow dyslexic Agatha Christie loved archeology. She spent hours volunteering at different sites in the Middle East with her archeologist husband. She must have enjoyed the slow unraveling of an ancient mystery.

All that delicate brush work, layers and layers neatly unfolding—no, thank you. I'm the first to rip open a gift. I am not one to save the paper for later. That's more the OCD crowd. See why we need all "types"? Why Helen Taylor is begging us to pay attention to complementary cognition?

It's dangerous for society to deem a type or a differently abled group *dis-abled*, *unnecessary*. Am I being wiped out evolutionarily because I have ADHD? Or dyslexia? That's what I suspected, sitting in Special Ed in high school, but now I'm learning that neuro differences are important—to the degree that we respect them, anyway. I love the sickle-cell anemia example. If we selected for (only mated with) non-sickle-cell genes, then that same gene that protects people from malaria would be obliterated from the genome. Maybe it's best we humans don't make too many big decisions about things like gene selection at this or any future juncture.

Take hunter/gatherers—it's one thing to assign roles, and it's another to be born into a role neurologically. Into that singular box defined by what you cannot do—like following-through, staying on task, sneaking up on prey—hunter. But... send me out on an exploratory mission, and my sidetracking, my inquisitiveness, my boredom, my ability to lose track of time and space may lead me to something important—gatherer. So, my ADHD makes me a gatherer or an explorer. It also helps me to hyper-focus—which is good and bad, depending on the situation. Like when I was filming the Iranian filmmaker, oblivious to the crowd gathering around to watch.

Back to binaries. And why aren't we part of that binary? Because binaries, things that are divided into two, like black and white, rich and poor, male and female, leave out the important in-between parts of society. Ahh, I'm off track, remind me to discuss the problem with binaries.

Here's a thought. Maybe we should stop teaching Aristotle? He wanted us all placed in neat little boxes. Categories, types—maybe it's time to move past all that? Haven't the human evolutionary biologists already done away with the idea of race? We are all the same race: human. There is an entire history of humanity that is predicated on how we treated each other arbitrarily based on visual and other differences, and now we need to make reparations, and engender real change, before simply dismissing history.

Anyway, the metaphysical idea of how and why we classify

to begin with becomes problematic. Sometimes I have more questions than answers, which someone once told me is a true sign of learning.

Chapter Twenty-Seven

"Wolves, osprey, hawks, foxes, and badgers all drink from the Yellowstone River, which runs just along the side of the road," Alex said, pulling the car onto a lookout. They got out of the car and Alex noticed that Kit appeared even more stunning against the Yellowstone backdrop with her bold-yellow cat-eye glasses and long green-velvet coat.

"I can't believe you brought party clothes," Alex said, taking out her phone and photographing Kit.

"I can't believe you didn't." Kit replied and smiled for a selfie of the two of them.

"Let's go," Alex said.

It was too dark to see anything of interest, and they were already late to Will's dinner party.

"I can't wait to see the pinhole photo," Kit said. When they had arrived at Alex's cabin from the airport the first thing Kit noticed was the soggy pinhole camera that Alex had made and forgotten about the day that she had found Marta in the Tinsley House.

Kit had picked up the camera and said, "There could be evidence in here." She insisted on taking it into town for the camera store to develop.

"They'll laugh at us," Alex said. But they had not laughed. The proprietor took the paper and promised to have it developed by the end of the week.

"Can't say there will be anything there, but we'll develop it," the woman promised.

Will was in the driveway pretending to take out his trash when they pulled up to his cabin.

Kit was finishing a call with her parents and waved a tentative hello from the car.

"I kind of lied and told her there was no reception in the house," Alex said, getting out of the car and following Will inside, where he straightened cushions and fiddled with the coasters.

"I was worried. What happened?" Will asked.

"Sorry. I wanted to show her Bozeman, and it got late."

Kit had insisted that they keep the pinhole camera discovery to themselves for now.

"You don't trust Will? —You haven't even met him.

Kit's logic was, "I don't trust anyone yet."

"I'm glad she was up for the party," Will said.

"Are you kidding? She's more than up for it. She's down-right excited. It's Diana that surprises me. I did not expect her to come—thought she was inconsolable?"

"Apparently Kamran has consoled her, and she is on her way."

Kit finished her call, walked around to the back of the cabin, and tapped on the glass door.

"Will!" Kit exclaimed as if greeting a long-lost friend.

"Kit!" Will replied and hugged her.

"Oh no," Alex half-joked. "He loves her already." Everyone loved Kit.

"Sorry about that. Needed to call my folks before it gets too late on the East Coast. No reception on that road. Good to see you have it at the house," she said, winking at Alex.

"It's patchy," Alex lied.

Kit threw her head back and gazed up at the night sky. She took in the vast expanse of snow and ice and declared it "Spectacular."

"No light for miles, clear sky. Perfect viewing conditions," Will reported.

"Are you the lone resident in the park? A city girl might feel a little nervous out here without anyone around," Kit said, and Alex gave her a sidelong glance.

"What is worse for a city girl—no phone reception or no people?" Will asked lightly, looking at Alex.

"The silence." Kit answered definitively. She pulled out a chunky bouquet of flowers from the brown paper bag she was carrying and handed them to Will. "For you."

"Thanks." Will smelled them. "Nice."

"Thank you for the dinner invitation."

"My pleasure. You're a brave soul to venture into the park this time of year, this time of night, and to meet a group of strangers no less."

"You mean a group of suspects in a murder investigation." Kit corrected him.

"Kit!" Alex was horrified.

"Only the ones I like," Will smiled warmly.

"Well, you know your friend Alex here loves a good murder mystery." Kit elbowed Alex.

"I do. Thought if I provided her one, she might notice me," Will joked, but no one laughed.

Kit changed the subject. "Seriously, this girl told me she's never skied. Imagine! I booked us a little weekend in the park. So, is this the edge of the park?"

"Close," Will said.

"Close?" Kit raised an eyebrow.

"Technically, we're right outside the park," Will explained.

"Really?" Alex looked confused.

"The Park begins across the road. We are still in Gardiner."

"It does?" Why had he not pointed this out to her before? "But we drove through the gate. The huge gate that Roosevelt built," Alex insisted.

"No, you circled around it. You go through it and then you come right back out." Will explained, matter of fact.

"What is with all the traffic circles? I'm always lost," Alex complained.

Kit and Will smiled at each other.

"Is that your excuse?" Will joked, but Alex was deep in thought.

"Were they trying to trip up the park visitors?" Kit asked.

"So, to be clear, we're not in the park?" Alex asked, confused.

"Come in." Will said before she could ask if his cabin was owned by the National Park Service. "You must be freezing. This way." He walked them around to the boot-room entrance, where Kit expertly kicked-off her duck boots. Alex shook her head. Of course, Kit would know to bring duck boots. When Alex told her about her duck-boot-buying debacle, Kit said she would not be caught dead in those rubber uglies. But apparently bought a pair anyway. Hers were a retro mustard-yellow that only a fashionista could pull-off. Kit and Diana would get along well.

Kit was as impressed with the cabin as Alex had been.

"Oh, my God, you have five different architectural innovations here. The metal sliders look like Gehry?"

"Yup."

"Frank Lloyd-Wright's fingerprints are all over this wood-panel interior," she said, sliding her hand along the oak panels.

"Wait till you see my bedroom," Will said.

"You've never invited me in there," Alex blurted out, then tried to verbally backtrack: "I meant..."

Kit squeezed Alex's arm—a signal to chill-out. "Let's see this showcase," Kit said.

Will's bedroom was built around a boulder.

"They couldn't move it?" Kit joked, continuing, "Now really, how did they insulate this?" Kit traced her fingers along the seam between the glass and the boulder, "Not a hint of cold air. Wow."

"Bathroom?" Alex asked, pointing to a thick wood door.

"Not quite," Will answered sheepishly. He opened the door and a strong whiff of cedar and eucalyptus wafted out.

"Will, friend, a sauna?!" Kit winked at Alex.

"Yeah, Will. A sauna? You've been hiding a sauna?"

"I haven't fired it up yet this season."

"Season? It's been sauna season since I got here," Alex insisted.

"*Ski* season," Will explained.

"Well, fire her up; the girls are going skiing. I'm sure we can add a third person to our reservation." Kit glanced at Alex for approval.

"There's no need for a tour. Cancel it. Let me take you," Will insisted.

"You ski?" Alex asked.

"Everyone here skis."

"I don't." Alex said.

"And, stay here. Forget the motel. Make yourselves at home, I need to attend to dinner." Will squeezed Alex's shoulder as he left the bedroom.

"This one has taste. Here I thought you were gaga over a guy in overalls with a gun," Kit joked.

"Gaga?" Alex laughed.

"Does this cabin belong to the park services? Bit of a Frankenstein project. As personal as it is ostentatious," Kit noted as they walked back into the living room. "I doubt our tax dollars paid for these double-paneled-glass sliding walls. I bet they completely open in the summer. Come on? An oak-paneled boot room? And what about that imported Swedish stove?" Kit asked.

Wait until she sees the Walker Evans photo, thought Alex.

"All the cabins have those; I have one," Alex said, referring to the stove.

"With green tiles like these? These tiles were individually frosted and fired. And don't tell me that you didn't notice these Gehry fish lamps; we saw these together at the Guggenheim."

"I'm going to see if Will needs help," Alex extricated herself from Kit's house appraisal. "Help yourself to a drink."

"From the authentic 'fifties drink caddy?" Kit called after Alex, who shook her head.

Alex paused at the kitchen entrance and watched Will gingerly lift the lid off his crock-pot and release the spicy warm aroma of sweet potato chili. Alex's stomach rumbled. Will bit his upper lip, in concentration, as he gave the chili a shake of cumin. She loved the way he whistled to himself as he sauntered over to the pantry and passionately scrounged around, moving aside jars of fig jam and mango chutney and a bag of freshly milled organic flour, in search of a vital ingredient. Perhaps the bottle of Mexican chili-lime seasoning that Alex gifted him? He was already shaking it on everything they ate.

Alex, who couldn't cook, enjoyed watching him drizzle the cauliflower with olive oil and then blindly reach for a spice, first mint and then a pinch of Japanese lemon pepper. He slipped the baking sheet into the oven and floured his hands to handle a waiting ball of dough when his phone rang. He tapped it with his pinky and Alex heard Scotty on the speaker.

"You busy?" Scotty asked.

She backed into the shadows to listen.

"Yes, but I have a minute, what's up?" Will felt around the counter for his air pods and Alex was thankful to see that they were out of his reach.

"I can't make it tonight. Picked up a bigwig from Washington." Scotty's tone was hush-hush.

"Here about Pete's murder?"

"Assuming, but not sure. His name seems made-up: Aaron Jones. He won't say who or what he's investigating. I've been assigned as his minder, chaperone, host. Not sure what my role is, or how long he's staying." Scotty sounded stressed, more so than he had been at the beginning of the investigation, during those crucial initial twelve hours when all the responsibility was on his shoulders.

"I'd say bring him with you, but not if he's a weird spy."

"Anyway, need to take him to the university tomorrow. He's got a meeting," Scotty reported.

"Can't he get a Lyft?" Will kneaded the dough.

"Apparently not. Asked for a police escort," Scotty said, proudly.

Will sprinkled a dusting of flour and rolled the dough out on a wood board. "Cheapskate needs a ride. You must tell people that you're a cop and not a chauffeur."

"It's a one-time thing. By the way, Pete was in Jackson Hole the day that Marta was found."

"Jackson Hole? That's not a place to shoot raptors, and it's in the opposite direction of Bozeman."

"Either way, he has an alibi, lest you think he hit Marta over the head."

"Who?" Will asked, distracted by the kitchen timer.

"Pete."

"No, I meant who's his alibi?" Will asked.

"The Raptor Rescue in the Tetons. A café in Jackson Hole."

"Raptors?" Will sounded doubtful.

"Yeah, you know: birds of prey," Scotty said.

"Yeah, funny. That's odd. You checked that out?"

"As best we could. He didn't stay the night anywhere," Scotty informed him.

"You sure?" Will asked, arranging a tray of appetizers.

"Needed to go see those raptors."

"Double-check, Scotty."

"I'm only one person."

Pete wasn't into birds, Alex noted. There wasn't a single bird photograph in the exhibit of Pete's Yellowstone photographs, not even an owl. Alex loved owls.

"Raptors?"

"Maybe he was branching out," Scotty joked. Will was clearly off his suspect list.

"Funny."

"Look, the raptor folks said they met him in the Tetons Lodge."

"When, what time?"

"He was there early afternoon."

"Enough time to drive back before the storm."

"It's not like he needs an alibi for his own murder."

"We are talking about Marta." Will reminded him.

"Right. Well, we can't exactly charge him now, so what's the point?" Scotty pointed out.

"What if there's a connection."

"That again?" Scotty sounded exasperated.

"Or what if he met someone in the Tetons? Someone significant, like his murderer?"

"What difference would it make? He was killed at the party," Scotty pointed out.

"Or so we think." Will said.

"We heard a pop and down went Pete."

"He was already down or slumped anyway. We need—" Will started.

"The coroner's report. FBI does not consider us part of this investigation. They throw me a crumb when they need something."

"What do they need now?" Will asked.

"Visitor list, party guests, etc. It could have been any visitor to the museum that day."

"Except that he was already down, remember? Time of death?" Will asked.

Scotty didn't answer.

"Scotty what is it?" Will asked.

"Well, I did get a big crumb. Autopsy says he was paralyzed

before he died. They still cannot identify the drug. They think it is something that in a large enough dose could kill someone within an hour without medical help. Some sort of paralyzing substance."

"Like a tranc for an animal?" Will suggested.

"Leave the poachers out of this."

"Why?" Will demanded.

"Anyway, the drug is nothing we can identify. No known poison."

"What does that mean?" Will asked. "Did someone slip something in his champagne?"

Alex's heart beat fast; she was the last person to have a drink with him, a drink he brought to her.

"Get this: they have no clue. And, before you ask, I checked with all the pharmacists. And the big-animal vets."

"Did you check with Raven?"

"Good point. The substance may have been locally sourced," Scotty said, thinking aloud.

"Want me to?" Will asked.

"Sure. Tell her Bigfoot was taken by a UFO."

"What?"

"She'll know," Scotty insisted. "And one more thing: Marta was a Polish worker. She's on the list."

The doorbell rang, and Alex startled.

"Later," Will said to Scotty, walking into the hallway and bumping into Alex who said, "I heard the bell."

"Let's go see who's here." Will said.

* * *

"Where's the Mrs.?" Will hugged Kamran.

"Jasmine's mom returned to LA."

"Your Mrs.," Will clarified.

"Right. Jasmine has a migraine. She flies back to LA in the morning. I'll have a single malt; the Japanese one I know you're hiding from me. Jasmine's mom made you Fesenjoon." He handed Will a casserole.

"With pheasant or duck?" Will joked.

"With tofu," Diana, who had come with Kamran, answered.

"The Persian kings are turning in their graves." Will joked.

"Oh, my God, it smells unbelievable. What's in it?" Kit asked, joining them.

"Pulverized walnuts, pomegranate paste, and secret ingredients that I'm not allowed to divulge," Kamran made a motion to zip his lip. "Kamran," he said and reached for Kit's hand.

"Kit," Kit greeted Kamran and Diana.

"I'm Diana, and this is dessert." Diana dangled a pastry box wrapped in ribbon.

"Hmm, I recognize these pastry boxes," Will said like an excited child.

"Chickpea-flour cookies with cardamom and rice-flour cookies with rosewater and that pistachio halva that you love," Kamran confirmed.

"I love your mother-in-law," Will said.

"Where did you find all this in Bozeman?" Kit asked, impressed.

"I didn't. I got a door-dash from Tehrangeles. LA's Iranian grocery stores are like walking into Tehran. Right down to the matchmakers trolling in the aisles for beautiful women to match with nephews, sons, grandsons, neighbors—you name it, they're on it."

"I can imagine that those shopping aisles must be downright hazardous for you, Kamran," Will joked.

"Hence door-dash."

"Seriously?" Kit was impressed.

"I'm joking. My mother-in-law came to help. With everything that has happened, Jasmine's a little off her game. Besides, she's less of a cook and more of a chemist."

"Did Marta cook for you? Persian food?" Alex asked, curious.

"Yes. Impressive observation. As a matter of fact, Jasmine taught her. My mother-in-law's Mexican cleaning woman in LA is an excellent Persian cook."

"Lucky Jasmine," Alex commented.

"It's been a hard week for her," Kamran did not elaborate. "I didn't mean to keep you all standing at the door. Let's enjoy that famous fireplace."

The smell of steamed basmati rice wafted through the air, and Kit declared, "This may be the best place on Earth to be a vegetarian."

"Right? Who knew? Right in the middle of all these bison and elk," Diana agreed warmly.

"You haven't lived until you've tasted an elk burger," Alex said.

"Sorry, Kit, I got your buddy here hooked on Elk burgers. Alex tells me you have a Smithsonian fellowship. That's impressive," Diana said.

"They asked her to stay an extra year. It's unprecedented." Alex beamed.

"I hired her to do my PR," Kit joked.

"You don't need it, Kit," Alex added, proudly.

Will ushered them to the fireplace. A cornucopia of brightly colored appetizers was arranged on a large silver tray: roasted cauliflower sprinkled with mint, pickled beets, kimchi fritters, miniature balsamic glazed fig pizzas, and Alex's favorite—sweet potato fries. Kit, whose parents were famous for their sophisticated dinner parties, was right at home.

"Mm." Kit bit into a shitake empanada. "I thought I'd be the only plant-eater in Bozeman."

"There are rabbits here," Alex said wryly, not that she had seen one. Too cold? Did they hibernate? She would have to ask Will.

"You're a vegetarian?" Will asked, thrilled.

"This spread isn't in my honor then?" Kit demurred.

"Nope. Vegetarian since kindergarten," Will declared.

Kit gave Alex a subtle thumbs-up and then gestured toward Diana and Kamran, who were deep in their own little party— and, by the looks of it, not altogether celebratory.

"So, Jasmine's getting migraines again?" Will addressed Kamran.

"Yeah, she left a note last night saying that she couldn't sleep, asked me not to wake her," Kamran said, breaking away from his tête-à-tête with Diana.

"She used to get them at school during finals," Will said. "What's stressing her out?" Will asked.

"Pete's death," Kamran suggested. "They were lovers, once," Kamran told Kit, all but admitting a strong motive for killing Pete.

"What wicked webs we weave," Will said.

"Nothing wicked about it," Kamran retorted.

"She's married." Diana added, as if she herself were not ensconced with that same married man. A man who was the most obvious link between Marta and Pete.

"Any more secrets?" Kit asked lightly.

"Who doesn't have a secret?" Kamran said, looking at Diana.

"Not to bring up the elephant in the room..." Will started.

"Oh, please do." Kit, giddy, was treating the murder like a party game.

"Was Pete supposed to be in the diorama during the opening?" Will asked Diana. "Seems overly hubristic, even for him."

"No," Diana answered definitively.

"What was he doing there, then?" Alex asked.

"Placing himself at the center of attention. What else?" Diana answered.

"Was anything moved or changed?" Alex asked, thinking of her miniature cabin and Will's question—"Was anything missing?"

"Aside from the gun that I had not placed in there, along with the addition of Pete... nothing else was changed," Diana answered, bitterly.

"What irony; Pete hated those things," Kamran remarked.

"Guns?" Will asked.

"Crittercams," Kamran clarified.

"How do you know?" Will asked.

"He made no secret of it," Kamran answered tersely.

"We fought bitterly about it when he was in town to mount his show," Diana glanced at Kamran—a warning.

"Who won?" Will asked carefully.

"Diana, of course," Kamran said.

"I do lose occasionally," Diana conceded.

Kamran stood and motioned for Will to follow him to the kitchen. "There's something you should know," Alex heard him say as they walked away.

"There's a lot I should know." Will answered, annoyed to be pulled away from the party.

Diana excused herself to "freshen-up," and Kit suggested that she and Alex help the men in the kitchen.

As they approached the kitchen, they heard Kamran say, "There's an agent here investigating Cloudsplitter. I wanted you to hear it from me. Just in case."

Alex pulled Kit aside, where they could listen in without being seen.

"In case what? What's this agent investigating?" Will sounded tense.

Kit whispered to Alex, "Colombo, the guy Scotty picked up, on my flight. 'Cloudsplitter' was all over the document he was working on."

"Kamran's company," Alex answered. It was printed on her fellowship checks.

"A trademark that I registered a week back is under investigation. Nothing to worry about—just FYI. They may question you," Kamran said.

"Me?"

"About Cloudsplitter. Lasers."

"Why?"

Alex sneezed.

"Kit?" Kamran saw her first.

"I came to see if you need any help?" Kit was quick to come up with an excuse.

Alex slipped back into the hall, unseen.

"We're good," Kamran replied curtly.

"Trash looks full. May I take it out for you?" Kit asked, playing the good guest.

"Sure," Will handed her the half-filled trash bag, and glanced at Kamran.

* * *

Alex followed Kit outside.

"It's beautiful. Too bad all anyone has on their mind is murder," Kit said and took a deep breath of the glassy air. She coughed.

Kit dumped the half-empty bag in the bin.

"Look," Kit pointed to the cars in the driveway; Kamran and Diana had brought separate cars.

"Why the big charade of arriving together?" Alex asked, as she and Kit walked down the driveway and away from the cabin.

Kit jumped at the sound of metal crashing. "What was that?"

"Sorry to scare you. Figured I'd bring out the recycling while we were at it." Will stood at the end of the driveway with his back against the recycling bin as if to guard it.

"No worries." Kit smiled at him broadly. He did not see Alex, who slipped back inside.

* * *

Diana pulled Alex to the side before she could sit and warm up by the fire, "I need to speak to you privately," she whispered.

"What about?"

"I don't trust anyone around here anymore," Diana admitted.

"Not even Kamran?" Alex asked.

"Especially Kamran. That's why I wanted to talk to you. Never trust a man in love."

"In love?"

"Isn't it obvious? He's still in love with his wife. She has him wrapped around her pretty little pinky."

"Isn't he also sneaking around with other women?" Alex regretted saying it the minute it was out of her mouth.

"What have you heard?" Diana cleared her throat and attempted to regain her composure.

"Woman, just one woman." It was too late. Diana looked like she might lose her lunch. Had Alex misread the situation between Diana and Kamran?

305

"Diana, are you OK?"

"I'll be fine—a little woozy, something I ate earlier," she lied.

Diana had said something to Alex at the opening of the exhibit that sounded odd and that made her uncomfortable, but she could not, for the life of her, remember what it was. Diana's criticism of Pete's hubris was hardly a motive for murder.

"Darn ADHD; you said something important at the opening, when I first saw you," Alex ventured clumsily.

"I thought you had dyslexia," Diana said.

"It's comorbid with ADHD, which makes me forgetful, and sometimes I'll remember after-the-fact that I put my foot in my mouth."

"Co-morbid? Is everything about death?" Diana whimpered.

"Yeah, learning differences are often compared to cancer." Alex hated everything about the way dyslexia was characterized from a disability to a morbidity. "It means that they occur together."

"I got that," Diana snapped.

"Sorry, you must be..." Alex searched for the right word or phrase.

Diana seemed ready to confide something but then changed her mind. Or did she want to ask Alex something? Did Alex know something she should not be privy to? She had asked a lot of questions in her research. She interrogated almost everyone at the museum in the effort to get a picture of life in Bozeman. Did she see or hear something that she should not have? Was there something that had escaped her attention? She opened her mouth to speak when Kit walked in.

"Where have you been?" Diana asked her.

"I was hoping to see a bear," Kit joked.

"No need to stand guard out there in the freezing cold

when you can visit the Grizzly Encounter," Diana informed her. Alex and Kit exchanged glances.

"The what?" Kit asked.

"The Grizzly Encounter. Surely, you've heard of it, Alex? It's right off the 91, before you turn on the 89 going toward the park, up the Bozeman pass. It's at the dip in the road where there might have been a freeway entrance or exit or rest stop. There's a little shack that serves as a ticket counter and gift store. The place is beautifully landscaped like Big Sky Country to make you feel that you're out there alone, up close and personal with the bears."

"And this is safe?" asked Alex.

"Dinner is served," Will announced, walking in with Kamran.

"Thought we were waiting for David?" Diana asked.

"No, didn't you hear? He left for England the day before Marta was assaulted."

"Does that mean that the paleo poet is in the clear?" Diana asked, disappointed.

"Looks that way."

"England?"

"Fellowship interview at Cambridge." Alex said. *Some people had all the luck.* "Oh, Fossil of Time," Alex intoned.

"Thou art mine," Kit added. No one laughed, and Kit said, "Tough crowd."

"Maybe she was with him the night before her assault," Kamran suggested.

"Why would she be?" Diana asked Kamran. "And why do you care? He's in the clear."

"Marta called me when I was with you all at the Back Barn. She was scared but didn't want to involve the police. She wanted protection. She told me she would be safe that night;

she was with someone. Could have been him," Will told them. "It could be important."

"Storm or no storm, someone managed to get to her," Diana said, looking at Kamran.

"Someone close by, who could walk over," Kamran suggested.

"Like me, or Diana?" Alex blurted out.

"Just thinking aloud," Kamran smiled at her.

"Or someone driving to Bozeman in a Jeep," Diana offered.

"'There is nothing good or bad, but thinking makes it so,'" Will recited from *Hamlet* and frowned at Kamran.

"Scotty should have us on 24-hour surveillance. We must be prime suspects in Pete's murder," Alex said and bit into a cracker.

"Alex, that's ridiculous," Kit glared at her.

"We could be."

"Depends on time of death and how long Pete was in the diorama." Will said soberly.

"So, it's occurred to you that I could be a suspect?" Alex turned on him.

"Everything has occurred to me," Will snapped.

"If you recall, he was busy spilling champagne on me right before the show," Alex reminded him.

"Champagne," Will said, "The poison Pete ingested had to be in his champagne."

"What time were you sipping champagne together?" Diana asked.

"Not good with time..." Alex muttered.

"Looks like I missed a killer party," Kit joked. No one laughed.

Chapter Twenty-Eight

The Grizzly Encounter was a little ticket-and-gift shack off the highway.

The young man at the counter gave Alex a thumbs-up for choosing the mug with the photoshopped picture of Brutus the Grizzly Bear.

"Good choice; he's our star. Got him when he was a baby, four years old," the man said, and rang up her purchase. "Couldn't be released to the wild, wasn't raised by a mama bear, knew nothing of the outside world. We saved him from a circus-type situation." He looked at his watch, "It's about feeding time if you all want to meet Brutus. Nine bucks a head for adults."

Kit looked around, "Where?"

"Out back," the man pointed to a door.

Alex handed him a twenty before Kit could swoop in and pay for their tickets.

He rang them up and then walked them through the door and out to the back where a large bear play pen sat at the edge of the forest.

"This is huge. You'd never guess from the road," Alex commented.

"Look!" Kit pointed at Brutus who was playing with a bucket and a small ball. "He's darling!" she said.

Alex snapped a picture of Brutus. She noticed that the clear blue sky made the world as visibly sharp as it did cold.

"He is huge," Alex remarked, less eager than Kit was to approach the short fence.

"Raised him from a pup. Found him out in the woods, injured. Now, he's a big Hollywood star. You've probably seen him in a movie. Great actor: super obedient, super gentle. Everyone loves Brutus. Well almost everyone; he wasn't too obedient for that big-shot photographer."

"What do you mean?" Kit turned back from the fence.

"Well, I don't know... If you ask me, it's a little like cheating. He wanted to take Brutus out into those fields right back there and photograph him like he's out in the wild. Of course, this is how they do it for movies and all that, but it takes a lot of prep, and he wasn't prepared to pay. We're living on a shoestring budget over here—hand-to-mouth, if you get my meaning, and that guy had seriously expensive gear. North Face, big old Nikon camera, and he's telling me he can't afford the shoot. I said it's not happening then. It's not like I can put a leash on Brutus and lead him out there. It involves a lot more than that. I got to hire extra handlers, you know, put up an invisible fence. There's a lot more that happens to make these things work without Brutus getting hurt—or anyone else for that matter."

"*Has* Brutus hurt anyone?" Alex asked, examining the short fence, and imagining Brutus taking it in one leap.

"No," he answered emphatically. "But you know how it is. We are required to have insurance on a site. And you can imagine insurance for a grizzly bear is high. You'd guess a man like that would know about all that. Especially if he's an animal photographer."

"A professional?" Alex asked, looking at Kit who was coming to the same conclusion.

"Not in the wild. Seemed kind of clueless," the man said.

"Could he have used animal rescues all along?" Kit asked Alex.

"I wouldn't put it past him if he was that desperate to get the bear out there in those woods," the man answered.

"Which would explain the raptor rescue," Alex whispered to Kit.

"Do they have wolf rescues like this?" Kit asked him.

"Oh, yeah: there's a bear-and-wolf center, the wolf-cub rescue, the injured-wolf home..."

They waved a last good-bye to Brutus. Kit shoved a fistful of fives in the donation box as they left.

"How about that?" Alex said as they drove off.

"About Pete possibly faking his pictures?"

"Yeah."

"I have no idea," Kit said pensively.

Alex remembered the postcard Jasmine gave her of the wolves.

"Could he have staged his most famous work without anyone noticing?" Kit asked.

"It's funny. I was telling Marta about Robert Flaherty and

the long tradition of staging or fudging a picture in documentary film. And that was well before photoshop came on the scene. The Soviets were fudging cinema in-camera in the nineteen-twenties before photoshop was invented. Fake news is nothing new."

"Makes you wonder what wasn't staged," Kit said.

"The red fox," Alex answered.

"What about it?"

"I'll never know if he caught her on our shoot unless they do a posthumous show of his work. For all we know, he may have missed every single shot," Alex says, "All I have to go by is the clicking of his Nikon."

"Come on; he was a photographer."

"An artist anyway—possibly a con artist," Alex said.

"Was," Kit reminded Alex. "We need to ask Will if we can see the photographs that were on Pete's camera."

"I was thinking the same thing. It's probably already with the FBI."

"Good point, but maybe we should at least tell the FBI. Why give the Bozeman boys all the credit?" Alex asked. "Especially Scotty."

"Why not? It's not like we are going into business here. You want to be a detective?" Kit joked.

"I have nothing else going on," Alex said heavily. Her phone was vibrating.

"It's the camera store. My pinhole photos are ready," Alex said.

"Let's go!"

Field Note

Cultural Colonialism is alive and well as what Antonio Gramsci called hegemony—when the ideas of a powerful culture dominate. Think McDonalds' golden arches replacing indigenous foods all over the world.

An anthropologist must be aware of her own power position. How she locates herself in terms of the culture she studies (this is called exteriority—positionality). Is she putting herself above other people? Her cultural identity—native or non-native, gender, language fluency, experience—all of it determines what she will be given access to. If I were Iranian, would Jasmine have been warmer, more welcoming—or, inversely even more on guard? The filmmaker should have been 'way more careful with me. I've been told that many Iranians who left in the '70s don't trust each other because they came from different political factions.

We are all liminal and never just occupy one position. We live in many different worlds. Who we are determines our access to data. Columbia University provides an official, embossed letter asking that the graduate researcher be granted access and aid in her research. It bestows the authority of a powerful institution. Some might laugh at this letter or see it as elitist; others will respect it. In some instances, it will open doors—in others, slam them shut. The key is to know which door to present it at. So yes, one of my positions is former SPED student; the other one is Ivy League researcher. Both positions mean something to someone, and I'll use either positionality or identity (and sometimes both) in the situation it's best suited for. There's something to chew on: we are always deploying our multiple identities in different ways, depending on the situation. Like my undergraduate roommate who wore a miniskirt to class but a long dress when her parents visited.

Back in the colonial days, anthropology, especially visual knowledge, was used to subjugate, to help colonizers rule more efficiently and sometimes more brutally. Identity cards are a great example of this. The penal system relies on them. You must be punished as someone. As an identity.

Chapter Twenty-Nine

Raven's house was like an upside-down wood octahedron that might roll off on its own if it were not for the thick conifers and pine that surrounded it.

"Geodesic dome, popular in the 'seventies," Will explained to Kit and Alex as they approached the front door.

"Raven is usually in her greenhouse this time of day," Scotty said, charging ahead.

The greenhouse was a long glass hallway that ran right up alongside the back of the main house. Tendrils of Chinese and native herbs threatened to choke the bright pink echinacea blooms that welcomed them at the door.

"Cool greenhouse." Alex remarked.

"Ingenious, right? Gets all its heat off the brick from the main house."

Stray pots, shovels, hoses, and the gray alley cat that adopted Raven could be seen through the glass walls, but no Raven. The cat followed them out of the greenhouse and then rocketed ahead to lead them into the boot room of the main house. They took off their boots and walked sock-footed into Raven's living room.

"You ought to lock your doors, Raven," Scotty yelled into the house by way of greeting.

"In Bozeman? Don't be silly," Raven answered, coming out of her office to greet them. She was a petite, bird-like woman who could throw down any of the primped Pilates crowd down-town. At seventy-five she still plowed her own drive. She was also soft, and gentle, and kind, and Alex liked her straightaway.

"Hi, boys. And you must be the anthropologists?" She smiled and hugged them each in turn. "Good timing; was just finishing my ESL class."

Kit looked around for the students.

"Online," she answered Kit's unvoiced question.

"Raven teaches botany and herbology online. Her avatar is this futuristic teen with punk pink hair and a mini dress that would have George Jetson blushing. Seriously, Raven, try to be more careful about locking-up."

"'Seriously,' Scotty?" she mimicked him, and pivoted toward the kitchen sink, "How long have you lived here, Scotty?"

Scotty looked confused.

"It's a rhetorical question, Scotty." She laughed. "I've

known Scotty since he was a wee one," she explained to the women.

"These attacks are new statistics. Places change," Will told her.

"Yup, ask any urban anthropologist." Kit said nodding to Alex. Scotty raised his eyebrows.

"Marta was not a burglary. And both she and Pete Holgan were attacked in museums. Doubt either incident has anything to do with unlocked doors," Raven said.

"She has a point, Scotty," Will conceded.

Raven smiled sweetly at Scotty.

"Besides," Kit added, "Alex tells me everyone seems to have a set of everyone else's keys here?"

"Are they connected?" Raven ignored Kit's comment, took the reading glasses from her head, and perched them on her long thin nose. They immediately slipped down. She peered up and trained her yellow eyes on Scotty.

"Can't see that they aren't," Will said.

"Did they know each other?"

"Does a serial killer pick people who know each other?" Scotty asked.

"No. But, really? A serial killer? And you think Big Foot's a hoax. Geez." She rolled her eyes. Will laughed.

She ushered them into her morning room and sat them down. "I've got this wonderful new dandelion tea." She poured hot water into her tea pot, covered it with a crocheted tea cozy and placed it on the table.

"I'll take some of that immune syrup that you store up," Scotty said.

"Sambuca? The bush gave—and gave—this year; made vats of syrup."

"Cool. Can I have a bottle for my vodka?" Scotty asked.

"Rather defeats the purpose, doesn't it, Scotty? You don't want to kill the medicine before it has a chance to go down."

Kit chuckled and Raven winked at her.

"So, to what do I owe the pleasure of your company? You boys must be busy, what with everything going on, to stop by here and see us. And you women are meant to be skiing, I'm told? What brings you this far out of town?"

"You guys are no longer out of town; you're practically in town these days," Will said.

"Alex, isn't that your area? Urban sprawl? By the way, we've been waiting for you to come and do a model of our house," Raven said.

"News travels fast," Alex said.

"Sure does when our favorite ranger is so—" Raven let her glasses slip down her nose as she peered at Will, "—involved."

"You do know that someone was murdered recently?" Will said, blushing.

"And that's why you want to talk to me? Please tell me I'm a suspect! That would be so much fun." Raven rubbed her hands together. "Things have been slow at work, and I could use a diversion."

"You know how it is whenever there's a murder; everyone comes to the local witch," Will joked.

"Seriously, what's the deal?" Raven channeled her professorial tone, the one she used when teaching her botany classes at Montana State.

"Post-mortem didn't find anything recognizable in his system. It's possible he had a grand-mal seizure or a heart attack. There were signs of a possible overdose."

"Hmmm. Drugged?"

"Must have been. Too coincidental that he'd have a seizure right before being shot," answered Will.

"Smart boy," Raven observed. "We are looking for a poison that would cause a seizure but leave no trace."

"Yup."

"Did he eat or drink anything before he was shot?"

"Champagne," Alex offered.

"That's not going to do it. But sweet enough to cover a bitter herb," Raven said.

"We're guessing a poison, native to the Bozeman Mountains."

"A local herb? *That's* why you need me," Raven realized.

"We need to know how long it would take to work. How easy it is to disguise. And what it's like to handle."

"OK, come with me. Bring your mugs." Raven led them back out into the cold.

* * *

Raven's medicine room was in the loft of the old barn that was otherwise used as a garage. Unlike the disrepair that marked the downstairs, the loft was newly redone in a beautiful cherry stain. It smelled like cedar and sage and other aromatic herbs that Alex had never smelled before.

"I had the herb drawers built right into the walls," Raven said.

"They look like the old card catalogues libraries had." Kit said.

"Yup, repurposed from the local library," Raven said proudly. Each compact drawer was outfitted with a thick metal clip that clutched an index card that explained the herb and all its medicinal properties. On the flip side was a faint pencil sketch of the plant. There were hundreds of cards: several were flipped to the picture side, others to the written entry.

"And there's the side-effects as well," Raven said, flipping the card to show the myriad ways an herb could interact with something. "Like a statin for example," she explained, and then asked, "Do you know if he was taking any meds?"

"No idea."

"Find out," Raven instructed them. "Bring me the toxicology report, and we'll get to work."

Chapter Thirty

Kit rang the bell on the counter and crinkled her nose at the sour-smelling potpourri satchels.

"Is this the right place? It's all floral and flounce," Kit frowned. "I don't see any skis."

"Hello, ladies!" A plump midwestern-looking woman in her seventies called out as she came barreling through a makeshift curtain of frilly streamers.

"We don't get a lot of visitors skiing in the park this time of year—which is why we double the gift shop as the ski-rental counter," The proprietor explained.

"Are we it?" asked Kit.

"Just about. There was a man in a bit ago."

"The day before Marta was assaulted," Alex said. The woman flinched.

"You know Marta?" Kit asked her.

"Oh, yeah, everyone knows everyone in the park."

"Of course they do," said Alex. "But she was different."

"She was, and she wasn't. Most folks around here are from around here."

"Where was Marta from?" Alex asked.

"Polish summer worker. She came with them and stayed on."

"When was that?" asked Kit.

"A year or so back now. Hard to say; one season leads to the next. When it was time to leave after the summer season, she came in and bought a little book about local flowers to send back to a friend in Poland. That's how I knew she wasn't going back with them. It was funny; she took her purchase outside and was back a minute later with a package all neatly wrapped and sealed. We do all that here—sure, we charge a little extra for wrapping—but she wanted to do all that herself. Save a buck, I guess. She took a marker and scribbled an address in Poland. She insisted on waiting and handing it directly to the Polish girl who worked here for the summer. Says she was hand-delivering it. The girl was on break, and Marta sat over there, in that chair. It's for our tired visitors during peak season when the lines are long. She waited a good hour. The girl came; Marta handed her the package, and that was that."

"Anything odd about the transaction?" Alex asked.

"Transaction?" The woman laughed. "People give packages to people all the time. You have any idea the cost of first-class mail to Poland? A book?"

"They were friends—Marta and the girl who worked here?" Alex asked.

"Never saw them together except that once. There was friendly chatter."

"How do you know it was friendly?" Alex asked.

The woman frowned, "What's this all about?"

"Just curious, given the attack."

"They said, 'Hello,' 'Goodbye,' 'What's up?' Friendly banter, like we are having now," the woman said tightly.

"In English?" Kit asked.

"Sure, what else?"

"Polish," Alex and Kit said at the same time.

"Where you girls visiting from?" The woman changed the subject.

"Washington, D.C," Kit answered.

"That skier might have been from Washington, D.C. Rascal still has my skis."

"Are you sure?" Alex's heartbeat quickened. She glanced at Kit who pretended to be engrossed in the postcard stand.

"If you're asking how good my inventory is, then yes, I'm sure," the woman snarled.

"No, I meant about D.C."

"Now, I'm not one to mind other people's business..." she looked at Alex, who tried not to smile at Kit, "But he did clear out his pockets on the counter—couldn't find his credit card. He had all sorts of museum cards; one said *National Geographic*. Isn't that in Washington, D.C.?"

"Yes," answered Kit looking up.

"What did he look like?" asked Alex.

"Tall, dark, and handsome, honey. Seriously, he was tall, darker hair, dreamy blue eyes. And in a big, huge hurry. Needed those skis ASAP, he said. And then—get this—another reason I remember him, is because he never returned them. Like I told you."

"Did you tell the police?

"By police, you mean Scotty. No. Poor boy has been running around like a chicken with his head cut off since that photographer got himself murdered. Nobody wants to bother Scotty right now. He's got enough going on with a murder and all. Especially over an old pair of skis that the insurance will cover." The woman casually ran her finger across the till.

"Have you seen a picture of the photographer who was murdered?" Alex asked.

"No. Pete Holgan, was it? I've seen *his* photographs if that's what you mean. Love the ones of the wolves. We have his post-cards on sale here." She walked over to the postcard stand and pulled them out. She handed one to Kit and another to Alex. It was from the same series as the one Jasmine gave to Alex.

Alex pulled out her iPhone and said, "No reception." She walked toward the door, and turned back, "Do you have Wi-Fi here?"

"No, can't say we do. Whole park's a bit of a dead spot."

"What about a land DSL? Do you have Internet?" asked Kit.

"Of course, honey we have Internet. How else do we do credit-cards?"

"Mind if we take a look?" asked Kit.

"What do you need?" The woman was reluctant to let them behind the counter.

"Pull up a picture of Pete Holgan. Google him on the web," Alex instructed her.

The woman sat down at the desk, put on her reading glasses, and typed.

"Lordy!"

"Recognize him?" Alex asked.

"That's him, all right."

"The man who rented the skis?" Kit confirmed.

"The one who stole them. No chance of getting back *those* skis."

"I wonder where he left them. We need to tell Scotty." Kit said.

"All right, if you say I should," the woman agreed reluctantly.

Alex knew she would not. "We can mention it to him. I'm sure he'll give you a call either way," Alex offered.

"That would be preferable. I like to stay out of other folks' business."

They paid for their skis and postcards and left.

"Good call," Kit high-fived Alex as soon as the door shut behind them.

"If she wants an insurance payment for her old skis, she'll need a police report."

"No kidding. Doesn't want them found, is more like it. She's waiting until that's an inevitability."

"The case of the rickety skis," Alex joked.

"Rickety skis? What's this?" Will came over to help them carry their equipment. "Already complaining about the skis?"

"I wouldn't know good skis from bad skis, but these do seem a little beat-up," Alex agreed.

Alex filled him in on what they had learned. "That must have been after I dropped him at the Wonderland Café," Alex concluded.

"Wonder who gave him a ride? No one mentioned it in their statements."

"Someone's hiding something," Kit said.

Will loaded the skis into the car and called Scotty as they pulled out of the parking lot and onto the barely plowed road.

"Well, that is a new development, for sure," Scotty said over the car speaker, "And this was Saturday afternoon?"

"It must have been. Right after we parted ways," Will said. "Why so secretive?" he continued "Was he meeting someone?"

"Maybe he was in cahoots with the poachers and making a ton of money on the side?" Scotty wondered aloud.

"I keep telling you, poaching isn't economic in that way; it's about cattle and land," Will argued.

"That's as economic as it gets. Folks will pay big money for land rights," Scotty said.

"True," Will conceded.

"One more thing," Alex interrupted, "Marta sent a package home with another Polish worker."

"I'll look into it," Scotty promised, "And, Will..." Scotty cut out.

"Let's ski!!" Kit exclaimed when the call dropped. But Will's phone immediately beeped. He pulled over to read his text.

"Even in death Pete's ruining my plans. Got to run back to Bozeman. Scotty needs me."

"Will!" the women complained in unison.

"You're our guide; I canceled the tour." Kit pleaded.

"I'll drop you at my place to get your car, and then..."

"There were two ..." Kit joked.

"Superstitious anthropologists on skis." Will said.

"Will, look," Alex pointed to the other side of the road.

"What is it?"

"Over there, on the shoulder. I thought it was a little white dog, like Jasmine's."

"Jasmine's in LA, and, besides, that animal never leaves her side. You probably saw a snow-covered skunk or something."

"A snow-covered skunk?" That sounded ridiculous enough, but more-so coming from a man who studied zoology.

Chapter Thirty-One

"What was that?" Alex readjusted her goggles and blinked.

"You saw it too? A flash?" Kit said, looking around.

"Something metallic, a reflection? It's probably nothing. It's deserted out here." Alex wobbled over on her skis to Kit and gave her a big squeeze. "I love that you are here, that you came," she said.

"Me too," Kit said.

Will had instructed them to stay on the ski path—an easy loop, which they were already halfway around.

"What is that?" Kit asked as they came upon a gorgeous pool of aquamarine-colored water that sizzled in the snow. "Shall we take a dip?" she joked.

"If you want to die. We would boil to death in there within a minute," Alex said. Kit appeared appropriately horrified.

"Weren't you skinny-dipping in one of these?"

"That was the river. And, if that was hot, imagine how hot an actual geyser would be."

"Let's get out of here, Alex. I don't want to be pushed in; do you?" Kit asked.

"By what—a bison?"

Kit held up her phone, "No reception."

"Of course not. We are dead center in miles and miles of snow, and not much else. Who's going to make a call out here? The bison?" Alex laughed and motioned for them to keep moving.

"Enough with the bison; aren't they dangerous? Don't they charge or something?"

Kit was usually the last one to sweat anything, so, if she was sweating, maybe there was something to be worried about. Alex turned to Kit, "Out with it. There's something you're not telling me." Alex broached the subject carefully.

"About the investigation?" Kit asked.

"You have a crush on Will," Alex blurted out.

Kit laughed so hard she snorted.

"What's so funny? What's wrong with Will?" Alex called after Kit who glided down the trail, laughing.

"Sorry," Kit stopped and turned to Alex breathlessly.

"If you don't have a crush on him, then why are you being weird around Will?"

"Weird?"

"Is it because we canceled your ski tour? Will promised to

take us, and now we are racing across a tundra unguided." Alex stopped to catch her breath.

Kit stabbed her ski poles in the ground, and said, "You're right. I've been a little weird, but it's not that."

"Aha, I knew it! There *is* something."

"Alex this murder situation is 'way more complicated ..."

"And this is news?"

"Well, we haven't had any privacy. You know, with Will around—"

"This *is* about Will? Spill it; only a stray bison will hear you. What's up?"

Kit turned to Alex, "For one, your mentor Diana is not having an affair with that gorgeous Iranian guy."

"But they were at his cabin together."

"So? Like I said, it's hard to get any privacy around here. If you wanted to conspire, you would have to go out into the wild. Look at us. My take: Diana and Kamran have the strongest motives. Pete was having an affair with Kamran's wife and trying to destroy Diana's work."

"OK. That's a bit extreme."

"These are facts, Alex, not feelings."

"He wasn't destroying her work; they had artistic differences. That's no reason to kill him."

"And Kamran? He hated Pete. Did you see his face when Pete was mentioned? And, requited or not, Diana has feelings for Kamran which might motivate her to help him."

"Help him what? Off Pete? That's crazy. But... hmmm. Maybe," Alex admitted. She filled Kit in on Kamran and Diana's conversation in the Bones Room. "But I doubt that they murdered anyone," Alex concluded.

"Well, someone did. Do you have any idea who is on Scotty's no-fly list?"

"No. Everyone, but me, lives here. So, it's kind of hard to tell if anyone's stuck here."

"Good point. Did Scotty tell you not to leave town?"

"Not in so many words."

"Then you could come home with me tomorrow?"

"That would look super-suspicious."

"Superstitious?"

"Suspicious," Alex yelled.

"What makes you a suspect, Alex? You didn't know these people a month ago."

"I *feel* guilty."

"That filmmaker's destiny was not your doing," Kit turned on Alex. "Stop it. Alex! What is with you and automatic guilt?"

"Years of Special Ed. Feeling guilty all the time that I needed people to bend over backwards to teach me what everyone else learned effortlessly."

"You needed no help figuring *that* out."

"A school psychologist pointed it out to me in high school."

"Right. Back to our murder. What would Margaret Mead do?"

"Seriously?"

Kit stared hard at Alex. She was serious.

"A genealogy," Alex laughed.

"Exactly. Let's treat this like a village."

"This is less a genealogy and more like a spider's web. They're all connected to each other, and not casually. Diana and Kamran, Kamran and Jasmine, Jasmine and Will—they were in school together."

"Really?" Kit raised her eyebrows. "You might have mentioned this earlier. Adds a new dimension to the ranger. This is starting to look less like a Margaret Mead village and more like Miss Marple's stomping grounds."

"But why try to kill Marta? She wasn't part of this web."

"Perhaps she didn't want to participate. She knew something and threatened to reveal it?"

"She's the one with the weakest link to everybody. I don't know. It doesn't feel right."

"And Will? He's surrounded by friends who all have strong motives. And you've known him for less than a minute," Kit pointed out.

"Yeah, a minute more than you have, so..."

"Knowing someone in the biblical sense obfuscates rather than illuminates."

"Obfuscates? Come on, Kit."

"OK. Romance clouds one's vision. It does not mean you know him better, but, possibly, less. Better?"

Alex slid one foot in front of the other, careful to stay clear of the creepy and potentially dangerous fumarole.

"Why didn't you tell me that you don't trust him?" she asked. She and Kit were gliding side-by-side again.

"It's not that I don't. It's too early to decide." Kit was panting. "Did we bring water?"

"Whoops."

"Snacks?"

"No."

"What if..."

"It's an easy tourist loop, we'll be fine."

"Well, let's not get out too far," Kit suggested. She stopped and took out the trail map Will gave them.

"It's a loop." Had it not been a loop they *would* be lost. Everything was so similar, and Alex had no clue how to read the sun, or any idea what direction they were traveling in.

"Instinct is overrated. We are scientists," Kit said, studying the map.

"Yes, social scientists. We rely on our guts to some degree."

"My gut tells me that we are out of our element."

331

"Anthropology is making the strange familiar, and the familiar strange," Alex recited the well-worn mantra when a hawk swept by.

"Making the familiar strange," Kit mused as she watched the hawk disappear into the sky.

"Kit! Look!" Alex slipped off her skis and used her poles to climb up to the edge of the embankment. "*No way!* Come look!" Alex called back to Kit.

"Alex?!" Kit followed her. "Don't leave the path. Or your skis. Will was adamant: do not veer off the path."

Alex pointed out in the distance, "Look—over there! You have no idea how rare this is."

They gazed out together at the great expanse, where all that was visible was the snow turning from white to a dusty grey in the darkening sky.

"Alex, is this safe? On the side of the road? It's getting dark; we could get hit." Kit pleaded with her to turn back.

"I haven't seen a car for miles."

"Because we've been on the trail, where it's safe," Kit reasoned.

"Come look; we have to tell Will!" Alex fumbled for her mobile. "No reception." She texted him a location pin, hoping it would send the minute they passed a cell tower.

"I like Will," Kit said.

"Who doesn't?" Alex didn't avert her gaze.

Kit squinted into the darkening distance and asked, "What am I meant to be looking at?"

"Wolves!" Alex announced, reverently.

"Wolves?" Kit asked, "Where?" Kit looked around, confused.

A loud bang reverberated through the cold, still air. Alex ducked. "Kit!" She grabbed Kit's hand and pulled her toward the trail. "Hurry!"

"Ouch," Kit winced. "Was that a gun-shot?"

"Sounded like it." Alex said.

"Where are we going? Alex—stop! We are headed toward the shooter."

"We need cell reception."

"Not in that direction we don't. We might as well be targets at a shooting range," Kit said, referring to their bright red and pink ski suits. "Let's go that way," Kit pointed in the opposite direction.

"Car's that way," Alex pointed away from the direction Kit was headed. Kit turned and followed, slogging along in her heavy ski-boots and cursing Alex's furious pace.

Finally, Alex stopped, and Kit let out a sigh of relief.

"Whoops," Alex said.

"Whoops?" Kit asked.

"Wrong way."

"What? How ...?" Kit was incredulous.

"How long have you known me? Have I ever known my right from my left?!"

"For God's sake, Alex." Kit threw her poles in anger.

"What did you do that for?" Alex asked, "Where'd they go?"

The women searched fruitlessly for the lost poles. Alex handed Kit one of her poles, and with one pole each, they stumbled their way back to the car.

Kit retrieved a bundle of maps from the glove compartment as Alex drove.

"What's this?" Kit asked, unearthing a small package wrapped in brown paper.

"Oh that. That was supposed to go to Jasmine ages ago. It's from the honey store."

"I could use a snack," Kit tore it open. "Bummer." She threw the package into the backseat.

"What is it?" asked Alex.

"Tea," Kit spat the word. "PG Tips," she said with a faux English accent.

"PG Tips? That's Marta's brand."

"Jasmine buys her maid tea?" Kit quipped; she was hungry and thirsty, and dry tea bags did nothing to appease her.

"She's like that, generous. She brought me that honey basket."

"Thank God you have maps," Kit changed the subject.

"Will shoved those in there. He insisted."

"And thank God for all-wheel drive. Jenny Lake will be the closest cell-phone reception," Kit reported, studying the map.

"How do you know?" Alex asked. Jenny Lake was the opposite direction of Bozeman.

"I've been around the bush enough to know where to find a phone tower," she said, adding in a more serious tone, "They may be following us. It's getting dark. At least in New York you know where to expect danger; so much for ethereal landscapes."

Alex's phone beeped, indicating that they had passed a cell tower. Her text and pin were on their way to Will.

"Quick," Alex threw her phone at Kit "Call Will."

Kit fumbled with the phone. "What's your password?"

"12345."

"No!?"

Kit punched the passcode into the phone and found Will's number in the favorites.

"Are you dialing?"

"I got his voicemail. I'll send a text. By the time he listens to a message, we'll be either shot dead or frozen to death."

The road and sky faded into a horizon of muddled gray with no safe harbor in sight.

"Unless they are tailing us with their headlights off, then

we are utterly alone," Kit said, pointedly eyeing the gas gauge. "Half a tank, Alex," she noted.

"They were probably poachers," Alex suggested, her eyes trained on the rearview mirror, "I don't hear an engine; do you?"

"Not sure if that's good or bad," Kit replied.

Alex's phone rang as they passed Jenny Lake.

Kit answered Will's call and put it on the car speaker. "Will!" Alex exclaimed.

"What's going on? Are you guys OK?"

"Someone tried to shoot us," Kit said.

"Shoot you?"

"Actually," Alex said, "they weren't shooting at *us*; they were shooting at the wolves. They must have been poachers."

"Did you see them? More than one person?" Will asked.

"We didn't see any wolves. Someone shot at us," Kit reported succinctly.

"Are you hurt?"

"They missed."

"Because we were not the target," Alex explained.

"Your glasses were fogged," Kit said tightly.

"Listen. Marta was released from the hospital this afternoon. Scotty put a tag on her cellphone in case she was in danger. Do not freak out—the last signal came from Gardiner, not far from that pin you sent me," Will said.

"When?"

"Last hour or so."

"Are you saying that whoever is after Marta shot at us?" Alex swerved.

"That's it! Pull-over; I'm driving." Kit insisted.

Alex's hands shook as she pulled over to the shoulder.

"I want you guys to get yourselves back to my cabin ASAP.

Break every speed limit. The worst that can happen is that you get a police escort."

"If you trust the police," Kit said under-her-breath.

"Or blow a tire." Alex said, as she and Kit slid over each other to change seats.

"Risk it. Burn rubber—get the heck out of there. If you are followed, go somewhere public—like a café. And send me a *find friend* request so that I can track you. Got to run; Scotty's calling. We *will* come get you," Will said and hung up.

"That sounded ominous," Kit treaded carefully. "Are you sure we can trust him? I don't know if it's such a good idea to share our location. He knows where we are headed; isn't that enough? I mean... "

"We have to trust someone," Alex reasoned. If Will had wanted to track them, he could easily have tagged a tracker on her car and followed them via Satellite. If he could do it to animals, he could do it to her Subaru. It was easy enough with an Apple Air tag.

"So where does this leave us? Alex," Kit asked.

"Trusting Will."

"I trust him; I do. It's everyone else in his orbit that I don't trust."

"I thought you liked him. You're freaking me out." Alex had teary eyes.

"Eyes on the road; keep a look-out. I'm just saying. We both know that Scotty doesn't have a handle on this case."

"I need to trust him. I like Will. I need one person that I can believe in, here."

"So, are we treating the fact that Will was alone when we were shot at as coincidence?"

"Yes... we are."

"Either way, I am putting us up in an Airbnb tonight, and I don't want you to tell Will where we are, OK? As far as he knows, we are going to be together until I fly out, which he does not know is tomorrow morning."

"Seems drastic, no?"

"Please Alex, just stay on there after I leave for a few nights until we can get more information on who shot at us. Until they find out what Marta is up to in Gardiner. I don't trust Scotty."

"Kit, you don't trust any cops."

"Can you blame me?" Kit swerved into the opposite lane.

"Let's drive. We can decide later." Alex said looking down at her phone. "No reception."

"Either way, Alex, we're going to a café and then an Airbnb."

* * *

Norah Jones swooned softly on the speakers, and the smell of freshly baked lavender scones saturated the heavy air at the Wonderland Café. The large picture windows were fogged from the breathless conversations mixed with the steam that puffed out from the kitchen, where the café's famous soups simmered away. A woman with a baby stroller vacated a table by the window, and Kit swept in to occupy it.

"Perfect place to keep watch," Kit said.

"And be watched." Alex added, placing her bag on the table. "The woman in the ski shop is not going to be happy; another pair—no, *two* more pairs—of lost skis."

"You know she'll be thrilled; more insurance money. Or, better yet, she'll make us pay."

"Great," said Alex. "Let's call Will."

"Isn't Gardiner out of Will's jurisdiction?" Kit asked, already knowing the answer.

"Wolves have no jurisdiction," Alex informed her.

"Alex, somebody shot a gun at us," Kit said. It was fully hitting her.

"At the wolves," Alex corrected her, "They may have been a bad shot. It's not clear where the bullet went. It could have been a warning shot," Alex explained.

"Do poachers usually warn their prey?" Kit was incredulous. "Alex, I stared hard out onto that wild expanse. I followed the finger you held up to my nose to direct my gaze and—nothing. Nada. No wolf."

"What else would they have shot at?" Alex asked.

Kit shook her head. And Alex added, "Because, if they had been shooting at us, we'd be dead. We were easy targets. They'd have to be a bad shot to miss us. We were bright-red sitting ducks."

"Was it a warning? The museum *must* be the link," Kit said.

Alex's phone pinged with a text from Will. "False alarm. Marta is safely back in her cabin. Her phone was stolen. It's turned-off."

Alex went to the bar to retrieve their hot chocolates. When she returned, Kit had laid out the blurry pinhole picture on the clean café table.

"Let's look at the pinhole picture again. Could the person have been on skis?" Kit asked and took a sip of her mint hot chocolate.

When they retrieved Alex's pinhole sheets, all they had was a blurry image of a figure in the field, and, given that the light was low that day, it could have taken minutes to hours to develop the image, meaning the person may or may not have been in the field as Marta was lying unconscious in the Tinsley House.

The image showed a blurry figure in motion, and, at first, they had assumed that the lines just in front of the figure's feet were shadows, but, now that they had been skiing, it was clear that these were skis.

"The person was on skis, which means that it's possibly the same person I may have heard come in and out of Marta's cabin the day I was snooping around."

"Who skis here?"

"Just about everyone."

"Alex, you're not safe here. Text Will that we are going to spend the night in a hotel down here. Lie to him that they wouldn't refund my ski package. Girl time—he can't refute that," Kit demanded.

"Ok," Alex said reluctantly and texted Will. She then turned to Kit and said, "Aren't you glad you came?"

"I missed you, Alex." Kit said, "Why in God's name are you playing Miss Marple with all these strangers? Let's go." Kit said, "We have a long drive."

"The ski lodge is down the road."

"We are going to an Airbnb in Bozeman. And we are not telling anyone, including Ranger Will."

"But..." Alex started to protest.

"Do not trust anyone. Including Will. I booked the Airbnb under my mom's maiden name. It's walking distance from your place, where you will leave your car parked, so that folks will think you're at home. Walk to the Airbnb and lock all the doors."

"Kit, don't be ridiculous; you're scaring me," Alex said.

"Alex, come home with me."

"You know I can't leave until this is solved."

"Don't trust Scotty, either."

"Kit, you're being extreme. And why Will? I thought you liked him?"

"I do." Kit paused, "Alex, Will's name was on the document that detective was typing on the airplane."

"What? You're telling me this now?"

"Didn't know his last name until I saw your phone entry an hour ago."

"You saw that document days ago. You mis-remembered."

"I just googled him. Do you know any other Cloudsplitter board members who are also park rangers?"

"Cloudsplitter? That's Kamran's company." Alex remembered Will's phone conversation with Scotty. He had called to warn Will that the company was being investigated and not to merely keep him updated on Pete's murder investigation. Scotty must have known that Will was a Cloudsplitter board member and that his name was on those papers.

"Harold William Duncan the Third?" Kit said to Alex who was already looking it up.

"This internet is so damn slow." Alex scrolled her finger along her phone to look at the Cloudsplitter website. "No wonder he goes by Will. If he's guilty of something, Scotty wouldn't entrust him with the case information."

Kit gave her a skeptical look and said, "Just be careful. Remember what we overheard at Will's party? When Kamran and Will were in the kitchen? They were talking about Will being implicated." Alex turned the word *implicate* over in her head.

"Relationships are built on trust. I do hope it works out for you guys. He's nice," Kit placated her.

"Yeah, he's great." Alex said with mock enthusiasm. This was what anthropologists called a public secret. The kind everyone knows but won't tell, lest it destroy the social equilibrium. They both knew that Will was more than capable of bashing in Marta's head and of killing Pete.

* * *

They paused under a streetlight while Alex unearthed the car keys.

"Now would be a great time to be a smoker," Alex said.

Kit didn't smile; her expression was pained.

"Kit?" Alex asked.

"I was thinking of him..." Kit met Paul, a photographer, at an Embassy dinner in Burkina Faso, after which they spent every waking hour together—until he disappeared a week later. "There was a dark side to him that I never told you about. It was sick, the adrenalin rush he got from going after a photo during war. Alex, a village was being blown to bits, and his goal was to get it on film," Under the streetlamp, Kit appeared haunted.

"You never told me..."

"I was ashamed to have feelings for a man like that."

It reminded Alex of Pete's story about the tiger and the villager. Alex hugged Kit tight. "Thank you for coming."

"Come on. It's getting cold; let's go." Kit turned toward the car.

"Wait," Alex paused. "Could Pete have been a war photographer?"

"Sounds like he had the emotional scars, the personality," Kit said.

"Shaky hands, too much drinking, no life partner. I did not put it together ..."

"Yeah, now that you mention it."

"Come on; let's go." Alex opened the door for Kit.

"Promise me the next time you almost get us killed that you'll do it somewhere warm." Kit asked.

Chapter Thirty-Two

Alex was surprised that she had never noticed the Airbnb before. It was only a five-minute walk from her own cabin and had a perfect view of the field, including Marta's cabin and the Tinsley House.

"We have work to do." Kit said as she carried a pot of tea and two cups to the living room table.

"Just like old times. I miss those late nights at Butler Library, sneaking in Sushi and being shushed by the librarians," Alex said.

"You're a visual anthropologist—let's solve this and get you home," Kit poured them each a cup of tea.

"And clear Will. But how?"

"Pete's body of work. What you said last night about war. Look at his entire portfolio. There has got to be a clue in there somewhere," Kit suggested.

"It won't be online. He has good and buried his past," Alex pointed out.

"Under another name, maybe. The internet is a garbage dump that never empties. There will be a trace of something somewhere. At least find out what he used to be called," Kit said.

"I'm on it," Alex assured her. "You'll miss your flight."

"Can't do that; I'm headed straight to the Nat Geo archives —I've already emailed them: access permitted," Kit reported. Alex gave her a final squeeze, and Kit slipped out the back of the Airbnb.

* * *

Alex spent the rest of that day and the next on her laptop, without much luck. Kit on the other hand thought she might have a lead at Nat Geo and was waiting for a call. Alex had a light dinner her second night alone in the Airbnb and checked her email one last time before bed. Her advisor at Columbia wrote to offer her a TA-ship for next semester. She had to be in New York in a week to secure it. She knew that her project here was in a shambles and that the TA-ship was her best option, but she was not ready to say goodbye to Bozeman or to Will.

She texted Will that all was well. She lied and said that she and Kit were having another girl's night in.

He texted back, "Rest-up. Call if you need anything." He did not sound concerned. Maybe she was imagining the danger. Either he dismissed the gunshot as a fluke, or he was stellar at boundaries. Besides, he did not know she was alone; he thought Kit was still there with her.

She climbed into bed thinking about Will's picture on the Cloudsplitter website and how Will's uniform wasn't typical of the other rangers, and how he rarely drove the park Jeep. A mid-century modern cabin in a turn-of-the century park; how had she not thought that odd? She assumed a National Park scientist earned a high salary. But what was he doing at Cloudsplitter? Had he helped develop the crittercam? He did say he was researching laser technology.

Alex drifted off to sleep dreaming of an older woman, in a calico chador, her face tattooed with henna. "A good anthropologist asks the right questions. You ask the wrong questions." The woman cackled wildly, exposing a mouth full of decayed and gold-capped teeth. Alex turned away, but the woman grabbed her with the force of the young. She pushed her down in a metal folding chair, "Sit. I'm not done with you." Then she turned toward her kitchen counter—to pull a knife, make tea? Alex did not wait to find-out. She bolted out the front door and across a snowy field, as if her life depended on it. She opened the door to her cabin in Bozeman—and woke panting.

It was a dream, a bad dream, she told herself. She sat up in the dark and deciphered the dream: the cabin was Marta's, which made sense given all the time she had spent reconstructing it and then analyzing it. The Henna-ed woman symbolized the Iranian filmmaker who was imprisoned. Her subconscious was speaking to her, making connections. But what was it saying? Marta? Danger? Was Marta in danger, or dangerous? Her gut told her the former. The police had not found her assailant, and, now that she was out of the hospital and away from their protection, Marta could end-up dead and buried in a snow drift, not to be found until spring. Dreams were either the clearing house of deeply suppressed feelings or prophetic warnings. *Which is it, Alex?* She begged her cryptic subconscious mind to reveal itself. She placed nightmares categorically with feelings; otherwise, she would never sleep. Like Marta calling Will because she had a nightmare. Maybe it was not so silly after all.

She switched on the bedside lamp and reached for her glasses and then checked her phone. Kit had texted her an image of a Nat Geo cover from a decade ago. There was no mistaking the intense hazel eyes. Alex had assumed that green eyes and honey-colored hair were Eastern European. She had committed the worst anthropology sin and stereotyped.

The perfect pieta. Kit wrote, and all the pieces fell together. He had staged it.

She would call Scotty in the morning. In the meantime, she was wide awake, and it was only 2:00 a.m.

The full moon lit up the kitchen through the large picture window. Alex turned on the kettle. The Airbnb had a perfect view of the Tinsley House. As her eyes adjusted to the dark field, she recognized a twist of dark gray smoke against the bright night sky. It could only be coming from one place. She cracked the kitchen window to get a better view. The Tinsley House was on fire. Alex's pulse quickened: *Marta.*

Alex texted Will to meet her there.

The cold air burned her lungs as she ran across the field.

She was panting heavily by the time she reached the front porch. The fire was a mirage, it was only smoke coming from the chimney. She paused to control her breath. All the curtains were drawn. It was impossible to know whether Marta was alone. But she was sure that Marta was in that house. She hoped that her theory about Pete attacking Marta was correct. But that left Marta with the greatest motive to kill him—and an unbreakable alibi. If Marta had not killed him, who had? And would they kill again to keep that secret? Was Marta next? Was she was hiding out in the Tinsley House? Or was she captive there? Alex had failed an informant once before, and she would not do that again. She tapped tentatively on the front door.

Marta opened the door as if she were expecting someone, ushered Alex in and swiftly closed the door behind her.

"You must leave; it is not safe," she said, shivering—despite the warm fire. Alex noticed a backpack by the door.

"Are we alone?"

"Yes."

Alex showed Marta the picture Kit texted her of a young Afghan girl lying in a ditch on the side of a road near Kabul.

"It's you."

Marta's eyes welled.

"Taken by Pete?"

"You found her."

Marta spoke as if the photo was merely molted skin shed after the fact. As if the camera, like they believed in parts of Africa and the Middle East, had sucked her soul.

Marta sat heavily on the couch and stared up at Alex with tears in her eyes.

"Photograph is more powerful than words. But words have a high price. My father was a poet—killed because of his words. My mother was killed because she didn't have any." Marta spoke articulately, finally dropping her long-worn-out act.

"What happened?"

"I came with my coffee tray. He is fighting with Diana. He does not recognize me. Mr. Mechanical Eye, the demon. Peter Demonica." Marta's eyes were bloodshot.

"I'm so sorry."

"He won big prize for this photo. In the museum I see him

after many, many, years. He has coffee. He wants cream. He looks right at me. He looks but does not see the same face that makes him so famous. But I remember him, and I am afraid. If he sees me, he knows I will tell everyone his secret. I call ranger for protection. I call my friend; she tells me Pete, he is in Yellowstone. I work late at museum, a storm is coming, storm will keep him away. But he comes and says he wants to talk. I call police, I do not want them to know me, so I tell them he is stealing camera. He throws his camera at my head to stop me. It hurts. I have big bump. But he runs away."

"Why didn't you tell the police?"

"I am nobody. No papers. Illegal. I am a ghost in this country. My power is disappearing."

"You must have been terrified when you saw Pete at the museum?" *That explains her bad mood on Friday.* "You could have told me."

"Dangerous man. Charisma and camera give too much power, lots of power. It is war, and he is telling people where to put things. Posing everything. All fake. Telling people where to stand, what to do, how to measure the light. He fights Diana about camera—about light. 'Measure the light in my eyes,' I want to say to him. 'I want the world to see it is distinguished.'"

"Extinguished," Alex whispered.

"All gone out. I want world to know Demon made me dark. But he scares me. I am silent. I put down tray with the coffee, and I run." Marta coughed. Alex brought the water bottle from the table and sat down next to Marta.

"He was going to leave. That's why he stayed, because of you? He recognized you?" Alex asked, handing her the bottle.

"He watched while soldiers, protectors ..." she faltered, "I do not believe in this security. Security comes with too high cost. He believes I am dead; he never check. He move me, pulls elbow, drags foot, drags me by my hair like a dog, kicking my hand."

An inch here, an inch there, the perfect pose, yes, Kit was right, the perfect pieta.

"And then he shoots."

Alex's heart jumped.

"*Aftermath of Taliban Attack* he calls it. He is like poacher." Her eyes were dry—she had used up her allotted tears.

"And Pete's death?"

"This is not murder."

"Of course not."

"You believe me? I only want to humiliate him. Like he humiliated me," Marta whimpered slightly.

"How?"

Marta pointed to the white flowers on the table.

"Always there. Waiting. They give comfort. Dried flowers for a heavy dream on bad nights, dried flowers to dream forever. Anytime I want."

Alex whispered, "Coma." *Koma*, Greek for deep sleep.

"Too many flowers in his drink." Marta sobbed. "I am not killer. My friend gave him same drink as me, to sleep here in this house, so police find me and send me to safe hospital." Marta's face relaxed, the last mask had fallen. "I measure the right amount," she continued. "I never mistake amounts, I can weigh in my hand, in my mind."

Someone mismeasured—or did they?

"Did you rig the gun?" Alex tightened the grip on her phone. Where was Will? Why had he not responded?

"Gun?" Marta was genuinely surprised. "Flowers killed Demon. It was accident, wrong measure."

"There was a gun in the crittercam. Was it a joke? Perhaps your friend?" If Marta had neither loaded that gun nor known it was there, then who had? She had an accomplice—maybe it was not an accidental overdose. Alex looked around nervously. "Are you expecting someone?"

Marta did not answer.

"Are you planning to go somewhere?" Alex pointed to the backpack.

"Home."

"Where? The cabin?" Alex stood and retrieved the bag. She handed Marta her battered leather coat.

"Friend's cabin. Hiding from police."

"Which friend, Marta? The same one who gave the flowers to Pete?"

Marta barely nodded.

"Who?"

"I cannot say. They are not a bad person. This was mistake."

They? Of course, Persian did not have gender pronouns, Alex remembered learning in a linguistic anthropology class.

"Put on your boots. We need to get out of here. If you didn't kill Pete, then someone else did, and they framed you. You are not safe."

Marta gasped; it had not occurred to her that she had been framed.

* * *

The women moved quickly and quietly across the dark field.

Alex punched in the code to the Airbnb, and Marta darted inside.

Kit was a tea drinker and had brought the PG Tips from the car with them to the Airbnb.

"Cup of tea?"

"Please do not call police."

"I promise." Alex said, deciding that, while Will was a

ranger, he did not count as police. After all, Marta herself had called Will once for help.

They drank their tea in silence. "You can trust me," Alex said.

"Trust?" Marta repeated as if Alex had said a dirty word. "American anthropologist comes to my village. She does not speak Dari; she uses me, young girl for translator. She works for soldiers. She shows soldiers where to cut ... you know on the animal the place with no protection?"

"The underbelly." Alex had agreed with the American Anthropologist Association's statement that the *Human Terrain System Project* that sent anthropologists to help the US military in Afghanistan with 'cultural sensitivity' violated that code of ethics which mandates that anthropologists do no harm to their research subjects. Frankly, it was a colonial project.

"Marta..."

"It is not my name. My name is Gol—"

"It's a pretty name; what does it mean?"

"Flower."

"Who is Marta?"

"Marta is the girl who visits refugee camp in Berlin. Polish girl, with her mother. She is crying and tearing math notebook. Her mother pays me to help her understand fractions. I know fractions. I know how to break things apart. We become friends. Three years. UN closed camp. Everyone sent home. She gives me Marta's Polish passport, she says, you go to Yellowstone with workers. Escape."

"You passed for the Polish Marta," Alex realized.

"Yes, I am same age."

Alex fought back tears. Marta was Alex's age.

Alex: "And you returned the passport in a book of flowers by way of another worker."

"Yes."

Alex filled a glass with tap water and unscrewed the plastic bottle of sleeping pills that Kit had left her, "Just in case." She gave two to Marta and took two herself. They needed to get through this interminable night when Will might finally wake and see his text. When it would be easier to navigate the harsh terrain ahead, and they could go home, wherever that was.

Chapter Thirty-Three

Marta had already drunk her tea and was sitting stoically, with her hands in her lap, studying Alex with the same placid expression that had not wavered from her face since they had arrived at the Airbnb. Alex took another sip of the scalding tea and regretted it. She examined the teabag, hoping for a little poem or inspiration. But PG Tips came without any words of wisdom.

"I sleep," Marta stood and Alex directed her upstairs. She instructed Marta to stay there until Alex came for her in the morning.

"I'll be up soon," Alex called after her.

Alex had planned on staying awake until she could call Kit, but the sleeping pill was already working. She turned off the light and headed toward the stairs when she heard a slight knock on the back door. Alex's heart pounded wildly. No one knew that she was here. She regretted taking the sleeping pills. She urgently needed to be awake, aware, and alert. She found her phone, turned toward the stairs, and froze. The large glass door in the back slid noisily along its track. Someone had managed to open it. She dialed Will. As their lines connected, a phone rang nearby. Alex's whole body froze. She fumbled and dropped the phone. The ringing stopped.

She would take a chance. It was safer than running.

Hey, Siri, call Bozeman police, Alex called out into the silence.

Calling boatman please, Siri replied. Alex lunged for her phone. But the intruder beat her to it.

"Drop it." The sharp and familiar voice sliced through Alex's sleepy brain.

A dog barked.

"What's that?" Alex muttered.

"That is the painful wail of separation. Surely, you've read Rumi's *Masnavi*: 'Listen to the Reed lament its separation from the field.'"

Jasmine's large dark eyes stared back at her from behind the strong beam of her flashlight. She wore the jacket Marta had insisted on leaving behind at the Tinsley House.

"Too bright? I never liked flash photography. Where is she?" Jasmine demanded.

"Who?"

"Marta."

"Why?"

"Good girl. Ask the right questions. Don't move." Jasmine stepped closer. "You're all the same. Anthropologists, photographers, studying us so that you can rule us, subjugate us, colonize us. Collect your evidence, collect your specimens, and then—bang!—take over." Jasmine held up a canister of bear spray. Whether she sprayed it at Alex or hit her over the head with it, the result would be the same. "Photography is dangerous. You said it yourself. Your stupid comment about guns and photographs. About shooting."

"I never—"

"Of course you did." Jasmine's breath was on her face.

"That was Pete's story."

"That man was a terrible storyteller. Don't you agree that what was missing in all those pretty pictures was a good story? He underestimated the power of a good tale. He only knew how to capture an image when his prey was most vulnerable. He was the worst kind of poacher. By the way, did you enjoy the way I changed your story? Adding a cross to lead you away from Afghanistan."

"*You* desecrated my nutshell."

"Did you like the little flint tool? It was the easiest thing to make in a pinch. It's a pebble from my driveway," Jasmine explained, pleased.

"You hit her?"

"No, but you all thought I did. That's the power of suggestion. Pete would have killed her; we needed to warn him to stay away."

"By killing him?" Alex battled wooziness the way a concussed person knew to stay awake.

"No..." Jasmine sounded tired now, deflated.

"It was quite an elaborate plan, must have taken some time," Alex slurred.

"We Persians are good storytellers. We excel at creating a picture, a visual. You should have appreciated that."

"Why hurt Marta?"

"You mean Gol—that's her real name' it means flower. To protect her."

"How?" Alex asked.

"I used the white flowers to drug her. She is a gifted herbalist, a real natural. Brilliant math mind. She can calculate a formula perfectly and accurately weigh a dried flower in her hand down to the ounce. Can you estimate the weight of a dead flower? The weight of a lost life? She knew a lot of the medicinal herbs in the mountains near Kabul, and Raven was teaching her how to identify the equivalent here in Montana. She lied to Raven and told her that the ones she knew were Eastern European." Jasmine turned and noticed the glass teacups and damp tea bags. "We Persians like to see the color of our tea. Where is she?" she demanded.

Alex slipped to the floor.

"Am I boring you?" Jasmine lowered the bear spray. "Isn't this what you wanted, anthropologist? A life story." She looked down at Alex, "How's this one: I'm sorry for being the lucky one. What stroke of luck would make Gol a maid and me a millionaire? I recognized her scars. They may not be the same shape or size or color, but they were inflicted by the same circumstance. I stroked her arm, circling my finger around each scar, tracing the little red slashes with my finger. 'What happened?' I asked her, and she pulled her arm away—mute, shocked that I could see the scars. They had become invisible through subterfuge—a second skin. She poured her story out to me shortly after she ran into Pete at the museum. She was terrified."

Alex flinched.

"When you live in a war-torn country, everything becomes about honor, revenge, and territory. Doesn't your religion tell you to turn the other cheek? But do you ever? No. Instead, you go colonize other countries for their oil, their uranium, their freshwater ports. And you destroy the place to the point where the survivors beg you to let them into your country for refuge. And refuge from what? From you. From what you've turned their citizens into—refugees from their homeland." Jasmine's anger and exhaustion were becoming primal, dangerous—something Alex feared she would not escape.

"She didn't want him dead," Alex reasoned.

"Neither did I." Jasmine lowered the flashlight. "But that won't make any difference to a jury in this country."

"You don't know that."

"No one convicted him. Until Marta told me her tormentor turned up at the museum, I had no idea about their past. I slept with him. A man who—"

"You couldn't have known."

"He was overdue his day in court. I lured him into the diorama and drugged him. I wanted to humiliate him and put him on display, the way he displayed her. I told him Diana wanted him as the centerpiece of the diorama. His oversized ego made him easy prey. 'She wants to celebrate you,' I cooed. That fool walked right into the trap. The only reflection that narcissist would see was his own face in a pool of blood. I handed him a drugged drink, and we chatted while it took effect. We had our trial. He told me everything. About how poor ole Pete could not claim his stupid prize once the committee learned of the nefarious way he got his shot. The guilty enjoy confessing."

"You were at the party?" Alex remembered Pete disappearing into the crowd, looking for someone.

"Nobody saw me in the dark. I rigged a fake wire along the back wall toward the kitchen, where I was coming and going with my tray. The remote control never left my pocket. Kamran took all the credit, but I am the one who invented that silly crittercam."

"Diana tripped on a wire," Alex pointed out.

"Misdirection. Diana thought she had tripped a wire, but it was all remote. Let's say having Diana trip allowed me to kill two birds with one stone."

Alex closed her eyes; she was fading.

"Wake up, anthropologist!"

"You were the waitress?" *Keep the story going,* Alex thought, reminding herself of *Shahrazad and the 1,001 Nights* —when the story ended, the storyteller would die.

"I wore a wig. Jack recognized me. Paleontologists are practiced at seeing beneath the skin. He saw through my make-up, my fake accent and blond wig. He sensed my Persian soul. Which is why he thought I was Marta." she paused, "Lucky me, the anthropologist was quick to jump on him for his mistake. Thank you, PC-police. Does that make you complicit? Something to gnaw on with your therapist. Surely you have one. Doesn't every Ivy League kid have a therapist cleaning up their deconstructed ego? Do you know what happened to Marta's father's university? The Americans blew it up. The same Americans who brought the University to Afghanistan in the 1960s blew it up 50 years later. You know what else they brought with them? The Taliban. They have not been as successful at blowing them up."

"Aren't you Iranian?"

"What's in a border? I used to be jealous of girls like you who thought childhood trauma was the wrong pair of jeans. Girls like you don't know what it is like to sleep with one eye open. I underestimated you. I liked you."

"I'm on your side."

"It's not about sides. It's about circumstances." Jasmine's voice softened, "It is easy to become someone in this land of opportunity, but it is also easy to fall. Gravity never sleeps, anthropologist." Jasmine raised the heavy and lethal canister of bear spray with both hands.

Gravity. Alex watched Marta come up behind Jasmine and whack her on the head with a frying pan.

A dog released a piercing howl.

Chapter Thirty-Four

Alex opened her cabin door to find Will.

"Your phone. It rang." Alex admonished Will before he was able to say hello.

Will looked at his phone, confused.

"Last night. I dialed your number, and I heard a phone ring."

"I never received a call."

Alex studied her call log. "That's weird. I called Marta. I was drowsy. A W is a sleeping M for me." Alex was relieved to exonerate Will. "Come in," she ushered him inside quickly, "I need to tell you something." Alex started—too late: Scotty was already upon them.

"Agatha Christie, our hero!" Scotty said, walking in.

"You do know she wasn't a detective? She was a mystery writer." Will laughed.

"Did you know she had dyslexia?" Scotty beamed.

Alex smiled; she did indeed know that.

"You sure did save this guy," Scotty said.

"How?" Alex asked, confused.

"Turns out the trip wire was a misdirection; it was a remote system of lasers based on a patent registered to Will," Scotty informed them.

"Wow," Alex said. So Will was the one being closely watched by the FBI.

"Poor Kamran; he's a mess. He had no clue that Marta spoke Persian or that it was her, not Pete, whom Jasmine was spending time with. We all thought she was Polish."

"When did Kamran get into cameras?" Will asked.

"He said, 'When that thug who called himself an artist slept with my wife.'"

"Revenge?" Will wondered, "He's not vengeful."

"Actually, Jasmine invented the camera," Alex told them.

"Now that makes more sense," Will said.

"Kamran wanted to put Pete out of business. He wanted the crittercam trademarked and on the market as soon as possible, which is why he drove through that awful storm to return to Bozeman. The call he received was from the museum guard, who reported the camera was stolen. Jasmine had to act fast when Kamran arrived at home, where she was hiding Marta. She sedated him with the flowers—" Scotty explained.

"Which explains why he stood up Diana," Alex added.

"Lucky for him that she didn't double dose him like Pete. Think she meant to kill him?" Scotty asked.

"No idea," Will said. "She's not a killer, but she's also extremely precise in everything she does. It doesn't make sense that she would have mismeasured the dose."

"Her lawyer asked for a coroner's report. He thinks Pete may have had a heart condition, and, if so, that will weigh heavily in Jasmine's favor."

"Poor Diana; was Kamran using her?" Alex asked.

"They go 'way back," Will answered.

"I'm confused," Scotty admitted, "Who tried to kill Marta?"

"Jasmine took Marta to the Tinsley House, gave her the sleeping flower, and lit the fire. Marta told me, when Pete found her on the side of the road in Afghanistan, she was playing dead to save herself."

"Playing dead?" Will asked.

"Yes, which she did again in the hospital until Jasmine administered more of the flower—the effect of which mimicked a coma on her vitals. Deep relaxation, in other words. Jasmine told her it was for her protection. She ate a petal a day. I followed Jasmine and saw her collect the petals right after telling her Marta was conscious," Alex explained.

"So that's why Marta's phone signal was picked up near Gardiner," Will surmised, "She was with Jasmine, who shot at Alex and Kit, who must have skied onto Kamran's property."

He turned to Alex, "Told you to stay on the trail."

"And that's why Jasmine was planning their escape. The cabin was too dangerous. She was not counting on Alex returning to Bozeman last night," Scotty said.

"How did she know about the Airbnb?" Alex asked.

"Jasmine slipped an air tag in Marta's backpack," Scotty answered.

Alex looked at Will. Had he and Jasmine worked together to develop the tagging system?

"Will Marta be deported?" Will asked. "She was barely an accessory. Her goal was to humiliate him, not to kill him."

"She's undocumented. Either way, I need to arrest her. But don't worry, Kamran says he'll get her the best defense attorney money can buy."

"You mean you did not arrest her with Jasmine?" Will asked.

"Alex said she'd taken a sleeping pill and needed to rest," Scotty said with a compassionate look toward the bedroom door.

"I had no idea she was here," Will said.

Scotty walked toward the bedroom, "Go ahead, wake-up Sleeping Beauty; time to rock-and-roll."

Alex nodded and braced herself for her performance. She opened the door to the bedroom, paused a beat, and then screamed, "She's gone!"

Scotty grabbed his coat. "Come on; we need to search the woods."

"She'll freeze." Will took his coat to follow Scotty, but Alex pulled him back, "Wait," she insisted. "You won't find her out there," Alex whispered.

"Jasmine was going to kill me with that bear spray; Marta saved my life. She hit her over the head with a pan. Remember when I was worried that the aura of the Nutshell Murders had seeped into my houses?"

Will nodded.

"Frances Glessner Lee's whole raison d'être was justice. Maybe the aura that I brought with me to Bozeman wasn't murder but justice."

"Right," Will encouraged.

"Glessner Lee's goal was to 'Convict the guilty, clear the innocent, and find the truth in a nutshell.' My failed fieldwork taught me that anthropologists do not merely watch life play out before them; we are *participant* observers. Life isn't a petri dish to be observed in a lab. *We* are the protagonists of our own stories."

"Right—" Will said.

"I do not work in a bones room. I work in a flesh-and-soul room."

"What are you saying?" Will asked.

"We place people in boxes because it is easier than dealing with the details. But, then, the devil is in the details. Anthropology is in the details."

"What detail am I missing here?" Will asked, confused.

"We can't turn people over to an unjust system that will send them back to an altogether criminal system," Alex said. "I let her go."

"What? She'll die of exposure; she'll appear guilty..."

"She has the Subaru, all my cash, and as much food as we could pack quickly—she's miles from here by now," Alex confessed. "I couldn't let her go to prison. I did not come here to construct a prison for her. A prison cell is easy to make; it's a box. She is much more complicated than that. She deserves more." Alex gazed in the distance, imagining one last question she would ask Marta. "Tell me about your house in Kabul. Were there lace curtains?"

"You did the right thing," Will said, taking her hands, "The first time you mentioned the Nutshells, I thought of *Hamlet*—a play about difficult decisions."

"About how indecision *is* action." As Alex who had a decision to make about returning to New York knew too well.

"Exactly. *Oh God, I could be bounded in a nutshell and count myself* ..." Will began the line from *Hamlet*.

"*A queen of infinite space,*" Alex concluded.

Acknowledgments

Thank you, friends, family members and fellow researchers who make the seemingly lonely task of writing a collective endeavor. As Margaret Mead says: *It takes a village!*

Three decades after Anthony Ambrogio and Anca Vlasopolos welcomed me into the Detroit Writers Group, Anthony's editorial guidance moved this work from draft to publication.

Tom Bowles and Robyn Klein, our Bozeman family, introduced us to everything from bugling elk to bubbling hot river dipping.

Alice Andreini, dear friend and fierce interlocutor, read and discussed and encouraged me through countless early drafts. As did Sam George, gifted editor, friend, hiking buddy and impromptu support in everything from 2E parenting to publishing. And thank you to his son Aiden, who brought us all together.

Charlotte Varzi taught me what tenacity looks like. Jehan, Kim, Jam and Manijeh are the kindest kin.

Susan Kolodziejczyk and Joanne spent hours hosting us at National Geographic, without which there would be no story.

Julia Lupton, friend and co-conspirator, for encouraging, supporting, and inspiring all my experiments. Namrata Poddar, OC writing companion, friend, and generous advocate thank you for championing women writers of color. Krista Nicholds, for so much. Claudia Shambaugh, and her magic microphone. Peter Sellars and Julia Carnahan for creative nourishment.

For all my early readers who added comments, commas, and encouragement: Alice Andreini, Kim Varzi, Charlotte Varzi, Naomi Chesler, Taly Marin, Robert Wood, Diane Fallon, Kate Wahl, Carolyn McAuliffe, Ilya Bernstein, Sam George, Anthony Ambrogio, and Dorothy Popp.

My dyslexia family of advocates, researchers, teachers, and writers: Brock and Fernette Eide who have offered support, advice, community, science, art, and the most precise diagnosis. Helen Taylor, whose work on complementary cognition and whose friendship have been a revelation. Jack Horner and Lisa Cupolo and the *Eye-to-Eye* team at Chapman University for supporting learners with dyslexia, especially Jack Horner who is the best of characters, real and imagined. Elayne Roberts and Karen Wieland who turned our book worm into a reader. Haya Sakadjian, Lisa Klipfel and all the parents in the Dyslexia parenting network, including the folks at Decoding Dyslexia. Christopher J Evans and Cathy Cahill who introduced me to stealth dyslexia and the work of the *Yale Center for Dyslexia and Creativity*. Jonathon Mooney for his advocacy and writing and a Zoom session on *Bright and Quirky* where he assured our budding writer that spelling was not a requirement for future authors! Johanna Young, parent, friend and 2E teacher of infinite patience. Dante Treggs. Jess Arce. Tim Weedon. Vanessa Hernandez, homeschool parents extraordinaire. Sahba Reza— family, friend, and dyslexia advocate. Christian Boer for his dyslexie font. Chris Arnold, for his sage advice and important disruptions. Tiffany Sunday for her advice and encouragement. Governor Gavin Newsome for changing the laws and showing the world what dyslexic leadership looks like. Gil Gershoni for lighting the way one interview at a time. 2E warriors, educators, doctors, researchers, and organizers: Lisa Reid, David

Palmer, Tom Kemnitz, Sensei Wayne Centra, Karen Boden Morrison, Chari Lewis, Heather Kaplan-Santos, Marc Lerner, Scott Murray, and Jake Greenspan—all of whom turn comorbidities into co-possibilities. Jenny Rankin, Mensa youth coordinator and gifted researcher and mentor, the late James Webb, pioneering researcher on gifted youth, who taught me the difference between a race car and a sedan. Randy and Kate Gremillion for bringing music into the mix. Jack Churchill and Scanning Pens. All the anonymous volunteer readers at Learning Ally. Susan Klein, Susan Claudia Lepselter, Aaron Fox and Theresa Truax, who teach, write, research, advocate, and parent. Adrian Southard, my Gen Z, ND creative consultant.

I want to thank the Anthropologists who during the years I was writing this work were (unbeknownst to them) encouraging my disruptions by publishing my experimental writing and inviting me to talk about my multi-modal practice, starting with Deborah A Thomas, who, as editor of *American Anthropologist*, solicited my essay, *The Knot in the Wood: The Call to Multimodal Anthropology*. Paige West inspired me from her first lecture and published *Hijacking the Elevator* in *Cultural Anthropology*, Rose Wellman who edited *Finding Home*, and all my other wonderful colleagues at the *Journal of Humanistic Anthropology*: Lucian Stone and Jason Mohaghegh did not bat an eye when I submitted a play to their collection in the *Journal of Comparative and Continental Philosophy*; Carole McGranahan and Nomi Stone introduced me to flash ethnography and published "*Mother Bard, Fight or Flight? An Ethnography of May*" in *American Ethnologist*; Grace Zhou and Jill Tan invited me to speak at Stanford and published the sound and text of "No Wings to Fly to God" in their Fieldsights in the *Journal of Cultural Anthropology*. Eduardo Hezara invited me to contribute what became a poem on dyslexia "Aristotle's Field Notes" in *100 Words for Katie Stewart* in *Anthropology and Humanism*. And again, I want to thank Carole McGranahan for publishing *Savage Minds* and bringing out *Writing Anthropology: Essays on Craft and Commitment*, where *Ethnographic Fiction: The Space Between*, my first essay on writing fiction, appeared. I want to thank all the anthropologists who have supported multi-modal work through the Society for Visual Anthropology, CAMRA at University of Pennsylvania, and Ethnographic Termanalia—especially, Deborah A Thomas. John L. Jackson Jr., Stephanie Takaragawa, Cam McDonald, and Harjant Gill, who nourished invaluable spaces for disruption. Thank you, Kim Fortun, for encouraging me to teach my multi-modal anthropology PhD seminar. Karen Holmberg for her friendship and for holding a space for me to write the next mystery. Wendy Shaw, for playing the angel. Sherine Hamdy, Harvey Stark, Nancy Um, Lola Martinez, Leide Porcu, and Mark LeVine for cheering me on. Laura Mulvey, for changing the way we look. For Sabine Parrish who invited me to discuss my novel at the *Oxford University Anthropological Society Book Club*, and Micro Gopfert who hosted me at the *Institute Für Ethnologie*, Anthropology Department, Goethe University, Frankfurt, Germany. For Pani Farvid, Chiara Bottici, and Jonathon Bach for bringing me back into the New York intellectual world post-pandemic. Thorgeir Kolshus, Alejandro Miranda Nieto, and Maka Suarez for starting a conversation in Oslo. Mark de Silva, for reviewing work that does not fit. And a big thank you to (former) president of the American Anthropological Association Alisse Waterston for her essay *Getting Credit*, in which she cites my ethnographic novel, *Last Scene Underground*, which, at the time (2017), was not getting credit as anthropology in some circles. All of this is to say that, despite Alex's difficulties in this novel, there are champions of experimental, multi-modal anthropology out there, and their support, creativity, and generosity has been invaluable. Brinkley Messick, Marilyn Ivy and Michael Taussig were the best possible mentors -- just saying, Professor Whiner is fictional!

Kasra Paydavousi for his amazing cover design, his logos, and all the beauty and art he brings to everyday life.

Author's Guild and Sisters in Crime for supporting writers, and the Newport Beach Public Library for supporting writers and readers.

And finally, museums and art institutions are instrumental spaces for education and outreach, especially for people who learn differently. I have had the pleasure of spending hours at The American Museum of Natural History and the Pitt Rivers Museum. I especially want to thank the Smithsonian Institute, where I first saw the Nutshells at the Renwick Gallery, and where my son spent three months in the Hall of Human Origins, culminating in a wonderful visit with Rick Potts and an intense interest in paleontology and human evolutionary biology, which led to sitting in on Jim Egan's wonderful anthropology classes at UCI and to the Museum of the Rockies, where the idea to write this book first hit me as I was standing in the Maiasaura exhibit listening to my eight-year-old son, who could not read, explain to me the significance of Jack Horner's work. Neither of us knew at the time that Jack Horner was a fellow dyslexic, that we would soon meet him and find out just how important his achievements are to the evolution in thinking of dyslexia as a strength. And what a generous and kind mentor he is to young learners with dyslexia who hope to follow in his path. And thank you to all the rangers and educators in our amazing national-parks system, especially Yellowstone National Park, one of my favorite places to wonder and wander.

For Rumi and Kasra, without whom my story is incomplete.

Made in the USA
Las Vegas, NV
11 November 2023

80600669R00225